Law School

FOR

DUMMIES®

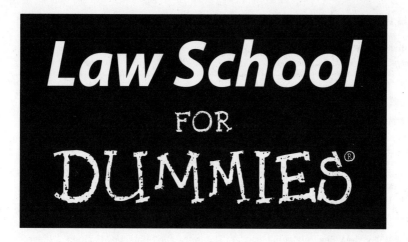

Law School FOR DUMMIES®

by Rebecca Greene, JD

WILEY

Wiley Publishing, Inc.

Law School For Dummies®

Published by
Wiley Publishing, Inc.
909 Third Avenue
New York, NY 10022
www.wiley.com

Copyright © 2003 by Wiley Publishing, Inc., Indianapolis, Indiana

Published simultaneously in Canada

No part of this publication may be reproduced, stored in a retrieval system, or transmitted in any form or by any means, electronic, mechanical, photocopying, recording, scanning, or otherwise, except as permitted under Sections 107 or 108 of the 1976 United States Copyright Act, without either the prior written permission of the Publisher, or authorization through payment of the appropriate per-copy fee to the Copyright Clearance Center, 222 Rosewood Drive, Danvers, MA 01923, 978-750-8400, fax 978-646-8700. Requests to the Publisher for permission should be addressed to the Legal Department, Wiley Publishing, Inc., 10475 Crosspoint Blvd., Indianapolis, IN 46256, 317-572-3447, fax 317-572-4447, or e-mail permcoordinator@ wiley.com

For general information on our other products and services or to obtain technical support, please contact our Customer Care Department within the U.S. at 800-762-2974, outside the U.S. at 317-572-3993, or fax 317-572-4002.

Wiley also publishes its books in a variety of electronic formats. Some content that appears in print may not be available in electronic books.

Library of Congress Control Number: 2003101865

ISBN: 0-7645-2548-4

Manufactured in the United States of America

10 9 8 7 6 5 4 3 2

About the Author

Rebecca Greene, JD, is a May 2003 graduate of Indiana University School of Law – Bloomington. A freelance writer, she is a contributor to the American Bar Association's *Student Lawyer* magazine and the 2003 edition of Peterson's *Law Schools.* She also is the author of *The Teenagers' Guide to School Outside the Box* (Free Spirit Publishing: 2001).

In law school, she was a staff member of the *Federal Communications Law Journal*, worked at the Environmental Protection Agency, Office of Regional Counsel, and the Center for Analysis of Alternative Dispute Resolution Systems in Chicago. She graduated from Carleton College in Northfield, Minnesota, in 1999, and currently lives in Chicago.

Dedication

This book is lovingly dedicated to my best friend and soul mate, Brian, who never fails to make me laugh and always is available for a spontaneous snuggle. He shares with me loving support and unfailing encouragement each and every day. Thank you for all you have taught me in our life together, Bri-Bear. I love you always.

Author's Acknowledgments

Many wonderful and talented people at Wiley Publishing helped make this book a reality. They include Acquisitions Editor Kathy Cox, who went out of her way to nurture a new author, and Project Editor Allyson Grove, who offered unparalleled editing expertise and countless useful suggestions that were right on target. A warm thanks also to Neil Johnson for his dynamite copy-editing, to Kurt Snyder and Jeff Cox for their brilliant technical reviews of the text, Holly Gastineau-Grimes for her expert endorsement assistance, and to everyone in Composition Services for turning words and thoughts into a reader-friendly and fun package.

Thank you also to everyone else behind the scenes at Wiley who contributed to making this book a success. A final shout-out goes to my trusty computer that stuck it out through 12-hour writing workdays with only the occasional crash and made writing this book such a joy — even with a missing shift key.

I also owe a huge debt of gratitude to the following people who generously shared their stories, wisdom, or encouragement, including my parents, Merle and Phillip Greene, my grandmother, Florence Manusow, Donald Gjerdingen, Leonard Fromm, Kevin Robling, Marshall Leaffer, Donna Gerson, Jef Richards, Sarah Zearfoss, Alan Dershowitz, Jen Weber, Michael Uslan, Robert Harris, Ingrid Anderson, Anita Rufus, Susan Palmer, Leverett Nelson, Amy Cook, Amy Liu, Pat Cain, Bree Kame'enui, Harold Davis Jr., Michael Pastor, Lyman Johnson, Eric Janus, Jeremy Hojnicki, Jonathan Greene, Shorge Sato, Kellianne Chancey, Ellen Deason, David M. Marquez, Matt Silverman, Scott Hairston, Donna Gerson, K. Bartlett Durand Jr., Wayne Schiess, and Mark Curriden.

Publisher's Acknowledgments

We're proud of this book; please send us your comments through our Dummies online registration form located at www.dummies.com/register/.

Some of the people who helped bring this book to market include the following:

Acquisitions, Editorial, and Media Development

Project Editor: Allyson Grove

Acquisitions Editor: Kathleen M. Cox

Copy Editor: E. Neil Johnson

Acquisitions Coordinator: Holly G. Grimes

Technical Editor: Kurt Snyder

Editorial Manager: Michelle Hacker

Editorial Assistant: Elizabeth Rea

Cartoons: Rich Tennant, www.the5thwave.com

Production

Project Coordinator: Erin Smith

Layout and Graphics: Seth Conley, Michael Kruzil, Jackie Nicholas

Proofreaders: Andy Hollandbeck; TECHBOOKS Production Services

Indexer: TECHBOOKS Production Services

Special Help
Jeff Cox

Publishing and Editorial for Consumer Dummies

Diane Graves Steele, Vice President and Publisher, Consumer Dummies

Joyce Pepple, Acquisitions Director, Consumer Dummies

Kristin A. Cocks, Product Development Director, Consumer Dummies

Michael Spring, Vice President and Publisher, Travel

Brice Gosnell, Publishing Director, Travel

Suzanne Jannetta, Editorial Director, Travel

Publishing for Technology Dummies

Andy Cummings, Vice President and Publisher, Dummies Technology/General User

Composition Services

Gerry Fahey, Vice President of Production Services

Debbie Stailey, Director of Composition Services

Contents at a Glance

Table of Contents

Introduction

· ·

Welcome to the wide, wonderful, and sometimes wacky world of law school! The book you hold in your hands will come in handy even more than that 10-pound casebook you just bought (or will soon buy). That's because it's an essential reference guide for those who want the inside scoop on getting into law school, staying sane while you're there, and graduating with the job of your dreams. (Sorry, acceptance letter to the school of your choice isn't included.) Everything you need to know to survive and thrive in law school is right here in this book. And what's a piddly $19.99 investment compared to $80,000 in student loans, right?

This book fits three (or four) years of blood, sweat, and tears into 384 pages. I funnel all the important information you really need to know into this book so that you can get started as quickly as possible on your path to successful law studentdom.

Why do I feel I have the qualifications to relate this information to you? That's easy. I just recently was a law student; I graduated in May 2003. It literally was only yesterday that I was pulling my hair out over finals, procrastinating on my studies, and dealing with the job search jitters. These kinds of situations are avoidable with the kind of support and encouragement you find here.

I know you're not a dummy. Heck, you surely can't be, because you've done so well in college and on the LSAT that you're either seriously thinking about or already in law school. You've already proven to yourself that you have the mental moxie and drive to make it in a competitive academic environment. So all you have to do is embrace the strategies of law school success I outline here, and look out world!

So sit back and follow me into the exhilarating world of law school, content in the knowledge that just reading this book puts you head and shoulders ahead of your law school (or future law school) classmates. Your GPA and résumé will thank you for it!

About This Book

I know that many law school books are competing for your attention. How do I know that? Because when I was in law school, I read all of them, cover to cover. But the following are several compelling reasons I think you need to choose this book instead:

✔ **It's written by someone who's been there, done that.** Some law school books are written by people far removed from the experience. They don't know the most significant topics affecting today's law student because they haven't been today's law student for awhile. This book is different because it's written entirely from the student's point of view. I rushed home to write this book *every day* during my third year. (It was much more fun than reading for class and studying for exams.) That's why you can count on this guide to give you the most up-to-the-minute information you need to get through law school.

✔ **It's every law students' book.** This book is aimed at students from every tier of law school, from lowest to highest. It covers issues most relevant to *all* law students, from older students to disabled students to people with previous careers. In other words, it doesn't assume that you're 22 and straight-from-college or that you go to an Ivy League law school and are in the top 10 percent of your class. This book addresses everyone, because today's law school classes are filled with bright, talented students from every undergraduate major, ethnic group, age bracket, and occupational background.

✔ **It's well-rounded.** This book doesn't *assume* standard law student protocol (for example, that you're going to opt for a traditional legal career, go out for law review, or even take the bar exam). Instead, I aim to present *all* your options, particularly the off-the-beaten-path ones that aren't talked about all that much in law school.

✔ **It's realistic.** When you're in law school, you hear plenty of myths, such as the ones that say only the top 10 percent of law school graduates get jobs or that you *have* to land a big firm summer job because everyone else is doing the same. This book cuts through the law school rumormill and gives you the real truth, straight up.

How to Use This Book

Use this book as a mentor, friend, cheerleader, prelaw advisor, career counselor, admissions advisor, hiring lawyer, and all-around reference. It's the equivalent of the upper-class student you never thought you'd luck out to know, the one who's willing to lead you by the hand and share battle-tested strategies each and every day.

But law students are busy; you may not have time right now to read the book from beginning to end. That's okay because whether you're a 1L or a second-semester 3L, you'll find everything you need to know by using the Table of Contents or the Index to look up what you're wondering about. Also keep in mind that each chapter in this book is self-contained and *modular*, meaning you can jump from chapter to chapter without needing to know information that came before or after.

Conventions Used in This Book

Throughout this book, you'll see words and phrases particular to the law school experience. Whenever I introduce an unfamiliar word or term, I immediately provide a definition right after it, to ensure that you have that information you need. One of the most important conventions you'll see is the shorthand of using "L" to denote your year in law school. For instance, if you're a first-year law student, I refer to you as a "1L," and so forth for the other years.

Foolish Assumptions

If you're an absolute beginner — you've never seen an actual lawyer up close or have no clue what the LSAT stands for — never fear, this book has everything you need to get started. If you fall into this camp, I assume that you have no prior knowledge of how to decide which law school to attend or what it takes even to apply to law school. I also assume that you may have heard a few law school horror stories, and I do my best to debunk them (or confirm, where appropriate).

However, if you already have an acceptance letter in your hot little hands (congratulations!) or are already knee-deep in a mounting backlog of torts reading, you'll also find this book to be a lifesaving resource. You'll discover how to choose courses that can benefit you down the road and select the right extracurricular activities for your personality. The bottom line is this book is for everyone who wants to understand the law school experience better.

How This Book Is Organized

This book is an easy-to-use, *nonlinear reference* — that's a technical way of saying you can start with any topic you want to find out about, anywhere in the book, and still find the information presented the way you need. But the chapters nevertheless have a rhyme and reason to them, all the same. (Don't you wish law school were this easy?) Here's how the order works:

Part 1: Considering Law School

The chapters in this part give you everything you need to know to get into law school. From weighing the pros and cons of the entire decision to the finer points of choosing the best law school for you, you can find everything you need to stock your mailbox full of acceptances.

Part II: Getting What You Came for: The Law School Experience

No first-year student can survive without getting a handle on the curriculum and learning how to healthfully balance law school and outside interests. The three chapters in this part give you the lowdown on getting though your first year with your sanity intact!

Part III: Studying Law: Secret Techniques That Really Work

In addition to showing you how to handle your coursework, I run through how to study productively, assemble the best study aids, ace your exams, and much more in Part III. On top of all that, I offer some helpful tips about what "thinking like a lawyer" really means and the fastest ways to get there.

Part IV: You're Halfway There (2Ls and 3Ls)

As all veteran law students know, the first year the professors "scare you to death," but during the second and third years, you already have a firm handle on the Socratic Method and how to navigate your classes with ease, so your energies turn to other things, such as choosing the best electives and extracurriculars. This part explains the best ways to make the most of your upper-class years.

Part V: Preparing for Your Future

Why is searching for a job (both summer and permanent) such an integral part of law school? These chapters tell the story. Regardless of whether you're more interested in a job at a traditional law firm or you prefer something more outside the box, this part contains all you need to know about finding and keeping the summer and permanent jobs of your dreams.

Part VI: Wrapping Up Your Law School Career

All good things must come to an end, and so will your three (or four) years of law school. But more fun is in store for you! Studying for the bar exam and getting through that last semester will be foremost on your mind, so I explain what you need to know to conquer both with style.

Part VII: The Part of Tens

This part consists of great law school party trivia and useful resources I wish I had known about sooner. Here, I list the ten best and worst things about law school, ten little-known law school secrets, and (more than) ten invaluable resources (hey, I couldn't resist).

Icons Used in This Book

If you're at all familiar with *Dummies* books, or you've skimmed through this book while debating whether to buy it, you probably noticed the charming little icons interspersed throughout the margins (why can't casebooks adopt these?). Here's the lowdown on what they mean:

This icon indicates juicy, hard-to-find advice from a seasoned upperclassman. Socrates would be proud!

When I draw attention to something that can be unfair to law students or negatively affect your law school experience, I use this icon.

Far be it for me to know something about *every* last aspect of law school; when I use this icon, I call upon the wise words of lawyers, professors, career counselors, admissions deans, and other law students, who provide you with advice straight from the horse's mouth.

When I want to reinforce practical or timesaving advice about the law school experience, I use this icon.

If you remember nothing else from this book, this icon signals an important tidbit to file away in your brain.

When I discuss an aspect of law school that can potentially reach out and bite you (an unequivocal tort), I use this icon. I also use it to point out things that may be dangerous to your GPA, social life, or wallet.

Where to Go from Here

By purchasing this book, you've taken an important step toward ensuring your success in law school. But where do you start? If you're still considering law school or you're in the midst of applying, start with Part I. If you've already passed this milestone and you're about to start your almighty first year, go straight to Part II. And if you're in over your head with all the work you have to do . . . start with The Part of Tens for a good chuckle. Go ahead and dog-ear the pages to your heart's content. That's what this book is for.

Part I

Considering Law School

The 5th Wave · By Rich Tennant

"Oh sure, my sister expects to get into any law school she wants. After all, she graduated from college, summa cum la-di-da."

In this part . . .

Deciding to go to law school is a big decision. In this part, you find out what the pros and cons are and who your fellow classmates may be. I clue you in on important considerations in choosing a law school and tell you how to wow admissions committees with your overall presentation.

Chapter 1

Exploring the Realities of Law School

Never before has a time been more popular for being a law student! Law school applications are up significantly, and law school seems to be the "in" thing to do across the country, regardless of whether you're a graduating college senior or a middle-aged career-changer. If you're looking to take that first step on the intellectual journey of a lifetime, now is prime time for doing it. At first, everything about law school can seem intimidating and intense, but rest assured that this chapter starts you out on the right path by offering an overview of the entire law school experience.

Demystifying the Law School Experience

Many prelaw students are confused about what law school entails, because they may not know anyone who's in or been through the experience (I surely didn't when I applied). So, in this section, I fill you in on exactly what you can expect as a new *1L* (first-year law student).

Preparing for three (or four) years of blood, sweat, and tears

No one denies that law school is a lot of work. You have three (or four, if you're a part-time or evening law student) years of challenging classes, approximately 100 pages of reading every night, and only one exam at the end of each class that determines your entire grade. On top of the academic load are time-consuming extracurricular activities, such as the law review or a law journal, moot court, and the myriad other organizations you can join (see Chapter 13 for complete details about law school extracurriculars).

And in your free time (who said anything about free time?), you'll be expected to send out résumés and cover letters while prospecting for your 1L and 2L summer jobs (see Chapter 14) and postgraduation permanent job (see Chapters 15, 16, and 17). Sound rough? It can be, but if you're up for it, law school can be one of the most rewarding experiences of your life.

Dealing with the law school setup

If one term were to describe how the law school experience is set up, it's "high school." With all your classes in one building, assigned seats, suddenly having lockers again, and the amount of gossip that spreads like wildfire, I'd have to say that high school is definitely an apt description.

Your first-year law school class is divided into sections, and you attend all your classes as a 1L with the same people. That can become trying when you have several *gunners* (people who constantly raise their hands, usually just to hear themselves talk) in your class. In time, however, you may grow to appreciate the comforting feeling of seeing the same faces, especially when it comes time to speak in front of 100 of them!

Surviving the Socratic Method

One of the horror stories you've heard about law school is true: Professors really do call on you in front of the entire class. The intense questioning that professors direct toward students is referred to as the *Socratic Method,* because Socrates (that famous Greek philosopher dude way back when) apparently liked to elucidate the responses of his students by asking them more and more questions rather than by providing answers.

The very thought of the Socratic Method petrifies most prelaw students (it sure had me jittery), because they're so unaccustomed to the idea. No college class that I ever heard of (or took) requires you to engage in a one-on-one interrogation session with a professor and sometimes even while you're standing up. Fortunately, by the 2L and 3L years, many professors tend to ease off the Socratic Method; courses are often taught in lecture or discussion format (see Chapter 8 to find out why).

But the Socratic Method does require you to really know your material; otherwise, you'll be embarrassed in front of the class while stumbling around for even a hint of the right answer. It also requires you to think quickly and challenge your previously held assumptions. Overall, I think the Socratic experience was a beneficial one for me. Although at the time it may have caused a few ulcers, in hindsight, it made me more comfortable about speaking in front of an audience (the class) and more appreciative of the verbal jockeying that lawyers do in the courtroom.

Thinking like a lawyer

The whole point of law school is training you in the fine art of problem solving and legal reasoning. Lawyers are said to look at problems differently than lay people. When lawyers hear someone talking about an incident, they listen for the ordering of facts and try to discern the precise issue without getting caught up in insignificant details.

The concept of *thinking like a lawyer* (see Chapter 8) is a subtle change that comes over you most likely at the end of your first semester or first year. Some law students swear that it's never happened to them, but your non–law school friends and family are likely to be the better judges of that. Listen closely to their comments after your first year. Do you find them saying things like, "You're so much more analytical or logical than you used to be"? Or, do you find yourself thinking about everyday situations like a banana peel lying on the floor of a supermarket just a little differently than you did before law school? If so, you'll know that thinking like a lawyer has begun to take hold.

Assessing Whether You Can Make It in Law School

At a minimum, you need to have a love for learning and a penchant for studying — plenty of studying — to succeed in law school. In addition, successful law students

- Manage their time effectively
- Don't succumb to procrastination
- Are strong writers (or willing to put in the time to improve)
- Get reading done in a timely manner
- Prepare for each day's class
- Juggle multiple tasks simultaneously
- Sometimes delay gratification (In other words, they put off going out for the evening to spend extra time getting their criminal law outline in better shape.)

Similarly, they (meaning full-timers) can put in time on an extracurricular activity like moot court or a law journal (see Chapter 13) without sacrificing the quality of their schoolwork. Extracurricular activities like these aren't required, but come highly recommended because they're great preparation for legal jobs.

Going part time versus full time

If you need to work full time to support yourself, avoid excessive post-law school debt, or pay tuition, you can consider opting to go to law school in the evenings or part time during the day. Most part-time and evening programs run four years, instead of the traditional three.

Part-time law students face challenges that their full-time peers don't. Part-time students need to make sure they have enough time to handle the often-overwhelming responsibilities of school, full-time work, and household and family responsibilities. Often, they have their hands too full to participate in some of the traditional extracurricular activities, such as law reviews/law journals and moot court.

Evaluating your study skills

Law school, like most other graduate programs, requires you to really buckle down and study. But studying in law school doesn't mean the kind of last-minute studying that may have worked well for you in college. Studying for law school classes is more of a little-bit-each-day-of-the-semester sort of studying that keeps you up to speed (prevents you from falling behind) and that enables you to absorb as much information as possible.

If you don't already have these kinds of study skills, you need to gain them quickly before law school starts; otherwise, you'll find yourself struggling to keep up. See Chapter 9 for some hints on developing successful law school study skills.

Managing the pressure

Being completely stress-free in law school is next to impossible (but see Chapter 7 for tips on not "sweating the small stuff" too much). If you're not looking for a summer job, you're worrying about your note (student article) for the law journal or finishing up your corporations outline (see Chapter 9 for more about creating outlines). On top of that, the pressure of one exam (see Chapter 11) determining your entire grade can become unbearable toward the end of the semester, when the stress *really* piles on.

Gaining a good sense of time management before entering law school is your best protection against this disabling kind of stress, because the pressure is constant while you're in law school.

Considering Other Important Factors before Deciding on Law School

Enrolling in law school isn't something that you can do on a whim (or because you don't know what else to do with your college degree). You must take into account whether spending three (or four) years of your life (and a bunch of money) engaged in the study of a discipline that realistically may not land you the job of your dreams right off the bat is really worth it.

Doing your research as a prelaw student is key. Talk to as many people — law students, lawyers, and law professors — involved in the law as you can. Actually go to a law school or two and sit in on some classes. Do you like what you hear? Do some job shadowing and/or informational interviewing (see Chapters 15 and 16). Find out what your hosts like and dislike about law school or their careers. Only by being armed with as much information as possible will you be able to make a well-informed decision.

Taking a hard look at your financial situation

While attending law school, not only are you faced with around $25,000 in tuition each year (depending on the school) but also with additional amounts for living expenses. You may even be faced with the costs (in time and effort and money) of moving to a new city, finding a new job for your spouse, or losing out on three years of traditional income.

Law school is certainly a financial sacrifice, but that sacrifice is mitigated when you're committed to taking advantage of the benefits of a legal education, including potential upward mobility, qualification for a broader range of jobs, and (sometimes) greater income.

Critiquing your reasons for becoming a lawyer

Because of the way many movies and TV shows portray lawyers, many people think all lawyers live glamorous, jet-setting lives. But the truth is that most lawyers fresh out of school earn what some people with bachelor's degrees make. The National Association for Law Placement (NALP) found that the median starting salary of J.D.s from the class of 2001 in legal jobs was $55,000. Also remember to factor in lost earning potential during the three years of school (for full-time students) and tuition and living expenses.

In addition, keep in mind that gigantic, posh law firms aren't where the majority of U.S. lawyers find work. Instead, many lawyers are employed by firms with fewer than 10 attorneys, in solo practice, or with the government (see Chapter 15 for a rundown of all the settings in which you can practice law). And many prelaw students don't realize that large student loans often preclude new graduates from taking lower-paying jobs they'd really like, in favor of the ones that will help with loan repayment.

That's why you need to make sure that a sky-high salary isn't your only motivation for wanting to enter law school (of course, that salary may come eventually, after years in practice). Identify the other reasons, such as your love of advocacy, desire to truly help people, or interest in a particular practice area that are driving your decisions.

When you think about why you want to enter the law, base your reasoning on your observations of real lawyers engaged in their typical everyday low-profile work and not on high-profile cases that come around only once in a great while.

Identifying who's really behind your decision to go

The decision to attend law school needs to be yours, and yours alone. You don't need to give in because of a persuasive parent, because all your friends are doing it, or because it's a respectable profession in society's eyes. Instead, you must have your own reasons for pursuing a career in the law that have nothing to do with anyone else's opinions. All too many law students are unhappy in law school mostly because they went into it for the wrong reasons. Make sure you're not one of these people; otherwise, you're in for a long and depressing three (or four) years.

Glimpsing the Law School Experience Year by Year

Traditional law school is three years long (longer for part-timers), made up of the first, second, and third years, each with its own particular characteristics. However, the 1L curriculum is pretty much the same across the board at all law schools.

First year: They scare you to death

The notion of scaring you to death comes from an old law school saw based on the terror that grips many 1Ls regarding the sheer amount of work they need to do and the fear of being grilled in the Socratic Method. Getting used to the workload, the professors' interrogations, and the single-exam format takes some time and effort. See Chapter 5 for some great hints to help you ease into your first year.

Second year: They work you to death

Your second year is often considered the hardest because you have many different commitments competing for your valuable time. You not only have your coursework to deal with, but you're also engaged in the long and involved process of finding a summer job in the legal profession (see Chapter 14). In addition, you'll probably be working on a law journal, law review, moot court, or other extracurricular involvements (see Chapter 13), which take up most of your spare time (part-timers may not have the time for extracurriculars).

Third year: They bore you to death

The third year is often the easiest, because by then you're an old-hand; you know what you need to do to get by, and you may not even care that much about hammering away at your studies when you already have a job offer in hand. More often, 3Ls are more occupied with their school-year part-time jobs at law firms or other legal organizations and job-hunting for postgraduation jobs than they are with doing the reading for class. With graduation (see Chapter 19) and the bar exam (see Chapter 18) right around the corner, they want to savor their last year of studenthood before moving out into the real world!

Charting the Law School Course

You pass through many milestones during law school, ranging from the first time you're called on in class to finding a summer job. Each one is important in your development as a future lawyer and each has its own triumphs and tribulations along the way.

Choosing an area of practice

Some but not all law students choose an area of practice, such as tax, intellectual property, or corporate law, to informally specialize in during law school. This informal specialization means they take lots of courses in these areas, work summer or part-time jobs in these fields, and generally try to get as much experience as possible. The purpose of doing so is to figure out whether they'd enjoy actually specializing in that area in legal practice (see Chapter 16 for more information about various practice areas).

Law schools don't require any sort of formal specialization (you typically don't graduate with a J.D. in a specialty or "major" unless you're involved in a certificate program [see Chapter 3], which some schools offer), but if you know early on what you'd like to go into, building up a résumé in that area as soon as possible never hurts.

Landing a summer job

You'll have two summers in law school — your 1L summer and 2L summer. Of these two, the job that you find for your 2L summer is by far more important, because it's the job that sometimes leads to a permanent offer of employment (particularly at firms). See Chapter 14 for detailed information about the summer job search.

What you do during your 1L summer is not as important, but getting *some* experience in a volunteer position (often for course credit) with a court or nonprofit or governmental organization is common. Part-time students may have a difficult decision regarding whether to switch from their current full-time position to something else in order to get the necessary legal summer job experience.

Searching for a postgraduation job

Finding any type of job that fits your personality and tastes takes time, particularly in a tight legal job market. Although graduating 3Ls without a job offer in hand may feel a lot of stress, with the right attitude and a good dose of patience, job leads should soon start heading your way. In Chapter 15, I point you in the right direction toward job-searching success and let you in on a variety of job-search tips. In short, persistence and a willingness to tell everyone you meet that you're looking for work are keys to landing a great job, whether legal or nontraditional (see Chapter 17 for more on nontraditional jobs).

Passing the bar with flying colors

Becoming a practicing attorney means that you must take and pass the bar exam in the state where you want to practice law. The exam, which is offered in July and February, typically is a two-day affair and varies in difficulty from state to state. Generally, you study for the bar exam, beginning right after you graduate from law school until the day of the test. If you don't pass on the first try, it varies from state to state on how many additional times you can take the exam before that particular state disqualifies you. See Chapter 18 for a complete discussion of the bar exam.

The bar exam isn't something to stress out extensively about (I know, that's easier said than done). But the truth is that most students pass the first time. Taking a bar review course (see Chapter 18) and diligently studying its material can make a huge difference in your confidence levels come test time.

Graduating and preparing for your life as a lawyer

Even when you graduate, your work is far from over. In your job, you need to spend your first few years extensively learning the trade, putting in long hours, and attending continuing legal education seminars. Your life as a lawyer may not always be easy, but it usually is intellectually stimulating and very fulfilling!

Chapter 2

Appreciating Diversity in Your Law School Class

. . . .

In This Chapter

▶ Recognizing different motivations for attending law school

▶ Understanding today's law school demographics

▶ Embracing diversity in your midst

. . . .

Characterizing law school as different from any other type of education you've undertaken isn't hard to comprehend. But did you also know that your fellow students may be a far more diverse and interesting crowd than any other student body you've encountered? Some new first-year law school students (1Ls) walk into orientation amazed to discover just how varied the backgrounds of their classmates are. If you're coming straight out of college, facing this kind of diversity can be a major reality check (particularly when you're in a part-time or evening program). When you're used to being in an undergraduate environment where everyone is 18 to 23 years old, the idea of sitting in classrooms with older students who have families of their own or high-powered careers can take some getting used to.

Exactly what types of students make up today's law school classes? You'll find 55-year-old grandmothers taking a civil procedure class with joint J.D./M.B.A. (dual degree students in the Juris Doctor and Master of Business Administration programs) students. You'll discover people embarking on second careers sitting next to fresh-faced, straight-from-college 1Ls, and everyone in between. This hodgepodge of people with diverse backgrounds makes for a challenging and stimulating classroom environment. Just ask anyone who's ever had a former police officer in her criminal procedure class. In this chapter, I discuss the many different peers you can expect to encounter during your years as a law student. Then I explore in detail how you can make the most of your experiences interacting with such a diverse student body.

Everyone Goes to Law School for Different Reasons

Classroom diversity is much more than racial and ethnic differences. A big part of the diversity you encounter in law school is the differing motivations of your peers for entering law school in the first place. For example, think about your own reasons and motivations for going to law school. Maybe you were like me and just didn't know what else to do with yourself. Perhaps your parents coerced you into it or you came from a family of lawyers and law school was the next logical step. Maybe your mission is more of a noble one: You want to use your law degree to help people whose voices can't be heard. Or maybe you're passionate about a particular cause, such as civil rights or the environment, and want to make a difference in the world. Whatever your reasons for choosing a career in the law, I'll bet they differ from those of the student in the seat next to you.

During your first few weeks of law school, take a few moments to meet the people sitting near you in class (before the realities of law school cliques set in). Talk to them about why they came to law school; you'll likely gain a whole new appreciation for the differences — and similarities — between people's motivations for pursuing a J.D.

Changing Times, Changing Demographics

A recent study, "Diversity and Legal Education: Student Experiences in Leading Law Schools," by Gary Orfield and Dean Whitla (and published in *Diversity Challenged* [Harvard Education Publishing Group: 2001] and released by the Civil Rights Project at Harvard University), found that 69.3 percent of Harvard Law Students and 73.5 percent of Michigan law students reported a "clearly positive" impact of racial and ethnic diversity on the quality of their law school educational experience. This study is evidence of the positive impacts that a diverse ethnic and cultural class brings.

In fact, gender and age diversity of the student body is an area where law schools often outshine other types of graduate education. Unlike top business schools, which sometimes have a female participation rate of only 30 percent, law school recently has become a 50-50 endeavor. And unlike medical school, which usually has only a small percentage of students older than 30, in law school, you're almost as likely to find study groups of 35-year-olds as you are of 23-year-olds. Additionally, many law schools have LL.M. (Master of Laws) programs for international students, and these students often audit courses with the J.D. students, which adds another unique viewpoint.

LEGAL EAGLE

My, how times have changed

Alan Dershowitz, a prolific author and professor of law at Harvard University, says that no one today would recognize a late '50s, early '60s law school classroom. The students — virtually all white and all male — generally wore suits and ties. They came to the classroom with open minds, open ears, and open eyes. They were like sieves waiting to be filled with the professors' knowledge — those great men in front of a classroom.

By contrast, he says, today's students are fully formed political and ideological beings. They know what they want out of life, and they know where they stand on the important issues of the day. They want to find out how to be good lawyers from their professors, but they don't want to be told how to live their lives. Dershowitz says the two changes are related. The increasing diversity of the student body and faculty have made it clear that law school students and teachers are different people with different values and that limits exist to what teachers can teach and students can learn from teachers. Much more learning these days is from student to student and less from teacher to student. That, too, he says, is a healthy development.

Providing perspective: Older students

Law school is a little like a traditional workplace in the sense that you interact with people of all ages. For the first time in your academic life, some of your peers are old enough to be your parents or even grandparents.

The time that the older students have spent away from the classroom can clarify their focus for attending law school, because they often have family or career commitments that make the decision to go to law school more weighty than for some younger students. When you have to leave an established career or do without the income to which you've been accustomed to pay for law school, you're making more sacrifices than a student straight out of college. Older students also tend to know what they want to accomplish because they've had the opportunity to sample the working world and discover their likes and dislikes about it. On the other hand, this time away also presents unique drawbacks for the older student, such as getting back into the swing of studying and finding the right balance between schoolwork and social life.

Capitalizing on previous job experience

If you've ever had a job with real deadlines, bosses, and two weeks vacation a year, you know that you learn pretty fast what you need to do to get by. That means figuring out how you can best accomplish what you need to do, when you're most and least productive, and how much you can do without burning out. These same traits bode well with the law school experience, and older students exhibiting many of these traits are worth emulating.

Older students (and particularly part-time and evening students), in general, handle tight deadlines and stressful situations that law school presents, because they've already "been there, done that" in their jobs and other experiences. Because they bring more maturity and experience to their studies, they're better equipped to take law school in stride. They're often not as shocked by the required workload, and as such, perhaps don't encounter as many setbacks and disappointments as 22-year-old 1Ls. So, when you hear them saying things like, "It's just a first semester exam; what's the big deal?" while you're biting your nails down to the quick, you'll appreciate their "don't sweat the small stuff" perspective (even if you can't quite imitate it).

Self-awareness also comes in handy when selecting your area of practice. From their on-the-job experiences, older students may realize valuable personal preferences such as their disdain for working in teams or, conversely, their penchant for research and writing or their passion for public speaking. Likewise, an older student's previous occupation, whether pilot or consultant, can help them choose an appropriate specialty, such as aviation law or a corporate practice. As a younger student, who hasn't had the opportunity to see what you're suited for in the real world, these choices may be harder to make. Harder, but certainly not impossible.

Getting back into the academic groove

Of course, being away from a school environment for many years can have its disadvantages. Getting back into the habit of studying and burning the midnight oil (keeping the irregular hours of a student) can be jarring, difficult, and something that older students may have forgotten about, especially when you're used to going home at 5 p.m. and not worrying about the obligations of your job until the next morning.

Many schools have student organizations that are tailor-made for older law students. For example, the OWLS (Older and Wiser Law Students) at my law school (and many others) is a group that meets regularly to talk about study skills, deal with life as an older student, and discuss how to parlay your former career into a legal one. To find out more about joining (or starting) your school's OWLS club, attend the student organizations fair (see Chapter 13) that usually takes place each fall semester or contact your dean of students. You can also check out the helpful Web site, NonTradLAW.com (www. nontradlaw.com), which is especially helpful for nontraditional prelaw students.

Balancing law school and family

Because law school alone is at times almost like having a full-time job, balancing it with a full-time job (for part-time and evening law students) and/or the demands of a family can be difficult, but that's to be expected in any type of professional program. For most single, straight-from-college students, however, this problem doesn't register. You come home after class, feed your goldfish, and head out for a night of studying or partying without giving a second thought to the needs of a spouse or child. For older students with a family life, however, maintaining this delicate balance between work and family responsibilities can be hard.

Students with infants or small children often find law school particularly rough. If an exam is coming up, explaining to your 4-year-old daughter why you can't play with her or why you need to study so much isn't easy. Having a partner or friend who helps you out during particularly stressful times is ideal. Otherwise, you can seek out other law students with children with whom you can form a playgroup and share responsibilities so that each of you has a chance to study undistracted for a few hours everyday or on the weekends.

Gay and lesbian students

If you're a lesbian, gay, bisexual, or transgendered (LGBT) prelaw student, you may have questions about whether you'll find a welcoming environment at your law school. In any educational institution, like any workplace or religious organization, some people simply are intolerant of nonmainstream viewpoints and preferences. That's just the way life is. At most law schools, however, LGBT students will likely find the majority of their peers and faculty welcoming and supportive. Still, you may wonder whether you'll encounter such support at the law schools you're considering. As you investigate schools, therefore, you may want to consider the following issues:

✔ **Deciding whether to be "out" in your application.** Of course, this decision is a highly charged and personal. You may want to just "be yourself" on your application, especially when your sexual orientation has a direct link with your desire to attend law school or practice law. Or you may decide that although your orientation is part of who you are, it isn't an important aspect of the law school admissions process. Whichever you decide is up to you.

✔ **Identifying schools that *are* LGBT supportive.** One way to judge the atmosphere of a law school is to inquire whether an LGBT student organization is active at the school, how many people are members, and what sort of activities or speakers the group presents. If it appears to be a thriving organization, it can be your best source for discovering the culture of a particular school and identifying openly gay or supportive straight faculty members who can answer your additional questions. Don't stop with the law school; however, check to see what organizations, if any, are available at the general university (if your law school has one).

Besides an LGBT organization at the law school, find out whether other thriving organizations seem to be supportive of diversity in general? If so, that gives you an idea as to the nature of the welcoming — or not — environment you'll encounter.

An excellent resource for prelaw LGBT students can be found on the Law School Admission Council's Web site, at (www.lsac.org/LSAC.asp?url=lsac/information-gay-lesbian-bisexual-applicants.asp). There, you can find results of a survey of law schools regarding five questions of importance to LGBT students, including whether the school has openly LGBT faculty and whether the school has a LGBT student organization, among others. LGBT law students can also go to The National Lesbian and Gay Law Association Web site at www.nlgla.org to take advantage of many resources for LGBT students (including the NLGLA Law Student Division electronic mailing list) and lawyers.

Students with disabilities

Law students with disabilities have conditions ranging from chronic health problems to blindness, deafness, and paralysis, and if you're a student with one or more disabilities, you're far from alone. Plenty of students with disabilities thrive in law school. The 1990 federal Americans with Disabilities Act requires law schools to make *reasonable* (determined on a case-by-case basis by your law school) *accommodations* for students who have disabilities. The disabilities covered under that law include any physical or mental impairment that substantially limits one or more major life activities.

Providing reasonable legal accommodations is your law school's responsibility to ensure that you're on equal footing with the rest of your peers, such as a special room for taking exams, the development of exams in a special way (such as enlarged print or read aloud), dictation equipment, special lighting in exam rooms, and extra time on exams, among others. The disabled student doesn't pay anything for reasonable accommodations.

If you're a disabled law student, you may have many questions about whether your law school can accommodate your disability, including:

- ✓ **When should I discuss my disability with the law schools I'm considering?** Many disabled law students simply wait until they've been accepted to speak with the dean of students, or they may alternatively mention their disabilities in their application.

- ✓ **What kind of medical documentation do I need to secure the accommodations I need?** Again, talk with your dean of students to get specific guidelines, but generally the more apparent the disability (like blindness), the less documentation you need.

- ✓ **How will the law school handle my accommodation requests?** Talking to the dean of students is the best way to find out whether the law school is able to accommodate you, or you can pose your questions to the university or law school's office of disability services. Discussing these matters well as soon as you're accepted is the best way to ensure that everything will be in place for your start date.

For example, Jen Weber, a 3L with cystic fibrosis at Indiana University School of Law in Bloomington, had trouble finding a job after college that was flexible enough to accommodate her frequent hospitalizations. She felt that a law career would enable her to be an advocate and still offer a degree of flexibility that she hadn't found in other careers. She entered law school at age 27, and met with deans to discuss her need to miss class frequently and to ask how accommodating professors would be toward her absences. Mainly concerned about fatigue and stamina issues, because she wasn't breathing properly, she found the law school to be extremely accommodating, allowing her to take exams in a separate room, to videotape lectures when she had to miss class, and to keep an oxygen tank at the school. Although her law school years weren't illness-free, she believes that her excellent time-management skills have enabled her to take advantage of her highest-energy times and get her schoolwork done efficiently.

Disabled students may want to look into the American Bar Association (ABA) Commission on Mental and Physical Disability Law (www.abanet.org/disability), where you can find the latest disability law news, research scholarship opportunities for law students with disabilities, and engage in a mentorship program for disabled law students that pairs you with disabled lawyers.

Part-time and evening students

Law school is time-consuming enough for a full-time day student. Students who go to school full time are in class only 12 to 16 hours per week, but they complain that they don't have enough time for the recommended standard of studying two hours for every one hour of time spent in class. For those who choose the commendable task of going part time or in the evening, the academic challenges are upped tenfold. Imagine working at your job 40 or more hours per week, and then going to class afterward four (or five) nights a week for two to three hours per night. When would you study — let alone cook, clean house, mow the grass, run errands, do the laundry, or walk the dog? A social life? Not on your life. Add a spouse or kids to the mix and what you have is Super Law Student!

Going to school part time or in the evening is undeniably more stressful than going full time during the day. The biggest questions you need to ask yourself when considering being a part-timer or evening student are

- ✔ Will I have enough time to attend to my studies?

- ✔ Do I have help to assist me with family responsibilities (such as a babysitter if you have young children)?

- ✔ Can I get the crucial on-the-job legal experience that I need for when I apply for jobs (see Chapters 14 and 15 for ways to deal with this)?

If you have well–thought out, positive answers to these questions, and are willing to complete school in four years, instead of the usual three, read on.

Juggling full-time work and law school

Discipline is key for any part-time or evening law student. Juggling work and school means that your time management system has to be top-notch. In other words, when other people are relaxing on weekends, you need to be studying or cleaning up your apartment. On the other hand, you're less likely to procrastinate when you're dealing with more that has to be done (multiple responsibilities), which, in turn, heightens the possibility that you'll excel in your studies. Part-time and evening students also tend to know more about what they're getting into, because they've conscientiously considered the consequences and decided to make the massive commitment to handling work and school. They usually enter law school with more realistic expectations.

On the plus side, many part-time and evening students report that their peers tend to be less competitive than the full-time day students, and thus more willing to help each other out. This can be crucial when you need to miss class for work-related responsibilities and want to borrow a classmate's notes.

Making time for extracurricular activities

As a part-time or evening student, most of your nonwork time is spent studying or taking care of errands. But some students manage to fit in an extracurricular activity or two on top of their already full plates, although some extracurricular activities just may not be feasible (such as committing to a journal, see Chapter 13).

Although adding more activities to your already full week may seem like the last thing you need, these activities can show employers that you're serious about practicing a particular area of the law or that you have an outstanding level of advocacy or legal writing skills, particularly when it's impossible for you to get legal experience during your law school years because of your commitment to your full-time job. Figure out what you have time for and, accordingly, try to incorporate it into your schedule.

Multicultural students

Multiculturalism is a big buzzword in America today. Everywhere you look, interacting with people of varied backgrounds is encouraged and celebrated. And that's no less the case in law school. Law schools, in fact, work hard to ensure that the educational experience is as strong as it can be for everyone.

When you combine people of different perspectives and backgrounds, your classroom environment is a much more stimulating and interesting place than if it was homogeneous. Although few people dispute that bringing diverse perspectives to the classroom is an unequivocal benefit for all involved, minorities may face a harder time adjusting to law school life than their majority peers. Here is a breakdown of some reasons why:

✔ Not many minority faculty teach in law schools, so finding role models is more difficult for minority students. In fact, the ABA reported that in 2001 only 837 out of 6,009 full-time law school faculty were minorities.

✔ Because only a small percentage of minorities attend most law schools, these students endure a period of adjustment and orientation to law school that their majority peers may not have to because they have a larger support group.

What can you do to ease your transition to law school as much as possible?

✔ **Choose law schools with supportive atmospheres, which you can judge by the existence and vibrancy of multiple minority organizations.** In addition, chat with minority faculty to get the inside scoop on the atmosphere at their law school.

✔ **Find mentors.** Your law school's minority organizations may help you set these up or contact the career services office (CSO) to get in touch with minority alums from your school.

✔ **Work to develop as many relationships with people at the law school as you can — not just other students but also faculty and staff from all backgrounds.** Getting as much information and knowledge about what law school entails as you can is the best way to succeed.

Check out the ABA's Commission on Racial and Ethnic Diversity in the Profession at (www.abanet.org/minorities/links/students.html# anchor-general-60262) for comprehensive information for students about minority organizations and scholarships, and other related information. Bookmark The National Bar Association, an association for black lawyers and judges at (www.nationalbar.org), The Hispanic National Bar Association (www.hnba.com), and The National Asian Pacific American Bar Association (www.napaba.org).

Beating the odds: A 62-year-old grandmother successfully tackles law school

Anita Rufus, a 62-year-old law student at California Western School of Law in San Diego, cites a life-changing line from an old movie as the driving force that inspired her to earn her J.D. In this particular movie, a middle-aged woman announces she's going back to school but is told by her unsympathetic spouse: "You'll be 60 before you graduate." She retorts back: "I'll be 60 anyway." Anita's unfailing motivation to achieve her dreams, without regard to age, has served her well throughout her life and her years in law school.

Anita, who graduates in December 2003 and plans to take California's February 2004 bar exam, decided to go to law school because she'd always been interested in politics, civil rights, and people-oriented issues. But the mother of twins and grandmother of five first needed to complete her bachelor's degree at the University of Redlands, graduating with a 4.0 GPA in 2000. Then, she applied to Cal Western, her first choice school, and got a generous scholarship. Anita decided to complete her degree part time, so that she could simultaneously maintain a personal life and spend time with her husband, who she says has been wonderfully supportive of all her law school endeavors. "I didn't want my life to be only about law school," she says.

Anita doesn't deny that law school has been more challenging than she originally expected, but she wouldn't have it any other way. Although she says the difficulty of law school work is definitely humbling, she tries to get as much as she can out of every class, instead of playing the competition game and focusing solely on grades. She says that one of the hardest parts about being in such a demanding program is that her memory isn't what it used to be, and she finds the tedious studying necessary to prepare for finals difficult. However, Anita clearly relishes studying the law. "A lot of the younger students understandably just want to get through law school and get a job. But that's not my perspective at all. I enjoy the law and want to explore how it relates to a broader realm of issues," she says. And she's done well, earning the highest grade in two of her classes, making Dean's List one quarter, and coming in second in her school's Gill Moot Court competition.

Anita says that another benefit of being a non-traditional student is that unlike many of her younger classmates, her broad range of life experiences more easily enables her to not sweat the small stuff. Her background includes a run for Congress, an award-winning radio talk show, her own secretarial and advertising service, and she was a cofounder of a highly successful telecommunications business (now known through a series of mergers as Sprint). Her extensive and varied real-world experience has enabled her to bring a perspective to classroom discussions that younger students don't have. She's also much more willing to ask questions and challenge professors than most of her fellow students. For example, she's had many younger students come up to her after class and say, "I really appreciated the questions you asked." Anita says that some of them are afraid to raise their hands, because they don't have as much experience challenging things, and they benefit from such role models.

Despite her already-busy schedule, Anita has found time to get involved with several organizations on campus. She has always been involved in activism and politics, but during the first two years of law school she avoided getting involved in anything because she wanted to devote herself fully to her schoolwork.

Entering her third year, however, she joined her school's public-interest law foundation, the women's law caucus, the local county bar association, and a local female lawyer's group. Her goal is to network in the local legal community and open doors toward what she wants to accomplish.

Anita plans to work in mediation after law school, which she says fits very well with her background in business. She's also very interested in constitutional law — particularly human rights, separation of church and state, and free speech. As for searching for jobs, she says she's not interested in associating with a firm: "I'm too old to worry about sitting in a back room doing research," but she is interested in part-time contract work in mediation or working with the American Civil Liberties Union (ACLU).

She'd really love to get back on the radio and find a way to combine politics and the law in a radio show. Although she isn't 100 percent clear about exactly what she'll end up doing, Anita says working with the issues she cares about and making a difference is all leading in a common direction.

What's next for Anita? This spunky lady doesn't sit still for long. After graduating with her J.D., she plans to get her Ph.D. at the University of California–San Diego in legal sociology, work part time in mediation, and get started on a book she's been itching to write. One overriding theme she's discovered in her successful law school endeavors: It's never too late. "If I did it, so can you. However hard you think it is, remember: The time is going to pass anyway, so you may as well end up a lawyer!"

Chapter 3

Choosing the Best Law School for You

In This Chapter

▶ Deciding which law school is best for your personality type

▶ Considering how many reaches, likelies, and safety schools to apply to

▶ Knowing what law school qualities to consider

▶ Making the most of your law school visit

A good law school isn't necessarily among the most prestigious in the country, located in a bustling metropolitan city, or endowed with a library bursting at the seams. Instead, a good law school is one that fits *your* individualized needs and is a place where you feel most comfortable and enthusiastic about studying the law. So how do you find out about what schools are the best match for your personality, budget, and geographical considerations? In this chapter, I cover the most important law school qualities that you need to consider before making your decision. By using the information here, you can visit the law schools and evaluate their qualities with an informed and inquisitive eye.

Deciding Whether You Want to Be a Big or Small Fish in the Law School Pond

One question that's important to ask yourself in choosing a law school is: Would you rather be a big fish in a small pond, or a small fish in a big pond? Many people who prefer the latter like the resources and opportunities available at a really prestigious law school, but they don't mind that they don't really shine there. Others prefer to be the big fish at a not-quite-as well-ranked school, where they can make the law review (see Chapter 13) or top 10 percent of the class with relative ease.

Harold Davis, Jr., an intellectual property lawyer at Katten, Muchin, Zavis, Rosenman in Chicago, didn't really consider the big fish/small fish dichotomy when choosing a law school. He just wanted to be *next* to the pond. He went to a relatively regional law school — the University of Miami — but his choice of a school dealt mainly with its proximity to South Beach. He loves Miami's warm weather, and thought, "If I have to deal with all the stress of law school, I may as well be able to study torts by the beach." Now, however, Davis prefers being the small fish in a big pond. This role gives him a platform from which to challenge himself and do better, which is exactly the situation he's now in as an associate at a large, national firm in Chicago. He also notes, the likelihood of getting eaten alive in a turbulent economy is less now that he's "part of a bigger fish in the school of sharks."

Making Sense of Reach Schools, Likelies, and Safeties

The competition for law school always is stiff, but in lean economic years, it often becomes even stiffer. Blame the poor economy for the increase in competition or simply the growing interest in law as a career field. Whatever the reason for the increase in applicants, having more *safeties* and *likelies* is even more important now than it was in the past. Here's a breakdown of the three types of law schools.

✔ A *reach school* is a school you'd love to go to (a dream school), but your qualifications are lower than those in its median range (which you can find out by looking at its Web site or browsing its admissions materials). For instance, if you have a 152 LSAT and a 3.4 grade-point average (GPA), and you're applying to a school with a 165–175 LSAT range and 3.6–4.0 GPA range, this school falls into your *reach* category. In other words, you're not at all sure whether you'd get in, but you want to give it a try. Reaches are great goals to strive for, and almost everyone has some dream schools that they long to go to. No matter how much of a long shot your dream school may be (Harvard, here you come!), apply anyway. You never know when that school may need another philosophy major/debating champion/resident of South Dakota type. They may be looking for someone just like you!

✔ A *likely* is just that — it's pretty darn likely that you'll be accepted. That's because your credentials are smack dab in the middle of the school's range — or are a tad higher or lower. You may also have some other overriding factor that makes it likely that you'll get in, such as it's a state school and you're a resident. Apply to as many likelies as you can, because that way you'll have a better selection when you begin receiving letters of acceptance.

> ✔ A *safety* is a school where your credentials are much higher than its
> range. You know you're a shoo-in, unless your clone has also just been
> accepted. Even if you're not too keen on ever going to your safeties,
> apply anyway — after all, who knows when your likelies will fall
> through? You don't want to be up a creek without a safety.

Many students wonder how many schools in each of the three categories
they need apply to. Generally, most applicants apply to an average of eight
schools total. Your strategy may be to apply to two reach schools, three
safeties, and three likelies. This strategy gives you a great selection from
which to choose. However, whenever your GPA or LSAT are out of sync with
each other — such as having a 3.8 GPA and a 150 LSAT, you may want to
apply to more schools, because this low/high disparity may puzzle admissions officers. See Chapter 4 for more on the admissions process and how
your LSAT scores and GPA figure in to the equation.

Weighing the Key Qualities of Law Schools

Law school is generally three long years (four for part-time students).
Compare that with average life expectancies and you're talking a considerable chunk of time. You don't want to randomly pick a school out of a guidebook or a state on the map, because you may be miserable there. So, your
best bet is doing a thorough job researching the schools. The following criteria give you a head start. Read through them and take note of which criteria
appeal most to you.

State school versus private

State schools are a great deal all-around, even when you aren't an in-state resident. Some of them, Michigan and Virginia come to mind, are even ranked as
the best of the best. In-state tuition usually is at least half (if not more than
half) of what you pay in out-of-state tuition. In general, you pay less at a state
school than at a private school, even if you're an out-of-state student. Some
states make it easier to become a resident for tuition purposes than other
states. For instance, in some states you must reside in the state for non-
school purposes for one full year before you start school to qualify as a resident; other states consider all professional students residents. How easy it is
to become a state resident may impact your choice of schools.

Most state schools have solid reputations, and if you're hankering for a large campus with many departmental, joint-degree, and extracurricular offerings, you've found your pot of gold!

Money matters

Tuition at many schools is $25,000 per year. Add living expenses, books, transportation, and housing into the mix, and you're looking at a grand total of at least $80,000 in debt postgraduation. Make sure that you pay particular attention to the cost of living because it impacts your budget significantly in either direction. That's why it pays to be smart about money matters before you apply. One key aspect to consider in terms of money has to do with the type of city you're in. Larger cities may have more opportunities for part-time jobs during the school year, which many students hold and which can be a significant source of income. Ask students what types of employment are available nearby.

For instance, in a small, rural town you're not likely to find an environmental or intellectual property law firm, but in a city you'll find many. And yet you'll also be able to live more frugally in a smaller city. In my law school town (Bloomington, Indiana), I was able to rent a great apartment for half of what I'd pay for the same type of apartment in a more expensive city like Chicago.

Financial aid packages

The debt shouldered by law school students can sometimes restrict what they do after graduation. For example, if you entered law school determined to do public-interest work (which traditionally is low paying), you may find out that you're forced to take a firm job just to bring your debt under control. That's why you need to apply for financial aid at all the schools you're considering and meet their specified deadlines. You never know when you may qualify for a needs- or merit-based scholarship or work-study agreement, instead of taking out pure loans.

Reputation

Schools are known to the legal profession (especially employers) in two general ways, by being a national school or a regional school.

✔ *National* law schools enjoy a reputation across the country, and they can find their graduates jobs nationwide, too. Whenever you mention the name of a national law school, like Harvard, Yale, or NYU, employers instantly recognize the name, whether they're in Boston or Boise, Idaho.

✔ *Regional* law schools, on the other hand, may not be well known across the country, but usually are well known in the states, cities, or regions where they're located. They tend to have the best success placing their graduates locally. If you're at a regional school in Maine, you'll have a much harder time looking for work in Florida or other distant locales than you would if you were at a national school.

When you want the most geographical flexibility, and can nab a spot, a national school is your best bet. Some employers may close their doors to you based on the reputation of your law school, especially when you aren't near the top of your class. But this practice is as much a fact of life at law schools as it is for undergraduate institutions.

Location, location, location

When you think about spending the next few years of your life somewhere, the location of the law school must be one of your prime considerations. If you're able to figure out where you want to practice *before* applying to law school, that can make your search much easier. Although I didn't know the particular city to which I'd eventually move, location was my number one factor, because I knew I wanted to stay in the Midwest after graduation. Additionally, I knew I wanted to go to a law school with a small-town, collegiate environment, and Bloomington, Indiana, fit the bill perfectly.

Another logistical factor to consider is whether you'll be happier in an urban or rural location. For students who attended an urban college, a rural or suburban law school may be a welcome change of pace, or vice versa. My school is in a small city, and I love the warm and friendly environment of a college town. If school spirit is what you're after, keep in mind that an urban campus may not have as much of a collegiate atmosphere when compared with a college town. So, if a swinging nightlife is what you value, you're likely to quickly tire of the same old bars in the same small city.

Likewise, be sure to take note of what surrounds the school. I visited some schools that had little in terms of restaurants, shops, gyms, and college hangouts around the law school. Others had a rich variety of cute sandwich joints, coffee shops, and boutiques. If the setting is important to you, visiting the schools gives you the most accurate reading. (See the "Visiting Law Schools" section later in the chapter for more information.)

Safety

Visiting the school is probably the best way to determine whether your school is in a safe location, although you can also check out crime reports for the area online. Do you feel safe walking around campus during the day? (I hope that your answer is yes; otherwise, you may be in trouble.) Find out what students say about safety at and around the law school at night. Are there campus shuttles, security personnel, and well-lit walking paths nearby? Because you'll likely be studying late at the library on more than a few occasions, finding out the safety record of a potential school sooner rather than later pays off.

Duration of law school

If you want to get done in a hurry, some schools offer the opportunity to graduate in two and a half years, rather than three. You can do so in one of several ways:

- ✔ Starting in the summer before the traditional first year of study begins (called *summer starters* at only a handful of schools that offer this option)
- ✔ Taking summer school to gain credits quickly
- ✔ Taking a heavier credit load each semester

Some people choose a combination of all three, so they take advantage of an earlier graduation date. Not all schools offer the opportunity to graduate early, but many do.

ABA-approved versus non-ABA approved

The majority of American law schools are ABA-approved (188 of them, to be precise). ABA stands for the American Bar Association, which is the accrediting body for law schools. If you're in an ABA-approved school, you have an easier path — you can take the bar exam in any state. If you're in a non-ABA approved school, you generally can take the bar exam only in the state where the school is located. However, there are sometimes workarounds to this rule, but they vary from state to state. Some states allow a non-ABA accredited law school graduate to sit for their bar exams after the graduate has been practicing law in another jurisdiction for a certain amount of years. Other states have other options, such as non-ABA approved graduates being eligible to sit for their bar exam after they have earned an L.L.M. degree (master of laws) from an ABA-accredited law school. For the most up-to-date requirements for your state, consult the national conference of bar examiners at www.ncbex.org where you can link to every state's bar admission office.

Keep in mind that some employers may regard a diploma from a non-ABA school with a bit of suspicion. The quality of your law school is often taken into account when making hiring decisions.

Joint-degree opportunities

If you're working toward a joint degree, you need to consider only law schools that are attached to a university or stand-alone law schools that have arrangements with other institutions. Many *joint degree* opportunities are available, combining a Juris Doctor (J.D.) with other disciplines. The J.D./ Master's of Business Administration (M.B.A) is the most popular. But some people work toward joint J.D./Doctor of Medicine (M.D.), J.D./Master of Arts (M.A.), J.D./Doctor of philosophy (Ph.D.), J.D./Master of Library Science (M.L.S.) degrees, and the list goes on. When enrolling in a joint-degree program, you usually either apply to both degree programs simultaneously or apply to the other program during your first year of law school.

Specialization in one or more areas

Some people know as prelaw students that they want to specialize in a particular area, such as environmental law, tax law, or maritime law. If you're one of those people, you may want to choose a school that specializes in your area of interest. What does it mean for a law school to specialize? It either offers a certificate program in the field or has a larger number of professors and course offerings than usual or clinics focusing on the particular area of practice. Some schools are synonymous with certain specialties. For instance, Vermont Law School is known for environmental law and Franklin Pierce is known for intellectual property.

Jeremy Hojnicki, a 3L at Vermont Law School, decided on Vermont because of its reputation as one of the nation's best environmental law schools. He was interested in environmental issues long before he had any thoughts about becoming a lawyer. However, he thought that going to a school that specializes in a particular area of the law can potentially pigeon hole a student, which can be good or bad. On one hand, it helps you because your résumé and transcript lean heavily toward one subject area and all things being equal, you'll be better suited for getting a job in a niche market than someone else. On the other hand, having a specialty can make exploring other areas of the law later on more difficult.

Teaching quality

The quality of your professors is a major factor in determining the overall quality of your education. You need to find out ahead of time how good the professors are at the school you're interested in. An outstanding professor makes the material come alive in ways you never imagined. I've taken several courses, which judging from their descriptions looked utterly boring, only to come away with an amazing educational experience, because the professor's enthusiasm and competence in an area made all the difference. Conversely, some interesting-looking classes with great potential have been botched by professors with poor teaching and interpersonal skills.

The first step in evaluating a school's teaching quality is browsing the law school's Web site. Check out the faculty biographies. What are their levels of experience? Have they written many publications, like textbooks or scholarly books? Are they fresh out of law school — or have they been practicing, clerking, or teaching for awhile? What's the ratio of full-time to part-time professors? Men to women? Diversity among professors? The best way to get the dirt on profs is visiting the schools and sitting in on a bunch of classes. Do the professors seem bored or lively? Do the students seem interested? Do the professors use many examples, overheads, or gestures? Or do they read from lecture notes in a monotone voice? When you're visiting, make sure to ask students for details about the professors. Who are the good ones? Are there more good than bad? Before you know it, you have an excellent idea about the faculty's strengths and weaknesses.

Course selection and breadth

One important thing you need to check with the law schools about is when you can start taking electives. Many first-year (1L) curricula are set in stone: You take certain required courses, and no electives are offered. Other law schools allow 1Ls to take one or two electives during the spring semester. The majority of schools allow all 2Ls and 3Ls to take entirely electives, but most require certain courses for graduation. For instance, my school requires a professional responsibility/ethics course, one writing course, one seminar research paper course, and one "perspectives" course to graduate.

Other schools may require clinical experience or a public-interest externship to graduate. Besides the typical courses, you may, of course, be interested in clinics, externships, and courses that prepare you for the business of law. (I discuss clinics and externships in Chapter 12.) You'll also want to look in the brochure, on the Web site, and talk to students about the availability of these types of classes.

Commitment to the public interest

For better or worse, many law schools focus on corporate law. Consciously or unconsciously, they send a corporate message to their students through course selection, guest speakers, and graduate placement. If you're instead interested in the public interest, you may want to find out about the school's commitment to it by

- ✔ Seeing whether the school's career services office (CSO) has a staff member who counsels students only on public-interest placement.
- ✔ Looking at the number of graduates who choose public-interest careers.
- ✔ Finding out how many clinical opportunities the school offers, whether they send students to public-interest job fairs, and whether public-interest organizations recruit on campus.

Overseas study opportunities

You've probably heard again and again the concept that law is becoming a global profession, meaning that it involves business and law in other countries, not only the United States. That may mean you'll need to supplement your legal education with opportunities to study abroad. Or you may just want to go abroad for fun. Either way, check out the study-abroad opportunities available at the schools in which you're interested.

Some schools offer a plethora of their own programs in addition to the opportunity to earn credit for programs sponsored by other schools. Study-abroad programs can be a year, a semester, or a summer in length. Some schools have strict rules about allowing their students to go only on their programs or on programs at a select few other schools. Other schools won't let you do any studying abroad during the year — only during the summers. The best strategy is to contact the dean of foreign studies to talk about what opportunities are available, or browse the school's Web site. See Chapter 12 for more about studying abroad.

Well-endowed library

A well-endowed library may be at the top of your list of school attributes. After all, you'll be spending a bunch of your time there. But the idea of a well-endowed library can mean more than the number of volumes in it. Sure, the number of volumes may be important, but how many of those tens of thousands of volumes are you actually going to use?

More important, in my opinion, is the number of computers and research stations. You don't want to be twiddling your thumbs on a regular basis while waiting to use a computer terminal. Other questions you may want to ask are: Is the library bright and airy or like a dank dungeon? And (more important), is food allowed? The answer to the latter question may be important to you, especially when you're the type who stays at the law school all night. My school's library permitted food, and I've seen pizzas ordered to study rooms in the library — it's a pretty great privilege!

Likewise, be sure to find out whether you'd actually be able to study in the library. Is it quiet? Do students respect certain areas as no talking? Are people using cell phones? Are the chairs comfy? This last point is crucial, because studying can take its toll and sometimes you just *need* a nap.

The number of graduates with jobs at graduation

Everyone is concerned about jobs these days, given the depressing state of the economy. When you go into hock for $80,000 total debt as an average law student, you want to make sure that you're going to be gainfully employed so you can pay off all that debt, preferably sooner than later. One way to gauge the reputation of a school is researching what percentage of its graduates have jobs at graduation and then at six months after graduation. The best way to do that is to inquire directly with the CSO at that particular school, but remember that CSO statistics sometimes are vague. To find out the entire picture, visit the CSO and find out what percentage of graduates are employed in legal jobs, what percentage in nonlegal jobs, and how many are unemployed or still looking for work. If the percentages of gainful employment are low, you may want to investigate a little deeper to find out why.

Visiting Law Schools

Visiting law schools — either before applying, or, more realistically, after being accepted — is essential to making an informed decision. When you visit law schools, the most important thing to do is ask questions. Talk to students, faculty, administrators, and admissions people. Have lunch in the cafeteria or student lounge and hang out in the library. Corral a few students and ask them in-depth, probing questions about their school. After all, wouldn't you love to speak your mind about the good, the bad, and the ugly regarding your undergraduate school? I'm sure you wouldn't have hesitated to describe in excruciating detail how bad the cafeteria food was or why prospective students absolutely must take particular classes. Law students are exactly the same way. So don't overlook this valuable resource!

Amy Liu, an associate director of admissions, and Pat Cain, an associate dean of admissions, at the University of Iowa College of Law, advise that taking a guided tour and sitting in on one or two law school classes are the best ways to gain a sense of what a particular law school is like for other students and what the school's teaching style is. They believe the feel and environment of a school are factors that you can observe only from an actual visit and that eventually sway someone to choose school A over school B.

Keep in mind that factors like the weather or a poor tour guide can erroneously color your impressions of a school. That's what happened to me — I visited one school on an awful, stormy day, and got a low energy feeling from the school and students that irreversibly colored my perspective. Had the day been bright and sunny, I'm sure I would have come away with a completely different perspective.

When you're visiting a law school, one interesting sociological phenomenon to make note of is how many students are wearing the school's T-shirts or other paraphernalia. I found at many schools a seeming but unscientific correlation between the amount of pride and school spirit students felt and the number who wore school T-shirts.

Figuring out the best and worst times to go

The best time to visit law schools is when classes are in session during the week. That way you can walk through the halls and get a read on the students: Do they seem stressed out or happy? Are people clustering and chatting during the break in between classes? Or, do they keep to themselves in a morose way?

The worst time to visit schools is during exams. I inadvertently did just that when I visited Indiana University, where I ultimately decided to attend. It never even crossed my mind whether exams were being held (even though it was prime exam season — the end of April). As a result, my visit wasn't that useful. I didn't get to talk to any students, because everyone was scurrying back and forth from the library like voles running for cover. I wasn't able to sit in on classes, because none were in session. All I was able to do was take a tour and walk through the silent halls, trying to make eye contact with stressed-out students. Try not to make this mistake — you'll get a much better picture otherwise!

You need at least half a day to visit each school. If you have time to do more besides just take the law school tour, sitting in on several classes, going for a law school and general campus tour, and having lunch with the students is better. If you have a little more time, be sure to check on the housing opportunities that are nearby.

Soaking up the atmosphere of the school

Doing a few specific things can greatly enhance the quality of your visit. Although these things aren't mandatory, they help you get a better feel for the school, the student body, and the quality of life there.

- ✔ **Deciding whether to schedule interviews:** The general consensus is that scheduling interviews usually has little effect on your chances of admission. In fact, practically no law schools even offer formal interviews. However, when you visit the school, you may be able to schedule an (informal) informational session with an admissions representative, just to gain information about the school. Although rarely do such interviews change your status from a no to a yes (or vice versa), playing up your selling points and presenting your sparkling personality sure can't hurt.

- ✔ **Sitting in on a class:** Sitting in on a law school class is always enlightening, especially if you've never done it before. Observe the formality of the class: Are people being called by "Mr." or "Ms."? Are they being asked to stand when answering questions? Are there enough seats for everyone? If you have a few hours, try sitting in on classes other than the typical first-year courses, which the admissions department usually arranges for you. Try to request one or two first-year classes and a few electives. Doing so helps you see the different class sizes, atmospheres, and teaching styles that the school offers.

When you're sitting in on a class, you may not understand a single word that's being discussed. In that case, don't strain yourself and become frustrated trying to comprehend. Instead, look around at the students, and observe their attitudes toward the class. When I visited my first school and sat in on a torts class, I'd never heard of a tort nor followed any of the discussion. Instead, I peered around at the students and tried to imagine myself sitting in that very classroom. Do the students seem engaged — or are they surfing the Web with their wireless Internet access? Does the professor seem to be enthusiastic about the subject?

- ✔ **Scoping out the city:** If you have a free afternoon, you may want to drive around the city, especially if you've never been there before. Does the city seem like your kind of town? Are there activities you enjoy doing there — whether that's skiing, doing art gallery hops, or eating out at a new restaurant every week? Is it a place that you'd feel comfortable in?

- ✔ **Scheduling appointments with key people:** One efficient use of your time during your visit is scheduling appointments with the financial aid staff, career services staff, any admissions staff you may want to chat with, and deans. You need to call ahead to schedule these appointments. Use your time with them to ask important questions and get a feel for their attitudes toward the school and prospective and current students. These appointments can be particularly helpful for gauging the law school atmosphere, if you're a nontraditional or minority applicant (see Chapter 2).

Querying your tour guide

Taking the law school tour (a narrated tour of the building usually led by a 1L) is your prime time for putting in some one-on-one time with a current member of the student body. As you're meandering through the hallways, ask all your most detailed questions, but keep in mind that this person is representing the school, so his or her answers may be edited. The following are some good topics to discuss with your tour guide.

- **Parking:** On most large university campuses, parking is a huge hassle. At my campus, students fought tooth and nail every day for the limited number of street spots. Your tour guide may have some insider tips about where the best parking can be found, may know of little-known nonuniversity parking lots that are convenient to the law school, or can tell you how to purchase campus parking stickers.

- **Housing:** Housing is always a major concern for the new 1L who has never been to a particular city before. You want to find out from your tour guide what sorts of housing most law students obtain — dorms or apartments? Ask where the prime real estate is located. Do many students live far out and drive? Are there any designated law student apartments, around which most of the social scene revolves? What are the average prices for housing? Where does your tour guide live?

If you're really digging this particular law school, it wouldn't hurt, when you have a free afternoon, to pick up one of those grocery store rental guides and drive around looking at the most appealing housing options. That's exactly how I found my law school apartment. After you get an idea of prices and overall value in that particular city, you'll be better able to comparison shop among the schools.

- **Student satisfaction:** Ask questions of your guide about the competitiveness of the student body. You want to find out how students generally behave toward other students — are they helpful or cutthroat? Furthermore, ask whether your guide thinks the law school seems isolated or whether it is well integrated with the rest of the campus. Are you able to take any courses from other departments in the university? Finally, ask your tour guide what made him or her choose this particular school over others. Is he or she happy here? The answers will likely be revealing, and you can find out what the school's strong suits are.

- **Social life:** Social life is important — you'll be at this school for three years, so the social life needs to fit your idea of a good time. Ask your tour guide what students do for fun. Are there many parties? Mixers? Law school-sponsored parties and dances? Does the social scene revolve around one sports bar — or is it more diverse? Are all students generally invited to student parties or are social circles overly cliquish? What is the dating scene like? Do law students date each other in large numbers, and if so, is it a taboo thing to do? Are there many intrastudent marriages?

- ✔ **Competency of the career services office:** Discussing the CSO will likely be one of your guide's favorite topics, because people generally either love their CSO or have horror stories about it. You'll want to find out whether the CSO is competent, what kind of assistance it provides, and how many career counselors deal with students. Ask whether the CSO is used in all aspects of the job-search process. Do they offer mock interview sessions? How many employers generally come to campus for on-campus interviewing?

Chapter 4

Using Battle-Tested Application Strategies to Succeed

. . . .

In This Chapter

▶ Understanding the application process

▶ Using your prelaw advisor to your best advantage

▶ Mastering the ins and outs of the LSAT

▶ Evaluating strategies for an outstanding application

. . . .

*W*hy is law so darn popular these days? It seems like every undergraduate student you meet wants to go to law school or has just applied. Some aim to improve their future employment prospects with a J.D. degree; others believe that a few more years of schooling will give them the time they need to "figure out what they really want to do." Either way, applying to law school certainly seems to be the "in" thing to do, but what does that mean for your chances of gaining admission?

The unfortunate truth is that snagging a spot at a law school is harder than ever. With thousands of law school applicants vying for a fixed number of seats, many students wonder what they can do to make their applications stand out. Having great grades, a sky-high LSAT score, and being president of the prelaw association no longer is enough. Everyone else has all that, too. Instead, you need what journalists call a *hook* — your own special angle that makes you memorable — and irresistible — to law school admissions committees.

This chapter introduces you to some simple, creative ways to overcome the admissions odds. I explain the essentials of the admissions process, including what you can do *now* to improve your admissions chances later. I show you how your prelaw advisor can help identify ways to increase your admissions chances. Then I walk you step-by-step through the art of assembling your application. Additionally, I give you the information you need to know to ace the LSAT and fill you in on how law schools weigh all aspects of your credentials.

Demystifying the Application Process

Many prelaw students find the law school application process intimidating, mainly because they're confused about applying for the LSAT, knowing who to approach for recommendations, and whether seeking an early decision is a good idea.

Some law schools use rolling admissions; others have official application cut-off dates. *Rolling admissions* means they accept applications beginning with a certain start date and evaluate them as they're received until the class is filled. In other words, with rolling admissions, no official end-date exists. As a result, whenever the class is filled and you haven't submitted your application, you're out of luck. On the other hand, those schools that enforce a strict cut-off date for applications require that you get yours in before that date. Even if you're the most promising applicant, your application won't get read if it arrives even one day after the school's cut-off.

Other important tidbits that you need to know when applying are the specific parts that make up the law school application. Generally, the application has several elements, including your

- ✔ Educational background, including your undergraduate (and graduate) grade-point average(s) (GPA) and transcript copies and analysis

- ✔ Law School Admissions Test (LSAT) score

- ✔ LSAT writing sample copies

- ✔ Personal statement and/or essay(s) (see "Making Your Application Stand Out: The Steps to Success" later in this chapter for more info)

- ✔ Extracurricular involvement

- ✔ College honors received

- ✔ Work record

- ✔ Recommendations from professors and/or employers

- ✔ Application fee (can be waived if you have financial need)

Although each part is important, most law schools say that the educational section is the most important, overall, because the admissions staff uses your GPA and LSAT scores to predict how well you can do in law school.

Setting a timely timetable

Regardless of whether the law schools you're interested in operate on a rolling admissions application schedule or have a set cut-off date, you want to make sure that you get your application ready to go as soon as possible.

Dates to remember

Start dates for applications to most law schools are usually around September 1, regardless of whether that school operates on a rolling or set cut-off date basis. Those schools that have cut-off dates usually set them around March 1. Schools with rolling admissions don't have closing (cut-off) dates. Start dates and cutoffs differ from school to school, however, so check with the specific schools in which you're interested to determine the appropriate dates.

Have your application ready to turn in as soon as you can, because you want it to be read sooner rather than later. But you don't need to be waiting in line at the post office the day the admissions cycle opens; many admissions folks recommend that you get your application in at least by December 1 to be considered early. Keep in mind that admissions people tend to travel during the fall months and generally start reading files around December 1. That means that even if you submit your application in early fall, you're still not likely to hear back until mid to late December.

The main benefits of being the early bird are twofold: Early on, admissions staff are still fresh and unjaded by the 100th "why I've always wanted to be a lawyer" personal statement that they've seen that week. Also, if the school you're applying to is on a rolling admissions system, you're better off if your application is read while plenty of spots are still open, as opposed to when only six seats remain.

With a first-come, first-served system, you definitely want to be in the first-served category. That means you need to set deadlines for completing the main components of your application and then stick to them. The main target dates that you need to scribble onto your calendar are when you must

- ✔ Register for the LSAT and LSDAS (see the section, "Navigating the Nuts and Bolts of the Law Schools Data Assembly Service (LSDAS)" later in the chapter for more information)

- ✔ Send a transcript request form (which you can get online at www.LSAC.org or in the free *LSAT & LSDAS Registration and Information Book* [found at your prelaw advisors' office]) to your undergraduate (and graduate) school's registrar, who will then send an official transcript on to LSDAS

  There is no set time that you need to send in the request form; a few months in advance of when you want to send in your application is a good standard

- ✔ Take the LSAT

- ✔ Write your personal statement/essays

- ✔ Contact the people from whom you expect to receive recommendations (See the section, "Making Your Application Stand Out: The Steps to Success" later in the chapter for more information on the last two bullets.)

Early decision

Another time issue that you need to be aware of is the option of submitting an early application for an *early decision*. Not every school offers this option; so if it interests you, make sure you inquire at every law school you're considering. Early decision is usually binding. With this option, you submit your application to one school (your first choice) by the early decision deadline, which is usually between November 1 and November 15. You must, however, withdraw your applications from other schools whenever you're accepted, and thus you're required to enroll where you've made the early decision. Under the early decision option, most schools will get back to you within 30 days of submitting your completed application.

In my opinion, early decision has its pros and cons.

- **Pro:** After you receive an acceptance, you no longer need to bite your nails worrying about whether you'll get into a law school — any law school. You'll have one acceptance under your belt, so you can dedicate the rest of your time to finding out what your first year of law school will be like (see Chapters 5 and 6).

- **Con:** Early decision is binding, and some people may be uncomfortable with making a decision so early in the year, before they've explored all their law school and geographical options. For instance, being bound so early in the game by an early decision may limit your flexibility if your plans suddenly change, like deciding that you'd rather be in New Mexico than Massachusetts.

Ultimately, it's a personal choice, and if it's an attractive option for you, you should discuss the pros and cons more thoroughly with your prelaw advisor (see the "Getting the Most Out of Your Prelaw Advisor" section later in the chapter).

Delving into the minds of admissions committees

Every prelaw student wonders exactly what goes on from the moment his or her application lands in the hands of the admissions staff. The first thing you need to know about the process is who serves on the admissions team. It's usually comprised of the dean or director of admissions, and several (between three and 12) faculty members (this depends on the school). At some schools, third-year (3L) students participate on the admissions committee.

The precise way that admissions decisions are made differs from school to school. But at every school, your file needs to be complete for it to be read. That means that everything has been received, including the LSDAS report (see the "Navigating the Nuts and Bolts of the Law Schools Data Assembly Service (LSDAS)" section later in the chapter for more info), letters of recommendation, and application.

At some schools, the director or dean of admissions may read through all the files first, deciding which files are *presumptive accepts* (most likely to be accepted) and *presumptive declines* (most likely to be rejected) sometimes on the basis of the *index number,* an amount derived from each respective school's formula for incorporating how much weight is given to the student's GPA and LSAT score. These decisions are the easier ones but these files are usually still passed along to the committee for a complete read-through (unless there is something glaring or wonderful in the file that the committee finds, they will be admitted or rejected).

However, many more files are designated by the dean or director to be sent to committee because they need more extensive discussion. These are usually the borderline files — the ones that fall slightly below the admit score but above the reject score. For example, if you have a disparity in your numbers, such as a high LSAT but low grades, your file will likely go to committee.

When your file is *in committee,* it is being discussed by several of the many committee members (for example, three out of 12 committee members may be assigned to read your particular file). At that point, your index number becomes less important than it was at first read, and your extracurricular achievements, work experience, and personal statement come into play because the admissions staff wants to find out more about you as a whole person. The committee members assigned to your file then vote to admit, deny, or waitlist. Whether you're told that your file is in committee depends on the school. You can try calling and asking; some schools will tell you; others won't.

Analyzing the ideal applicant

Many students are concerned about what they must do to be considered an ideal applicant by the law schools. In a perfect world, an ideal applicant

- Has great grades
- Comes from an academically rigorous school
- Scores high on the LSAT
- Participates in a bevy of fascinating extracurricular activities
- Submits a strong personal statement (and/or essays) exhibiting unique personal characteristics
- Submits glowing letters of recommendation, detailing how and why the student excelled academically and personally in all coursework

Of course, many mere mortals fall short in one (or all) of these ideal criteria. But the majority of applicants have an asset in at least one of these areas that they can play up. Whatever your particular strength, be sure to let it show through! Write about it in your personal statement if it isn't your grades or LSAT score. When your strength *is* your writing skills, show them off in your personal statement. The key, just like in fashion, is to accentuate the positives.

Amy Liu, an associate director of admissions, and Pat Cain, an associate dean of admissions, at the University of Iowa College of Law, describe how they choose their entering class by two different methods. Half the class is chosen primarily by numbers, and the other half is chosen primarily by outstanding personal characteristics. The half that's chosen by numbers alone is held to very high standards. For example, the admissions committee likes to see an LSAT score of 161 or above and a GPA above 3.5 or better. For the half chosen by less tangible qualities, the most competitive candidates have solid academic credentials and experiences, such as working full time or part time in a law firm, governmental, or public-interest organization; traveling internationally; serving in leadership roles for a college club or organization; or exhibiting a firm commitment to public service. Files in this category — *the numbers plus pool* — are read by three faculty readers who look for interesting personal facts that make a candidate stand out from the crowd. Most readers go directly to the applicant's personal statement, so keep in mind that demonstrating unusual achievement in a particular hobby or outside interest may pique their curiosities. In recent years, faculty readers favored admitting a concert pianist, an applicant who had worked in a foreign embassy, a White House intern, and applicants who possessed a demonstrated commitment to public service by either working for an AIDS foundation or serving in the Peace Corps.

Charting challenging coursework or playing up your work history

Law schools tend to prefer people who earn not only good grades but also take more challenging courses. They want to see that you excelled not only in all your introductory courses but also in your major. They want to know that you did well in upper-level electives and often look toward courses that require you to think analytically, write long papers, do research projects, or give class presentations for indications of your abilities.

The best gift that you can give yourself before entering law school (and potentially floundering during that first year) is a course of study in which you can learn the fine art of critical analysis. Courses that require advanced reading comprehension, like English, history, philosophy, and many others, are excellent for gaining that skill. Just like science is the main medium that doctors use, language is the art of lawyers. If you're a science or art major, for instance, you want to make sure that you're comfortable with language and analyzing it in complex ways. You may want to take several extra challenging core humanities courses to make yourself ready.

If it's been years — or even decades — since you received your undergraduate diploma, you may be asking how you can avenge all those C's in your major back when you were young and foolish. All is not lost for nontraditional applicants whose performance in college was poor or mediocre. Many admissions committees will overlook substandard college performance somewhat if you have a strong showing on the LSAT. Additionally, if you've succeeded in a demanding job, your work-related accomplishments will also weigh into the admissions decision. Your B– in freshman physics becomes less important than the major deal you helped secure or the building you helped design in recent years.

What if you're in a double bind: You have bad grades and you didn't do so hot on the LSAT? All is still not lost. You probably still have a shot at gaining admission to a law school (especially if you've succeeded in a demanding career), but you will generally face a tough time in the admissions process. As a result, you may need to apply to schools that are more realistically within your grasp.

Solving the "major" problem

It's a myth that law schools favor history or political science majors. (While I'm on the subject of myths, there's no such thing as graduating with a major in prelaw either.) It often just happens that students *self-select* — think they need one of these two majors to be attractive law school candidates.

Law school admissions committees don't seek any preferred law school major, but that's not to say that you shouldn't major in history or political science if it really floats your boat. When your interests tend toward art history, biology, astrophysics, or environmental science, by all means pursue those majors. That way if you apply for law school, you'll most likely stand out from the crowd and perhaps be viewed as adding diversity to the class.

The key is pursuing what you're interested in, because you're more likely to get better grades in subjects for which you have an affinity. Besides, at the undergraduate level, college is prime time for dabbling. In law school, you'll be limited largely to law courses, so think of college as one of your last chances to experiment intellectually.

I was an English major in college, and I found that major to be quite helpful when analyzing cases, which is pretty much the bulk of what you do in law school. I found that the skills I used to analyze a D.H. Lawrence novel are similar to the ones I used to study Roe versus Wade. Likewise, my experience writing long and involved English-major papers came in handy when it was time to write long and involved papers for law school (particularly in my 3L required seminar course). Furthermore I believe that philosophy can be a very useful major, because it teaches you the intricacies of logic, which is great preparation for law school.

Finding out that majoring in a science (such as chemistry or physics), computer science, or engineering makes you very much in demand if you decide to go into one particular practice area (patent law) may surprise you. (A *patent* is the exclusive right to make, sell, or use an invention for a certain period of time, if the invention satisfies certain criteria.) Intellectual property (of which patent law is a subset) employers tend to be much more interested in folks whose undergraduate degrees are in science or technology than they are in folks with backgrounds in humanities, primarily because intellectual property law, in large part, deals with patents. You essentially need an undergraduate science degree to sit for the patent bar. Thus, because many law practices that deal with intellectual property concentrate on patents and your background is in a field that produces intellectual property, you're bound to be highly sought after when you choose that area of legal practice. So, all you science majors take note: You'll have an additional area of practice welcoming you with open arms when you're interviewing for summer or permanent legal jobs.

Getting the Most Out of Your Prelaw Advisor

Prelaw advisors help you navigate the law school admissions process; they're like your personal law school counselors. These lifesavers can inform you where you're likely to be accepted based on your numbers, how people from your school did when they applied to the same schools in the past, and, more important, how students with grades and LSAT scores similar to yours fared at those schools.

How do you procure a prelaw advisor? Most undergraduate institutions have a designated prelaw office, where students just go on their own to talk with the one or two officially designated prelaw advisors. Schools that don't have formal offices have one or more professors designated as prelaw advisors. You aren't assigned a prelaw advisor the way an undergraduate course advisor is assigned to you; nor do you select a random professor on your own. Instead, you make an appointment to see the predesignated prelaw advisor whenever you feel the need. Some students choose not to make use of their prelaw advisor at all; others only do so sporadically throughout the admissions process. The decision is up to you, but forging a relationship with this person can help you survive the admissions process with greater ease.

Asking an advisor to recommend you

Traditionally, professors write your letters of recommendation, but prelaw advisors can also write a letter for good measure. Sometimes a letter of recommendation from a prelaw advisor can make the difference if the advisor has especially good connections with a particular law school's admissions committee or if many past alums of your college were successful in gaining admission to that law school. Three additional reasons that you may consider having your prelaw advisor write one of your recommendations are

✔ Your advisor can compare your credentials with those of other students who are applying to the same school.

✔ You and your advisor have been meeting on a somewhat regular basis to discuss your personal statement, goals, and application strategies. He or she may thus know you for a longer period of time (and better) than some of your faculty recommendation writers.

✔ Your advisor may be better equipped for offering insight into your motivations for choosing law and your overall academic competency than a professor for one particular course.

If you want your prelaw advisor to write a letter of recommendation for you, be sure to provide all the necessary accoutrements. This may mean offering a résumé, your personal statement, and perhaps even sitting down to brief your advisor on anything else you think he or she needs to know (like your Apache heritage or your proficiency in watercolor painting).

The following are some productive ways that you can make the most of your relationship with your prelaw advisor.

✔ **Showing your personal statement to your prelaw advisor.** Ask for helpful comments and feedback. Find out whether you're conveying what you want to convey in the statement, and whether any changes in content are needed. See the "Making Your Application Stand Out: The Steps to Success" section later in the chapter for more info about personal statements.

✔ **Asking which professors whose classes you've taken might be good at preparing law school recommendations.** Prelaw advisors can steer you toward professors who they happen to know write extremely detailed and lively recommendation letters. Conversely, they can steer you away from professors who don't tend to put much effort into them. Your advisor can also help you select a variety of professors to write your letters (for instance, advising that you get recommendations from professors who taught two seminar-type classes and one regular lecture).

✔ **Taking advantage of your advisor's counsel.** Advisors are a shoulder to cry on when you receive rejection letters and a source of support when you're undecided between several schools. Sometimes having a neutral third party like an advisor helps you through the process of making emotionally charged decisions.

Making Your Application Stand Out: The Steps to Success

With today's increased competition for admission to law school, ensuring that your application presents the best possible picture of you and your accomplishments is more important than ever. This section covers what you need to do to make sure your application is an instant success.

No. 1: Gathering great recommendations

One of the purposes of letters of recommendation is to enable law schools to find out, from a third party, how you compare with other students taking your same classes. Law schools hope that people making the recommendations write about your academic promise, your performance in their classes, how you compare with other students they've taught, and your overall intellectual curiosity.

Of course, some recommendation writers are brief and to the point. They may write something like, "Bill was in my class and did well," and that's about it. This type of recommendation, however, isn't much help. Law schools are looking for something meatier. That's why the best recommendation letters are personal, based on a knowledge of your personality and academic successes.

Most schools want between two and three letters. The first step toward gathering great recommendations can be done years before you apply to law school by figuring out who the prime recommendation writers are and forging personal bonds with them. Choose professors with whom you've had several classes within your major. You may also want to choose people who've served as your advisors or with whom you've worked on special projects. Look for people who know you well. The professor of your freshman biology class, in which you were one of 250 students, may not be the best choice, even though you earned an A in the class. The professor of an upper-level seminar, where you wrote an outstanding research paper on the history of jazz dance, would be a better choice.

When you've been out of school for a while, make sure that you follow these same procedures, but substitute "employer" for "professor." Law schools prefer to see someone familiar with your academic work write on your behalf, but this may not be feasible if you've been out of school for eight years. Instead, an employer may be able to speak to similar abilities, like your ability to meet deadlines, master complex subject matter, or propose innovative solutions to your company's problems. Law schools understand that what you're doing now speaks more to your abilities than what you did years before as an undergraduate.

Some students hesitate when approaching professors for recommendations, because they think they're asking for something too time-consuming of them. However, professors are used to being asked to write recommendations, so don't feel like you're imposing. When you've identified potential recommendation writers, approach them well in advance of the application deadline. Give professors at least five weeks to work on your recommendation. Putting things aside or getting swamped by other types of work is just human nature, but you don't want your recommendations completely thrown by the wayside, so leave plenty of time for them to be written.

When you actually ask someone to write a letter of recommendation, make sure that you watch closely for the professor's reaction. If the response is anything less than an enthusiastic "Yes!" watch out. Any hesitancy suggests that professor may not be able to write you a great recommendation and may be nonconfrontational, not wanting to give you an outright "No." You don't want a recommendation that speaks negatively of you, so whenever you encounter any hesitancy, just thank those people for their time and leave. A good way to dispel any doubts is to phrase your request like this: "Would you be willing to write me a strong recommendation?"

When approaching your target professor, ask for a time that's convenient for the two of you to meet for a briefing session. You want to sit down, explain your reasons for going to law school, discuss your academic record, and answer any other questions you professor needs to know to be able to write your recommendation. Provide a résumé and your personal statement, whenever you think they will make writing good things about you easier.

When you receive a commitment from your professor, be sure to follow up like a hawk in pursuit of a field mouse. Check on the people writing your recommmendations every few weeks just to be sure they haven't forgotten about you. Sending an e-mail along the lines of, "I was wondering whether you needed anything else to help you write my recommendation," is a tactful approach. And, of course, make sure that your recommendation writers submit your recommendations on time, either in a sealed envelope with their signatures across the back) to you (so you can send them to the law schools) or directly to the LSDAS, along with the official LSDAS recommendation letter form (see "Navigating the Nuts and Bolts of the Law Schools Data Assembly Service (LSDAS)" section later in the chapter for a detailed discussion of using the LSDAS recommendation service). A single late recommendation can keep your file from being reviewed.

Last, and surely not least, send a gracious thank-you note to your recommendation writers. Handwritten is always preferred, though typewritten is okay, too. Thank the writers for their time and energy in writing your recommendations, and let them know that you'll keep them abreast of how things turn out.

No. 2: Writing a sparkling personal statement and/or essay

Writing a *personal statement* (an open-ended essay where you tell the admissions committee about yourself) or an *essay* (where you write on a specific question) doesn't need to be a chore, especially when you leave yourself enough time to do a bang-up job.

The crucial part about writing your personal statement is choosing what you want to write about. (You have a designated topic with the essay.) When you choose a topic, make sure that it has what journalists call a *hook* — your own unique spin. In other words, if you have an extraordinary event in your background that makes for interesting fodder, write about that. Maybe you spent a semester in Bali and it really influenced your outlook on life; write about that. As one admissions dean I spoke with said, after they finish reading it, you want only one reaction: "Wow!"

Admissions committees see their fair share of the typical "why I have always wanted to be a lawyer" essays, so make sure whenever you choose a similar topic that you take great care in making your statement stand out. Additionally, admissions people advise against simply regurgitating your résumé into your personal statement. Instead of listing and briefly describing everything you've done since freshman year of college, focus on one or two standout experiences and write about those.

There's generally no length requirement for personal statements or essays. Some law schools will specify a length requirement in their applications, but if yours doesn't, assume that any reasonable length is fine. In other words, two to three double-spaced pages is the norm; six may be okay, as long as you have something important to say in every single one of those six pages.

Allow at least a month total for writing, editing, and proofreading your essay. You want to have enough time to put it away for a few days so you can distance yourself from it and gain additional perspective. Similarly, you always want an extra set of eyes to look at your work when it's finished. You can find willing readers at your college's writing help center, from your prelaw advisor (see "Getting the Most Out of Your Prelaw Advisor" earlier in this chapter for a detailed discussion of prelaw advisors), in professors, or your friends.

No. 3: Proofing your application

After your application is complete, you must go over it again, checking for any typographical errors. If you're so inclined, one way of preventing most typos is making a photocopy of your application, filling it out, examining it for any typos, and then transferring the same information to the real application. By filling it out this way, you can figure out whether you need an additional sheet of paper, and you can catch any silly mistakes, like spelling the name of your city wrong. Keep in mind that a sloppy application really rubs admissions folks the wrong way. Take particular care, for example, not to talk about the "school of law" when it's really the "college of law." Make it clear that you've done your research.

No. 4: Deciding whether to include attachments

You may want to submit a published article, a few slides of your artwork, articles written up about you in a local newspaper or magazine, or any other information that fits into a manila envelope and supports your case. Although you don't want to overburden the admissions committee by sending 100 slides of your best paintings, your senior honors thesis, or your treatise on amphibian history, a few noteworthy samples may make you stand out more favorably from the rest of the competition. The key to remember with attachments is: Be reasonable.

Admissions folks generally recommend against sending CDs and videotapes — they just don't have the time to hear or watch them, as much as they'd love to see you win the gold in your ice skating competition.

No. 5: Filling out all financial aid applications

Make sure that you don't overlook this step when you're seeking aid. If you're applying for federal aid, you must complete the Free Application for Federal Student Aid (FAFSA). You can file this form any time after January 1, but ideally between January 1 and March 1. If you're applying for private sources of loans, these programs have their own applications and deadlines. Some law schools also require you to complete additional information (besides the FAFSA) to be considered for aid. Contact each admissions office to determine what you'll need to fill out for each school.

Many law schools consider all applicants for *scholarships and fellowships* (grants which you don't have to pay back). Check in the school's brochure, or call the school directly to find out when you need to submit your admission application to be considered for scholarships and fellowships. Some schools have cut-off deadlines, beyond which you won't have priority consideration for these attractive forms of aid.

No. 6: Making sure your application is complete

Last but not least, do not consider your job done as soon as your applications are in the mailbox. You need to remember to call on each law school, making sure that all your applications are complete (including recommendations and LSDAS reports). Don't wait for the law schools to contact you about missing information, because not all of them will. Many, however, send out postcards when your application is complete. No action can be taken on your application until everything is received.

Improving Your LSAT Savvy

Nobody enjoys taking standardized tests. In fact, most people would rank them just before public speaking and spiders. However, this is one phobia that you'll need to triumph over if you ever want to get into law school. *LSAT* stands for the imaginatively titled Law School Admission Test. You can pronounce the name of this test either "el-sat" or "el-es-a-tee". The Law School Admission Council (LSAC) is a nonprofit corporation that creates and administers the test. Here are some quick LSAT stats (hey, that rhymes):

- ✔ **Length.** This beast lasts a half-day, and is comprised of five sections of standardized multiple-choice questions. Each section consists of one 35-minute set of multiple-choice questions. Only four of the five sections will actually factor in to your score; one section is the unscored experimental section, and won't count for anything. You'll be notified of the start and stop time for each section.

- ✔ **Writing sample.** At the end of the test, for 30 minutes, you'll be required to produce one writing sample. This writing sample isn't part of your overall LSAT score; in fact, it's never even scored. Instead, it's sent to the law schools you apply to, but how much weight it's actually given is determined by each school's admissions committee members. In short, don't sweat this part too much.

- ✔ **Dates offered.** The test is offered four times a year, in June, October, December, and February. For more details, see the section "Deciding when to register for and take the LSAT" later in the chapter.

When you approach the test with a positive attitude, you're more likely to do well on it than you are when you approach it with fear and loathing. Remember, the LSAT is not out to get you — it's just a test, waiting to be aced.

Discovering what's tested on the LSAT

You can't study for the content that is included on the LSAT in the same way you can take an undergraduate course in the necessary sciences to improve your Medical College Admissions Test (MCAT) score. The LSAT tests verbal reasoning and reading skills that you've acquired up until this point, including the ability to analyze and evaluate arguments and draw inferences from complex information. Although you cannot take any specific college classes to improve your LSAT score, practice does make perfect. By practicing actual exam questions, you can become more familiar with the way questions are asked and thereby increase the potential for improving your score.

The following is a breakdown of what is tested on the LSAT. Keep in mind that each of the four parts counts equally towards your score (although there are technically five parts, one is an experimental section, and does not contribute to your score; but you won't actually know when taking the test which section is experimental):

- ✔ **Logical reasoning.** You'll have two 35-minute logical reasoning sections, but they won't necessarily follow each other. In each section, you're tested on your ability to criticize, understand, and analyze short arguments. You read through written arguments in short passages, which the *LSAT & LSDAS Registration and Information Book* explains are taken from sources including newspaper articles, speeches, and editorials, among others. Following the arguments are a question and five answer choices. The question will ask you to detect reasoning errors and recognize issues, among other abilities. One important point to remember about the logical reasoning sections is not to use any information outside the passage to answer the question. In other words, take what's written in the passage at face value, even if you learned something different in class about the topic or don't agree with the argument. I found logical reasoning to be the hardest part of the entire exam.

- ✔ **One reading comprehension section.** At first glance, you may think, "What's so hard? I can read, can't I?" But the reading comprehension on the LSAT is much more difficult than it sounds. The main purpose of this section is finding out how well you can read, accurately digest, and reason with complex information. You read four passages that can range in subject matter from early Flemish painting to the Harlem Renaissance literature movement. The passages are followed by a series of five to eight questions that ask you things about how the passage is organized, the author's attitude or the main idea of the passage, among others. These questions often require you to look something up in one of the passages. The passages are usually long and complex, so it's hard to remember what you've just read by the time you get to the questions. What makes this section so tricky is the tight time limit — 35 minutes. Answering five to eight questions per passage is quite a bit of work in that amount of time. Attacking this section by working on your speed is best, because speed really counts when time is at such a premium. I also found it helpful to read the questions first, so I had an idea of what to look for when reading the passage.

✔ **One analytical reasoning section.** Analytical reasoning (also known informally as the "games section") requires you to make deductions from a set of conditions or rules. You're drawing conclusions about the nature of relationships; some questions involve people swapping seats at a table or arranging colored jars on a shelf. The point is to figure out who's left sitting where after they all swap seats or to determine which jar is left facing north. I found myself drawing many diagrams to answer these questions.

✔ **One experimental section.** Only four out of the five sections tested on the LSAT count toward your official score; one section is unscored, because it's experimental. This section can be the same as any of the three types mentioned in the previous bullets. In other words, you can potentially have three logical reasoning, one reading comprehension, and one analytical reasoning section, but one of the logical reasoning sections won't count. However, figuring out which section is experimental can be tricky, and you're better off not wasting any time trying to do it when you're actually taking the LSAT. Save that for when you're dissecting the test with your friends afterward. You don't want to guess wrong while you're taking the test and end up blowing off a section that actually turns out not to be the experimental one after all.

✔ **One writing sample.** The handwritten writing sample is sent directly to the law schools by LSDAS without being scored. You have 30 minutes to complete the writing sample. Whether, and to what extent, the law schools use the writing sample in making their admissions decisions is anyone's guess. Don't worry too much about this section, because its significance on your chances of gaining admission to law school is likely to be negligible. Concentrate on writing neatly and legibly, and whatever you write will probably be fine. Just make sure to answer the actual question asked.

Figuring out the best way to prepare

Taking the LSAT is painful enough the first time around, so you don't want to take it more than you have to. The best policy for getting the score you want on the first attempt is trying your best and using one of these three preparation options:

✔ Preparing on your own using commercially available study guides

✔ Taking an expensive test-prep course

✔ Doing absolutely nothing and seeing what happens

Because many law schools weight your LSAT score at least as heavily as your GPA, and sometimes slightly more, I highly advise against the third option in the previous list. When you do nothing, you risk blowing any shot you may have at being admitted to the law school of your choice if your score is very low. However, some people try this option and do very well. Although the choice is up to you, the rest of this section focuses on the more reliable — and far less risky — first two options.

Going it alone

The benefits of preparing on your own are costs and flexibility. Studying by yourself is less expensive than taking a prep course that can cost you into the hundreds of dollars. You can buy — or borrow — a few of the commercially sold books and study at your leisure; that's where the flexibility comes into play. You won't need to go to class, do homework, or sit down to take practice tests at any particular time — as long as you actually study.

If you go it alone, you should definitely incorporate a few timed practice LSATs into your studying curriculum. Taking a practice test under time pressure can help you really diagnose your strengths and weaknesses. There's a sample LSAT you can take under timed conditions in the free *LSAT & LSDAS Registration and Information Book* (which you can find at your prelaw advisors' office, your college career center, or a law school admissions office) or download the sample test from LSAC's Web site at www.LSAC.org. Otherwise, you can find sample tests in commercial prep books at your local bookstore or library.

Although the going-it-alone approach may work for you, the reason this approach can never work for people like me is that you're left completely to your own devices. You can buy all the study books on the shelf at the bookstore, but if they're left sitting untouched on your desk, they're not going to do you a whole lot of good. If you're very motivated, and can act as your own taskmaster, then this method may work wonders for you. But for procrastinators like me, it's a dismal prescription for failure. When you have the inner motivation to sit down a few hours a day with these commercial books, let alone actually take one or more timed practice tests, then more power to you.

Getting some help from the pros

Because the do-it-yourself method never worked for me, I decided to take one of the popular prep courses. I found the prep course that I took to be helpful in identifying my strengths and weaknesses, and it actually increased my score by 20 points from the first diagnostic test that I took to my score on the real LSAT.

Like any course, however, it's only as good as the work you're willing to put into it. A prep class won't do you much good when you fail to show up, don't do the homework, and take none of the tests. You won't learn much by just signing up.

I did most of the assigned homework and attended every scheduled practice test. By far, taking the practice tests helped increase my score. Besides the most popular, well-advertised prep courses, many universities or community education centers offer their own versions of LSAT classes. Or, you may be able to find a law student who's willing to tutor you privately. Just make sure that student did well on the LSAT.

Deciding when to register for and take the LSAT

You want to register for the LSAT one month beforehand so that you don't risk having to take the test anywhere other than your preferred test location. If you don't register until the last minute, you may find yourself driving four hours to a remote testing location, and nobody wants that. When you register by the regular deadline, you're more likely to get your first choice of testing sites. There is also a late registration date, but its deadline is only a week or so after the regular registration date (registering late also incurs you fees).

You can take the LSAT in June, October, December, and February. Most schools recommend taking the June or October tests, because if you don't do as well as you'd like, you can take the next available testing date without being late in the applications process. In other words, taking the February test for entrance in the fall of the next academic year is too late for many law schools whose cut-off dates are March 1.

You can register for the LSAT via phone or mail, by using the information and forms in the *LSAT & LSDAS Registration and Information Book*, which you can pick up free at your undergraduate institution or at any law school admissions office, or you can do it online at www.LSAC.org.

Navigating the Nuts and Bolts of the Law Schools Data Assembly Service (LSDAS)

At the same time that you register for the LSAT, you also want to register for the *Law Schools Data Assembly Service,* or *LSDAS.* There is no specific deadline for registering for the LSDAS, though the general guideline is to register with the LSDAS a few months before you want to submit your law school applications. Most law schools require you to use the LSDAS, because it — and not you — sends transcripts, your LSAT score, and (sometimes) recommendations directly to the law schools.

The LSDAS is administered by the LSAC (Law School Admissions Council), an organization that coordinates the law school admissions process. That makes the LSDAS a sort of clearinghouse that processes certain parts of your application, like the transcripts and LSAT scores.

Running down what an LSDAS report includes

Basically, LSDAS compiles a special report that it sends to every law school to which you apply. The report includes

- ✔ Copies of your undergraduate and (graduate) transcripts
- ✔ A summary of your undergraduate grades to date, which are converted to the LSDAS's standard 4.0 system, so that law schools have a standardized basis for comparing candidates
- ✔ A report regarding your LSAT score
- ✔ Your letters of recommendation processed by LSAC (if the school allows it, you can send these letters directly to the school yourself)
- ✔ The writing sample from the LSAT

Each law school you apply to (those that require you to register with the LSDAS) needs one of these special reports. All you need to do to have them prepared and sent is to register with the LSDAS, by following the instructions online at www.LSAC.org, or by getting a hold of the *LSAT & LSDAS Registration and Information Book* (available free at your prelaw advisor's office, your college career center, or any law school admissions office).

Registering for the LSDAS is one fee (separate from the LSAT fee), but if you're applying to more than one law school requiring you to register with LSDAS, you'll need to pay additional fees for each LSDAS law school report you order. The initial LSDAS registration fee includes one LSDAS report. For example, if you're applying to ten law schools total, you need to order nine additional reports (because one is already included in the initial LSDAS registration fee).

The other important thing to remember about ordering law school reports is that you don't give LSAC the names of the law schools where you want these reports sent; you simply indicate and pay for how ever many reports you want (corresponding to how many schools you plan to apply to). Then, when the law schools receive your applications, they themselves will request an LSDAS report directly from LSAC. So if you plan on applying to 12 law schools (and order 11 extra reports), but actually end up applying to 13, one lonely law school will be left out in the cold, and be unable to process your application, because when it contacts LSDAS for your law school report, there won't be any left. I found it helpful to order one or two extra law school reports; that way, I knew I'd be covered if I applied to an extra school later on in the process.

Requesting transcripts

After you've registered for the LSDAS, use their transcript request form to get one *official* transcript sent from your undergraduate and any graduate institutions directly to LSAC. Keep in mind that the registrar needs to send the transcript; it can't be given to you and then sent by you to LSAC. The forms can be found in the current *LSAT & LSDAS Registration and Information Book* or they can be downloaded from www.LSAC.org.

Transcripts of graduate/professional work, after you've obtained your bachelor's degree, will not be summarized on the LSDAS law school report; but copies of these transcripts will be sent on to law schools.

Processing recommendation letters

Using the LSAC recommendation letter service is purely optional, unless the law schools to which you're applying require that you use it. You can find out what each school's policies are on this matter by looking through its application materials or calling the admissions office directly. Otherwise, you can just have your recommenders send the recommendation letters directly to the law school, or go through your undergraduate institution's recommendation service.

The way LSAC's service works is that you have your recommendation writer write and sign the letter, and send it directly to LSAC along with the completed special Letter of Recommendation Form contained in the *LSAT & LSDAS Registration and Information Book* or downloadable from www.LSAC.org. Both the form and the recommendation letter go in the recommender's own envelope (regardless of whether you go through LSAC's service, you can provide your recommenders the envelope with postage already affixed, as a courtesy). You need to make sure each recommender gets a copy of the form. It's important to send the LSAC's Letter of Recommendation Form along with the actual letter, otherwise LSAC will not be able to match up the letter to your file. And you sure wouldn't want someone else to benefit from your glowing recommendations!

Glimpsing What LSAT Scores Can Get You into Law School

So you've taken the test, and nervously await the results. Your LSAT results are available approximately five weeks after you take the test; your scores will be mailed to you. If you are chomping at the bit, and can't wait that long, about 20 days after the test date, you can call the LSAC's TelScore, which is a telephone score-reporting service and find out your score. The TelScore number is 215-968-1200. I certainly couldn't wait the five weeks, so I called TelScore the first day it became available. To find out the telephone score release dates for each test date, consult the *LSAT & LSDAS Registration and Information Book* or go online at www.LSAC.org.

LSAT scores range from 120 to 180. You get a 120 for signing your name on the answer sheet. It's rare to get a 178–180, except, of course, for Reese Witherspoon in the movie *Legally Blonde* (her character scored a 179).

The best way to find out what scores you need to get into a particular law school is to check out a guidebook — one that lists the law schools and their criteria for admission. In general, you're considered competitive for a law school when you score is at or above their median. Anything more than that, and you're golden. Anything less, and you may have a tough time without a great GPA or other compelling personal characteristics

When should you take the test more than once? Because retaking such a major test is an ordeal, it's best to seriously consider your chances of raising your score. If you were sick on the original test day, didn't have time to study for personal reasons, or were distracted by the marching band playing outside the testing center, those are good grounds for taking it again. But if you're not confident that you can increase your score by several points, or aren't willing to put in the time the second time around, it's best not to risk getting a lower score the next time.

Law schools generally won't penalize you for taking the LSAT more than once, but remember that it conversely doesn't look too good if your score goes down significantly. Most people who take the LSAT again do so only one other time; fewer people take it three or more times. But one admissions person I spoke with recalled a student taking the LSAT five times! Many schools will average your LSAT scores; others look at the highest score, but specific practices differ among schools. Your best bet: Whenever you're looking to take the test more than once, be sure to check with the individual schools about their policies.

Playing the "Weighting" Game

Many students wonder how each component of their application is weighted in the admissions staff's decision. Because the admissions process has become more competitive and crowded through the years, many law schools no longer have enough time to spend a leisurely session evaluating every nuance of each candidate's application.

That's why some schools use index numbers. *Index numbers* are special formulas that give different weights to the LSAT and GPA. They're helpful to admissions staffers because they offer a quick way to grasp the credentials of a particular candidate. Many schools use the index number to formulate a score above which applicants are presumptively admitted, below which, presumptively rejected.

Gauging your GPA and LSAT score in the application picture

A sad fact about law school admissions is that you can be summed up by a single number. For some schools, your four years of hard work as an undergraduate are weighed exactly against your performance on a one-time, half-day test. Some schools give the LSAT even more weight, claiming that because so many colleges grade differently, they can't possibly judge between a 4.0 GPA at one school and a 3.8 GPA at another. So, instead, they rely on the LSAT as the great equalizing factor. You may find this news outrageous. After all, how can four years of blood, sweat, and Professor Smith's advanced physics class be the same as a few piddily hours of multiple-choice questions?

You can look at some informative charts showing numbers of applicants who applied to law school and those who were accepted nationally based on their GPA and LSAT percentile in the Law School Admission Council's *The Official Guide to U.S. Law Schools*.

When you're applying as a college student or recent graduate, law schools are likely to place more emphasis on your GPA and LSAT. With nontraditional students they may look at whether you've taken several years off or had significant work experience, because a nontraditional student's work achievements tend to speak louder for his or her present ability to do well in law school than 6-year-old grades. Regardless of how many years nontraditional applicants have been out of school, admissions committees tend to place more emphasis on the LSAT, which is of course a more recent accomplishment, than on the older GPA.

Susan Palmer, an associate dean for admissions at the University of Virginia School of Law, in Charlottesville, Virginia, explains that the LSAT is the one factor in the admissions process that is standardized for nearly every applicant, which is unlike the tremendous educational variation among undergraduate academic programs. That said, although the LSAT is a good indicator, it isn't infallible. Standardized tests historically have over-predicted or under-predicted classroom performance of some candidates. When an applicant presents a widely disparate LSAT score when compared with undergraduate grades, most admissions professionals want to know how well the SAT or ACT predicted college performance. In the case of an applicant with a 3.9 GPA in an academic major with a 50th percentile SAT score, a lower LSAT may not be accorded as much credence. Similarly, a candidate with a 98th percentile SAT score and a 2.9 GPA may find that the admissions committee is more skeptical of a high LSAT, because the high standardized test score did not accurately predict college performance.

Recognizing how extracurriculars help

Citing your undergraduate or personal extracurricular activities provides the most help when you're not a presumptive admit or reject but somewhere in-between. When an admissions committee actually begins reviewing your application, it looks at many factors, including your work experience, extracurricular involvement, recommendations, and your personal statement. Even if you're a nontraditional applicant, you still need to include any extracurriculars you're involved in, such as a writing society, a political association, or a religious group.

When it comes to extracurriculars, law schools prefer quality over quantity. They'd rather see two or three extracurriculars in which you've held leadership roles or won accolades than a list of ten where it looks like all you did was attend a meeting or two.

Handling the Outcome of the Application Process

Law schools vary on how long they take to decide which students to accept. The time frame can be anywhere from three weeks to several months. The official reply date, for traditionally accepted students (those who are not wait-listed) is April 1 to April 15. During this two-week period, if you've gained an acceptance, you need to let the school know that you're enrolling. After the school figures out how many of its accepted students will enroll, they can go to their waitlist, and start contacting those students.

Celebrating your acceptance

Don't think that a thick envelope in the mail is the only sure sign of good news. When I received my letter of acceptance to Indiana University School of Law–Bloomington, it came in a thin envelope with only one piece of paper inside — the acceptance letter. When I first saw the envelope, I was sure that it was a rejection, and I briefly considered just tearing it up and throwing it away without even opening it. Good thing I didn't! This demonstrates that you shouldn't be too quick to judge an acceptance letter by its thickness.

Some schools include your school-specific scholarship or fellowship aid award letter in with your admissions letter; others don't. Some send scholarship or fellowship application forms with their acceptance letters. You probably won't find out about your federal loan aid until later in the summer; contact your specific school's admission office for specific details.

After you receive your letter, celebrate! Go out with your friends — heck, even order yourself a cake! It's been a long, hard road, and you've earned it!

Deciding between two or more schools

If you're in the enviable circumstance of being accepted at two or more schools, you need to decide which school to attend. Generally, most schools require your response between April 1 and April 15.

Visiting the schools again (or for the first time) after you've been accepted is always a good idea. Doing so enables you to take a good hard look at them with the eye of an admitted student. When you're there, try to imagine yourself actually attending. Can you see yourself fitting in with the environment? You may also want to ask each admission office about what types of aid you can expect to get at each school — both scholarships and fellowships and federal aid.

If you're still having trouble deciding which school to choose, enlist the help of your prelaw advisor, who can help you better hash out the pros and cons of each school.

Handling the waitlist

Some students who weren't accepted are put on the waitlist. If you land on the *waitlist,* it means that you're qualified to do the work at that school, but there were more qualified people ahead of you who were accepted first before the school ran out of seats. Don't give up — you're still potentially in the running! As the cancellations come in (after the April 1-April 15 candidate reply deadline), you may find yourself getting a phone call or letter with wonderful news. Generally, law schools don't start contacting their waitlisted candidates until May or June, and sometimes as late as the end of August.

If people who said they'd enroll don't show up for orientation, waitlisted candidates may even be notified after law school starts that they're in! If you get such a call, be prepared to change plans at the drop of a hat, if you're so inclined.

Dealing with a rejection

If you weren't accepted anywhere, you have some tough decisions to make. You can either take a year off and reapply or decide that law school isn't for you and pursue another career path. If you decide to take a year off and reapply, contact the admissions committees where you weren't accepted and ask about the reasons why you were rejected. They may be able to give you a lead that you wouldn't otherwise have considered, including factors like your application was full of typos, your grades didn't survive their index number cutoff, or you were an out-of-state resident hopelessly competing at a state school with in-staters for acceptance.

Regardless of what you find out, make sure that you incorporate corrective measures into your strategy for next year's application season. If you have an opportunity to improve your application for the next round, such as working on an interesting project, taking a legal-oriented job, or retaking the LSAT, do it. Or, if you'd rather not, you may simply want to apply to a different set of schools next year. Either way, remain optimistic that the next application season will work out for you.

If, on the other hand, you decide that if getting into law school is this hard, you don't want any part of it, then consider other careers that are law-related but that don't require law school, such as paralegal work, mediation, or nonprofit advocacy work.

Deciding to Defer

Taking time off between college and law school is the gift that keeps on giving. Many schools allow you to defer admission — usually for one year — after you've gained acceptance. *Deferring* means that you gain admission but take a year off and keep your seat in that class until the next academic year. Schools generally grant deferments on a case-by-case basis.

Generally, the procedure if you want to defer is that you write a letter to the law school admissions dean stating your reasons for deferring. Then, the admissions committee decides whether to grant it, and sends you a letter back for your files. You'll usually need to put down a seat deposit to hold your place.

If you want to take a year off, some people find a greater peace of mind by applying and then deferring enrollment for a year (instead of taking the year off and applying at the end of that year for the next fall). You simply apply for law school during your senior year of college, and then if (or as long as) the school allows it, you can choose to defer your enrollment at the school for one year. Using this method means that instead of taking the year off and then applying, you can apply right away, be accepted, and then wait a year before enrolling. The main benefit of deferring your enrollment in law school is the unparalleled peace of mind that results. Deferring enables you to really enjoy your year off, because all the hard work of applying and taking the LSAT has come and gone.

What can you do during your year off? Some students who defer want to have fun, take an easy job, and hang out with friends. Others want to get a taste of the real working world, take a challenging job, and find out what real dead-lines are like. Some want to try something adventurous, so they live for a year in a foreign country, work aboard cruise ships, or work as seasonal workers. During my year off, I worked a series of short-term jobs as a waitress, a book-store cashier, and a secretary. I also took several classes like drawing and ceramics for fun. My year was an enjoyable one, and I gained the experience of living in my first apartment in a lively city, Minneapolis. The real payoffs were evident when law school began. That's when I realized that I was able to focus on my studies instead of lamenting the concept of three more years of school. Many of my peers who didn't take time off burned out after the first semester.

In short, deferring can refresh and reenergize you for the challenges of three difficult years of professional education.

Part II

Getting What You Came for: The Law School Experience

In this part . . .

Your first year is the most important of your entire law school career. In this part, I help you make the transition to a law school mentality, show you how to ace your courses, and tell you how to best achieve a healthy balance between work and leisure.

Chapter 5

Getting Into the 1L Groove

Congratulations! You've made it to law school after a grueling application season. You conquered the LSAT, and now's the time for you to get everything ready so you can hit the ground running during your first year of law school! Before you officially begin the school year, getting your life, lodging, and law school lingo up to speed is a wise idea so you won't have so much to worry about as the semester gets underway. Moving to a new city, starting a new school, and opening a new chapter of your life often is scary and uncomfortable — at first. However, soon you'll be armed with all the tricks of the trade to make your transition as painless as possible. This chapter discusses some of the best ways for new 1Ls to acclimate themselves to the law school mind-set and start the year leaps and bounds ahead of their peers.

Performing Five Crucial Tasks before School Starts

Think about the month or so before the school year starts as being the prime time for you to get all your affairs (everything) in order. Yep, you need to start packing up your old place, confirming your new place, and reading about your new city. This section describes five key actions that must be taken *before* your classes start, because that's when you have plenty of time and energy to deal with them. The last thing you need as a 1L is to be worrying about things that you can easily take care of beforehand.

Take control of your personal life

First-year law students don't have much time for dating. The reason: Almost all their free time is devoted to staying on top of reading, freaking out about exams, and trying to figure out exactly what this thing called law school is all about. But the problem is especially difficult when the angst of a relationship back home already causes you mental anguish. Everyone goes through tough times with his or her sweetie, but you need to iron out any significant relationship issues before going off to law school.

Doing so, however, may mean deciding that that you need to break up or separate before you start law school. Although breaking up is hard on you, remember that you're starting a new phase of your life, so you need to make sure that your relationships are prepared to withstand the time commitment and stress of law school. Most of my peers who had an *HTH* (hometown honey) at the beginning of law school broke up during the first semester. Many of them cited the same reason: The other person just couldn't relate to what the 1L was going through. On a happier note, however, many new 1Ls decide that heading to law school is the perfect time to solidify a relationship. You're starting a new chapter of your life, and getting engaged, marrying, or starting a family may be a wonderful way for you to begin your new path as a soon-to-be law student.

Even when your relationship is in great shape, I recommend explaining to your significant other that you're not going to have as much time to spend with him or her for at least the first year of school. You need to explain that law school may mean putting a cap on nightly four-hour marathon conversations or twice weekly dinner and movie dates. But be sure to reassure your partner that this 24/7 time commitment to law school is only temporary — after the first year is over, and you're better able to gauge how much time you need to put into your studies to get the grades you want, you can probably devote more time to all the areas in your life, including your partner. Of course, part-time and evening law students, who will likely work full-time during their entire law school careers, may need to explain to their partners that their free time probably won't increase appreciably from the first year to the rest.

Put your finances in order

No one likes worrying about money, especially when you have a million other things to think about. You don't want to be halfway into your first month of law school only to find out that your loan check won't be arriving on time because you forgot to fill out the required paperwork. As soon as you arrive on campus, check in with the financial aid office and go through the following steps:

✔ Read all the materials that you get from the financial aid office closely, and double-check that your information is correct on every document you receive.

✔ Resolve any snafus right away and don't hesitate to contact the financial aid office with any questions.

✔ Determine how you want to receive your living expenses checks (if you decided to take out loans for living expenses) before school starts and arrange for the checks to be mailed to you or direct deposited to your bank account.

Secure comfortable housing

In the same way that a comfortable bed helps you sleep much better, which in turn enables you to work more productively (when you're not falling asleep at your desk every five minutes), a comfortable apartment is another key to success in law school.

When your neighbors are a bunch of loud fraternity or sorority members, unruly townies, or other forms of around-the-clock party animals, you're unlikely to arrive at law school adequately rested each day. This also holds true if you have an inconsiderate roommate, who insists on keeping odd hours. The presence of annoying neighbors and roommates or loud bass thumping through your walls at 4 a.m. may also negatively affect your ability to study undistracted at home.

To avoid these unfortunate circumstances, securing your housing well in advance of your arrival in town is a good idea. (I went on one trip to Bloomington looking for housing four months before school started.) Doing so enables you to aim for the best housing selection, which is particularly important when you're in a university-town where move-ins and move-outs are often timed to the start and end of the school year. Otherwise, when you show up without housing or any clue as to where you're going to live, you may be forced to move into whatever housing is left over, or get stuck with a roommate you may not be compatible with. Some hapless 1Ls end up with apartments that have rodent problems, broken appliances, and inattentive and uncaring slumlords. Doing some advance research into what housing complexes are quieter and better maintained greatly adds to your peace of mind when school starts.

Asking around is the best way to find plum housing, and you need to accomplish this either as soon as you send in your acceptance notice or sometime during the spring or summer before your first year. Some good places to start are

✔ **The law school admissions office.** Notices of rooms to rent or people seeking roommates often are posted here. You can find good housing on these lists, or the admissions staff can alert you to popular law student housing complexes. If you do decide on a roommate, make sure you do adequate research on the person; find out his or her sleeping and waking habits; how clean he or she wants to keep the place, whether he or she has any pets, and what his or her policies are on visitors. The last thing you want stressing you out during your first year is roommate troubles.

✔ **The free rental guides at the grocery store or gas station.** Pick one up and drive around to as many apartments as you can fit into your schedule. I chose this approach, and managed to see ten different apartments in one day; at many places, no advance appointment is necessary.

✔ **The university's graduate dorms (if applicable).** Some law schools offer students the option to live in university-owned apartments or dorms earmarked for graduate students. You may or may not be entitled to a meal plan if you choose this option; inquire at your law school admissions office for more information. One of the benefits of dorms is that most of them come furnished. But be sure to ask other residents living there about the quality of dorm life. Dorms can sometimes be notorious for boisterous neighbors, insect problems, and lack of air conditioning. Check them out thoroughly before you sign.

When looking at any housing option, always ask questions about the age of the complex, the availability of maintenance, noise levels, heating/air conditioning, and other amenities. Find out about the frequency and number of break-ins or other crimes (if any), whether graduate student discounts are available, the percentage of undergraduates residing there, and any insect or rodent problems. Noisy neighbors are bad enough, but the last thing you need is a colony of ants or the resident mouse destroying the serenity of your new pad.

Coordinate your move

A few weeks before moving into your new place, you need to develop a plan for getting out of your old home that includes

✔ Setting a packing timeline

✔ Scheduling movers

✔ Turning off the phone, water, electricity, and other utilities

✔ Changing your mailing address

In preparation for moving into your new digs, be sure to inquire whether they'll be ready by the time you arrive in town. Having to stay in a motel with all your belongings while waiting for former occupants to move out is a huge hassle.

How long before school starts should you plan on moving into your new pad? A good guideline is two weeks at the minimum; otherwise, you'll be in a rush to get everything done. I moved in three and a half weeks before school started, and found this timeframe to be ideal. I had plenty of time to furnish my apartment, get household supplies, and learn my way around town. When you arrive at your new place, make sure that your telephone, electricity, and other utilities are turned on, that your mail is being delivered, and that your cable can be hooked up.

All law students need home Internet access (to check e-mail, complete any online legal research and writing assignments, and do at-home legal research). If you desire high-speed Internet access, be sure to make arrangements for this as well, but first check to see whether your new apartment or dorm is wired for it and that your city or town is eligible to receive it. Many law students just use their regular phone lines and modems and get a special connectivity package from the university that enables them to dial in to the university's modem pool at no charge. The cost of the connectivity package is usually minimal, and it enables you to dial up free (as long as you're in the same area code) to the university for all your years as a law student there, even during summers. This is a huge bonus, because it means you won't need to sign up with a commercial Internet Service Provider.

As long as you've taken the time for planning how your move will go, you won't get caught by any nasty snags. And even if you do, because you had the common sense to move in a few weeks before school starts, you'll have enough time to straighten out any problems.

Establish a routine

A couple of weeks before law school begins, figure out what sort of routine you need to establish so that everything gets done. Some people may equate the notion of *routine* with a boring, predictable life. But when you're faced with so many new experiences and the time-consuming study requirements of law school, you'll be hard-pressed to do everything that needs to be done on a daily basis without a routine.

For instance, when you've taken the summer off and slept until noon every day, you need to get back into a routine of rising early. Ask yourself about the following factors to determine what variables are going to be part of your new routine:

✔ **Sleeping patterns:** Will you need to go to bed at 10 p.m. to feel rested for the next day? Will you get up early enough to get all of your studying done, or will you try to cram it in the night before?

✔ **Exercise:** When will you fit in your exercise regimen? Before dinner, three times a week? Or by getting up early in the morning and hitting the gym before classes?

✔ **Food:** Will you shop for groceries once a week? Or will it save you time, money, and cleanup hassles by eating out at inexpensive places for lunch and dinner?

After figuring out what I need to plan for during the day, I've always found that making a rough weekly schedule is helpful, penciling in class and study times, workouts, meals, and fun. Developing a rough plan now of when you'll do things helps you feel more at ease later on when law school is in full swing.

Tips for Taming Your Transition

Almost every transition is stressful, regardless of whether it's starting a new school, moving to a new town, or starting a new job. It's a life change, and getting used to life changes takes time. I've always been more comfortable when early on I feel as much in control of a situation as I possibly can. Arriving in your new city two to three weeks before school starts is an ideal amount of time for

✔ Moving in

✔ Decorating your new pad

✔ Figuring out where key places like the post office, self-service laundry, bars, and so on are located

✔ Generally, getting your bearings before law school begins

If you're a part-time or evening student who's about to start a new full-time job, you'll have additional changes in your life. Starting any new job takes some getting used to, particularly if it's in a brand new field or in a new city. You can help ease your transition by

✔ Talking to as many employees in your new job as you can before work officially starts

✔ Visiting your employer to find out how you can get started on the right foot

✔ Reading up on trade or industry publications

If you have concerns about juggling full-time work with school (and who doesn't?), chat with other part-time or evening students at your school to find out how they've managed. If your school has a part-time or evening students' club or organization, call up the president and chat about your concerns. When you hear from other people who are successfully doing what you want to do, you'll feel more confident in managing your time and transitioning to your new job.

Getting your bearings

I have the world's worst sense of direction. It always takes me a few months — not weeks — to get to the point where I don't feel lost in a new city. But if you fare slightly better where directions are concerned, you can find the fastest routes to bookstores, drug stores, movie theaters, pet stores, and other places that are important to your routine by

- ✔ Arming yourself with maps of the city and of the campus so you become acquainted with where the nearest hangouts, restaurants, museums, auditoriums, student unions, and gyms are located

- ✔ Heading out on foot, by car, or other means to figure out how to get to where you need to go

- ✔ Checking with the city's chamber of commerce or tourist office to stock up on any activities brochures, coupons, or other benefits they may offer

Although it sounds really obvious, you'll probably want to make sure you know all the nuances of getting to the law school from different parts of town, especially when you're living away from campus. The reason I mention this is because during my first semester of law school, I knew only one way to get to the law school from my apartment. When there was construction blocking that particular route one day, I had no idea of what new detours to take. Thoroughly knowing all possible routes from the beginning would've saved me countless wrong turns and panic.

Additionally, knowing where you'll park is also important given the scarcity of parking spaces at most large universities and big cities. You'll want to figure out your parking options well in advance, including university-owned parking and private parking. If you don't want to deal with university parking, ask around at the admissions office to find out about any out-of-the-way private lots near the law school.

Perusing the law school bookstore

If you've never before seen a *law school casebook* (a thick hardcover book filled primarily with appellate court cases), you may find that taking an advance trip to the bookstore to check one out is educational. Sure, you're risking a heart attack finding out just how much these babies cost (and weigh), but you can at least flip through one, contemplating the vast amounts of knowledge it holds.

Although most law school bookstores offer new and used books, some law schools operate a student government–sponsored bookstore that sells only used books. These books are often priced at whatever the sellers think they can get for them, so it pays to make a beeline for this particular bookstore, because its prices are usually much less than the ones at the regular law school bookstore. The selection, however, is necessarily hit or miss. You can also find great deals on a variety of study aids (see Chapter 10).

Finding out what the university offers

One advantage of attending a law school that's attached to a university: You have access to all the resources that the university offers. You'll also be surrounded by a multitude of departments — graduate and undergraduate, research institutes, resource offices, and specialized libraries. Grab a copy of the most recent university course bulletin, and read through all the department listings. This information may come in handy whenever you want to audit a course for personal interest or when your law school allows 2Ls and 3Ls to take some non–law school courses for credit.

You'll also want to take a tour of the university campus (if you haven't already) that points out areas of interest like the health center, playing fields, gyms, and auditoriums. Ask the tour guide where you can pick up the campus newspaper, which always provides a wealth of information about current happenings, from theater to movies to sporting events.

Meander through the student union, and check out the activities desk, where you can often find brochures and schedules of fun classes offered by the union. Many unions offer inexpensive classes like massage, drawing, photography, or Italian, all for students who want to try something different in a no-stress atmosphere without grades. While you're at the student union, you may want to find out what restaurants or food courts are available (and when), the location of any movie theaters, and recreational activities that are offered, such as racquetball, bowling, or billiards.

Regardless of whether you're at a big university that offers these kinds of amenities, you may also want to find out what kind of student organizations the university offers. Most universities have a student organizations fair at the beginning of the year; however, signs and posters advertising the times and locations may not be posted in the law school. Check the campus paper to familiarize yourself with various organizations and what they do.

Selecting the Right School Supplies

For some people, the thrill of buying new school supplies wore off after the fifth grade. For me, on the other hand, shopping for new highlighters, note-books, pens, and binders still has the same exciting feel in law school as it did as a youngster. There's just something about the fresh start of a new aca-demic year that I always found inspiring, even as a 3L! Before you run out to your local office-supply store and load up on highlighters and printer car-tridges, think about what supplies you need right now and which ones can wait. What follows is a rundown of the main school supplies that you'll need from the start during your first year.

✔ **Computer:** A personal computer is essential for your law school years. Many law schools actually state in their academic regulations that all students must have a computer; check with your school to determine its policies.

Many students wonder what type of computer to buy. Law schools gen-erally send out flyers discussing the make, model, and minimum specifi-cations of the computers they recommend. I kept the computer I got long before law school ever started and didn't encounter any compati-bility problems, even though mine wasn't on the recommended list. Because my computer worked well, was relatively new, and had plenty of storage space, I didn't see any reason to buy the law school's sug-gested computer. As long as your current computer is in fairly good working order, and doesn't crash too often, it should be fine to last you through your law school years.

Some law students wait until they arrive on campus to buy their comput-ers, because many university bookstores offer good discounts on comput-ers and computer peripherals. However, remember to get there early — the lines can grow long closer to the start of classes. Don't forget to pick up a campus connectivity package from the bookstore, so you'll be able to connect to the Web from home right away.

✔ *Black's Law Dictionary:* The day was rare during my first year that I didn't pick up my old friend *Black's Law Dictionary* and use it to look up some foreign-sounding bit of legalese (see Chapter 8 for more on legalese).

You and your dog-eared *Black's Law Dictionary* will even become partners in crime as you furiously flip through it during class, trying to keep pace with the lecture or looking up a word when you're called on. But, as the first semester wears on, and you become more proficient in legal lingo, you'll rely less and less on your dictionary. Nevertheless, this book is an absolute necessity for getting through your years of law school. You can find the dictionary at your law school or regular bookstore.

✔ **Notebooks and folders:** With only a few exceptions, one way that law school classes differ dramatically from undergraduate classes is that you'll receive far fewer handouts. Before my first year, I dutifully bought five folders, one for each class. Out of the five, I ended up using only one folder, and that was for legal research and writing, which had a plethora of handouts. The other four standard courses relied exclusively on the casebook and *casebook supplements* (an affiliated book of the newest cases/statutes that have come out since the casebook's printing). So buying a heap of folders may be unnecessary.

Notebooks, on the other hand, are crucial. I used three 70-page notebooks in each of my five 1L classes, writing on both front and back sides of the paper. Between briefing cases, taking class notes, and writing casebook notes, you'll need a bunch of notebooks (unless, of course, you take your laptop to class).

✔ **Reading lamp:** When you're sitting in your carrel late at night, hunched over your property casebook, and squinting at the tiny font sizes, you'll wish that you had a clip-on reading lamp. Most carrels have built-in lights, but they're sometimes broken or just not bright enough. You can buy cheap, clip-on lamps at any office-supply store. Save your eyes while you still can — you'll need them in good working order during your three years of law school!

Attaining the Law School Mind-set

As newly minted 1Ls, you may need some time to get used to doing things the law school way. When you're a 1L, everything is new to you. You may find practices like the widespread use of seating charts unfamiliar or speaking in front of 100 other people disconcerting. Relax. Because none of your classmates (presumably) has been a 1L before, you're all in the same boat. By supporting each other and joking around about this new culture, you'll get the hang of things before you know it.

Communal living 101: Too close for comfort or all happy together

Attending law school is a little like you're back in high school again. All your classes are in one building, you have lockers that usually aren't big enough to hold more than a few books and a jacket, and most people eat lunch in the same lunchroom. For some people, especially older students, this blast from the past takes some serious getting used to. A couple of ways of breaking up the feeling of communal living include having lunch outside the law school and studying someplace other than the library. Instead, try finding a local coffee shop, bookstore café, another university library, or a quiet nook in the student union.

A chair of one's own: Identifying with the seating chart

Another way law school is like high school is the assigned seating. I can't remember a single college class where I had assigned seats, but I haven't taken a single law school class where I didn't have one. The forbidding thing about a seating chart is that seats are assigned the first or second day of classes, so you need to choose where you sit carefully. Strategize where you'll sit by getting to classes early on the first and second days, because if you choose a poor seat — or seatmate — you're stuck there all semester.

The way the seating charts work is that on the first or sometimes the second day of classes, professors pass around large paper maps of their room's seats, and you're expected to sign your name on the space that corresponds with where you're sitting. A day or two later, professors are likely to have taped photos from the class viewbook to the charts next to each corresponding signature, making it easer for them to identify everyone in the class.

If you don't want to be called on too often, choosing a seat that's out of the professor's direct line of sight sometimes helps. I've had much success with this technique, especially by sitting on extreme sides of the first row. The professor almost never looks directly at the first row or the extreme sides of the room in any location, so you're safer in those areas. When you actually want to get called on, however, be sure to sit right in the middle — rows 3–6 — and in the center. Beware of sitting in the very last row. Many professors become annoyed by students who do so when plenty of other seats are available in the room.

Michael Pastor, a clerk for a federal judge in the District of Maryland, advises that no matter how carefully you choose your seat, you sometimes just can't predict where your professor's gaze will fall. Pastor remembers one particular administrative law professor who repeatedly called only on people in a certain row, despite the fact that plenty of students hadn't been called on even once. The professor never seemed to remember that he'd already called on those same people just the day before. Luckily, Pastor wasn't in that particular row (and never was called on in that class), but he pitied his fellow classmates who got nailed, without fail, each and every day. He muses that students in that row probably studied harder for that class than any other, because they knew they'd get called on.

Preparing for the formalities

One aspect of law school that took me completely by surprise is the tendency of most professors to refer to students by "Ms." or "Mr." rather than by their first names. A few of my professors used first names, but by far the majority used courtesy titles in all three years of law school. One amusing consequence of this formality is that 1Ls in the hallways often call out salutations to each other using their respective courtesy titles. "How're you doing Ms. White?" or "Do you want to meet for lunch, Mr. Freeman?" are frequent student exchanges. By the end of the first semester, I still didn't know most of my peers' first names!

Understanding how your class is divided

Unlike college, where each class that you take is made up of a different set of people, as a 1L, you attend classes with the same set of people for virtually the entire year. At most schools, each 1L class is divided into sections. At some schools, a class of around 200 to 220 people is divided into 8 to 10 sections, each with about 25 people. These groups of 25 often meet individually for legal research and writing classes. For the other standard 1L classes, each individual group is usually melded with between two and four other groups.

Before I started law school, I'd heard of this practice and worried that being with the same people day-in and day-out would become highly annoying. To my surprise, I never once felt that way. Instead, seeing the same faces every day was somewhat of a comfort, during those times when law school was such a maelstrom of uncertainty. As 2Ls and 3Ls, the division system no longer applies, and you're with different people for each class again. I rarely had the same people in any of my 2L and 3L classes, and some classmates from my first year I never saw again, because we must have had completely different schedules.

Sanity-Saving Ways to Survive Orientation

Orientation is usually a two- to three-day event preceding the start of classes. Most orientations are set up the same way, with introductory comments from people in all the major facets of law school life. For example, you may hear a representative of the career services office (CSO) and the various deans speak, followed by meetings with various faculty members and lunch with your peer advisors. Many schools assign small groups of new students to 2Ls who serve as *peer advisors.* Your peer-advisor group will meet for meals, go to social events together, and serve as a support group through the early weeks of the semester. Members of these groups often become long-term friends. If you want to get the most out of your orientation, follow these tips.

✔ **Attend every meeting.** Most law schools mail out an orientation packet to you a few weeks before classes are slated to begin. This packet usually details everything you need to know about attending meetings. Remember that going to everything during orientation is always best, no matter how tired you are or how lame you think it may be. You never know when you'll miss out on an important piece of law school trivia or find out something interesting about your classmates.

✔ **Tag along on tours.** When you're new to law school, and don't know where anything is, be sure to go on as many tours as you can, including tours of the law school, main university, career services office, and law library. Library tours are important because they give you a general overview of where everything is, but many of the books the librarians point out have such complicated-sounding names that you may not remember them. Still, when you have a general idea of where the reporters, legal encyclopedias, and law reviews are located, you'll be a step ahead of the game when classes start.

✔ **Go to all the social events.** The first few weeks in law school are critical for meeting new people and forming friendships. Social events during orientation — either organized by the school and/or put on by students — are great ways to mix and mingle. I recommend going to everything — the welcome picnic, lunch with your peer group, and the late night party hosted by your new neighbor. Cliques tend to form fast in law school, so you want to meet as many people as you can initially and try to keep an open mind. Often, the people you meet during orientation will still be your friends when you're 3Ls.

When you're an older student not planning to do anything more with the law school social scene, getting out there during the first few weeks is especially important in order to meet new people before the frenzy of law school life kicks in.

✔ **Involve your family in orientation.** Orientation is great for you because you get a solid snapshot of the school that reveals its mission and its offerings. However, your spouse or family usually won't be so lucky. Although some schools formally involve families in orientation, many more don't. So, in that case, letting your loved ones know what you've discovered in orientation and what services or aspects of the school may be beneficial to them is up to you.

Chapter 6

Surviving Typical First-Year Classes: A Crash Course

- -

In This Chapter

▶ Making sense of your 1L courses

▶ Getting a feel for how classes are organized

▶ Maximizing classroom time

▶ Developing good relations with your professors

▶ Knowing what to do if you're unprepared for class

- -

You may have heard people say that law school is the most rigorous and intellectual education of all the professions. Why, you may ask, is that true? Because you're *constantly* being challenged. Law school isn't like memorizing the anatomy of the body by rote; you're actually finding subtle weak points in an argument. In class, you're not passively taking notes in a huge lecture hall; you're bombarded at every turn with your professor's relentless Socratic questioning (see Chapter 8). Instead of dozing off when an overhead projector switches on, lively debates among your peers keep you on your toes, and the pace of the class forces your brain to be in constant overdrive.

If that isn't enough to stimulate you, well, perhaps 100 pages of reading per night or that shot of adrenaline you feel when you're caught unprepared will do the trick. The good news: If you follow the advice in this chapter, you'll be ready to gracefully hit any kind of pitch that law school or your professors throw at you out of the park. This chapter describes what courses you'll take, how they're organized, and how to avoid falling behind. Want to know when to perk up your ears in class and how to know what your professor considers important? It's all here, so bust out your syllabus, start flipping through your casebook, and prepare to discover what your first-year classes are all about!

Understanding the 1L Curriculum

Most law schools offer the same seven required courses (including legal research and writing) that comprise the standard 1L curriculum. How many credit hours and semesters the respective law schools allot to each course varies, however. For instance, some schools require two semesters of contracts, whereas yours may require only one (or vice versa). At some schools, you may take one or two of these required 1L courses in the second year, instead of the first.

Although all law professors have their own perceptions of what material within a single course deserves more or less coverage, the basic substance of 1L classes is similar from one law school to another.

Although schools differ on how many semesters you take each of the following courses, rest assured that all 1Ls are pretty much learning the same material.

For part-time and evening students, the concept of a first year falls apart to a certain degree, because they don't take all of the following courses during their first year. At many part-time and evening programs, students take the traditional 1L courses during their first *and* second years, taking fewer credits each semester than full-time students. The third and fourth years of part-time and evening programs are when upper-class electives are taken.

Torts

If the only tort you've ever heard of is the kind (spelled: torte) that goes well with coffee and a scoop of ice cream, you're far from alone. Basically, tort is the French word for a wrong. More specifically, *torts* are civil wrongs where some sort of remedy (usually damages in the form of monetary compensation) can be obtained. Torts class covers many of the same things you'd imagine that personal injury lawyers handle — car accidents, erroneous amputations, battery, and heavy objects falling out of windows and injuring people, just to name a few.

I liked torts class the best because reading about the cases was so much fun. Reading the details of horrific surgical mishaps, train wrecks, defective products, wild animal attacks, and slips and falls was a refreshing change of pace from drier courses like contracts. One thing's for sure: After a stimulating semester of torts, you never look at a banana peel lying on the sidewalk in the same way again!

Civil procedure

Civil procedure (or *civ pro*) is all about how to sue someone for noncriminal penalties. The course shows you the steps you need to go through to begin proceedings against a defendant in state or (more frequently) federal court, the structure of the court system, how to determine which law (state or federal) controls, and under what circumstances a case can be brought in state or federal court. Many law schools use the most recent edition of the *Federal Rules of Civil Procedure* as one of the main teaching tools for the course. You also find out how to file a *complaint* (which signals the start of a lawsuit), how to handle responses to complaints, and how lawyers use a host of motions and counterclaims to stymie the proceedings.

One of the most surprising tidbits I got out of civ pro is the tiny percentage of lawsuits that ever make it to court (most are either settled or otherwise terminated). Think about it for a moment: In the litigious society you're familiar with, as many as ten times more lawsuits are initiated than are actually ever tried in court!

Criminal law

If you're fascinated with the criminal mind, or have an image of the criminal lawyer as the prototypical attorney (you know, like the ones you see on TV shows), this course is sure to captivate you. Here, you discover the notion of *mens rea* (the guilty mind), endlessly discuss the concept of punishment, and focus on the notion of intent. You find out about the significance of the due process clause in the Constitution and examine the insanity defense in depth.

I think criminal law is the most practical and useful of the 1L courses, because the concepts are easier to relate to everyday life. It seems that criminal law is the one law school course that is useful for everyone to take, because, for the most part, everyone knows at least a little about it. After all, crimes are an unfortunate part of everyday life in America, and knowing how they're classified and how the prosecutorial system works is valuable knowledge for anyone.

Contracts

In *contracts* class, you work on the nuts and bolts of your garden-variety contract. You glean what makes up an *offer* (an attempt to initiate a contract), an *acceptance* (agreeing to the terms of the offer), and *consideration* (something of value required for an enforceable contract); what constitutes a transaction; and when you can revoke a contract without penalty. You also find out about *breach of contract* and how to interpret contracts.

After taking this class, you're much more informed and capable of dealing with routine things, such as your apartment lease, health insurance contract, or employment agreement. One result of this class: You'll never again sign your name to anything without going over it with a fine-toothed comb!

Property

Property is the course that's all about the relationship of rights and duties to land or objects. In this class, you talk about issues such as rights in personal-property and landlord-tenant issues and how people's estates are divided up after death.

Property, however, involves more *abstract thinking* (heavy on the theory) than other law school courses and is harder to relate to on an everyday basis. That's why I considered it to be by far the most difficult first-year subject. For example, you learn about complicated concepts such as *future interests* (where possession of property occurs in the future) and *adverse possession* (getting title to property through possession under certain circumstances). You also draw plenty diagrams, which may help you conceptualize some of the more theoretical ideas (particularly future interests). You'll certainly learn some interesting new vocabulary, like my all-time favorite: the ridiculous-sounding *fee tail* (a particular type of estate).

Constitutional law

Constitutional law (or *con law*) is all about the law that comes from the Constitution. In this course, you talk about governmental powers (the three branches), due process, and the Bill of Rights. You also delve into topics such as separation of church and state, equal protection, and the commerce clause. One of the great things about con law class is that you touch on many important issues facing American society today, including racism, civil rights, abortion, school prayer, and the death penalty, just to name a few. You read landmark cases like *Roe v. Wade,* the *Bakke* case, and *Marbury v. Madison.*

Con law is unique in its emphasis on a *"balancing" approach.* Many con law cases have no clear-cut answers, so the courts attempt to weigh the competing interests to arrive at reasoned (or balanced) solutions. When you finish the course, you'll have a greater appreciation of the difficult jobs that judges have.

Legal research and writing

Ah, the joys of legal research and writing. You can aptly call it "the other white meat," because legal research class is one of your required 1L courses, but it's very different from the others.

At my school, legal research class was graded pass/fail (which is common at many law schools), yet it often took up more time than all my other graded classes combined. How can a (usually) two-credit, pass/fail course take up so much time, you ask? For one thing, legal research is the only law school class that actually has regular homework (other than reading) assignments. (I know, the mere mention of the word "homework" may summon bad memories of high school.) Almost every class features *citation exercises* (where you find out the correct legal citation style for sample cases and other works cited in legal memos and briefs) to hand in, research exercises to perform with library reference materials, and many long reading assignments to work on how you perform various legal research tasks. You also must complete several large writing assignments, ranging from writing several analytical memos to researching and writing a *brief* (a persuasive document in which a lawyer advocates for why the client should prevail in a lawsuit) and then arguing that brief in the spring before a mock judge panel.

Beware of blowing off legal research class! Many students are tempted to do just that, because the class usually is ungraded and often only one or two credits per semester. However, it's one of the all-time most important classes you ever take in law school. The concepts that you discover are crucial to your success as a lawyer — and they come into play heavily during your summer legal jobs (see Chapter 14). So, do yourself a favor and treat legal research class as if it were like the graded, five-credit class it deserves to be.

Of all the law school books you want to sell, don't sell your legal research and writing books. They'll come in handy during your summer legal jobs. I took all my books from legal research and writing to my 2L summer job at the Environmental Protection Agency, and consulted them almost every day as I wrote memos and conducted legal research. Rereading them, or at least skimming them, prior to starting your summer jobs (as a review) is also a good move.

Reviewing How a 1L Course Is Organized

Unlike many of your college courses, a 1L class is fundamentally different in terms of pace, structure, homework, and expectations. Probably the biggest difference between law school and college is the lack of traditional homework (except for legal research and writing class; see the previous section). You almost never have a single nonreading homework assignment: no papers, quizzes, midterms, or any other sort of non–final exam evaluations. In my entire law school career, the only pieces of homework I ever had to do were a short writing assignment or two in torts class and several short papers (two to three pages) for two upper-level electives. In general, the only homework that you have is reading.

The problem with the lack of traditional homework is that many people become lazy about keeping up with the reading. They take a few days off, and suddenly they're 100 pages behind. It's so easy to do, and I recall that the desire to slack off crept up on me every semester. You may be tempted to think of reading as not real work, but after you fall into that dangerous mind-set, everything goes downhill. You fall so far behind that you can't keep up in class very well and you become really nervous when you're inevitably called on and haven't glanced at the material in days. Keeping up with the reading always makes your law school coursework go easier for you.

The syllabus: Just the facts, ma'am (or sir)

The only real handout you're likely to receive during an entire semester (except in legal research and writing) comes the first day: the almighty syllabus. In your college classes, you probably got a several-page, detailed, descriptive syllabus (perhaps even on bright-colored paper) that featured a perky explanation of the course and its goals. In law school, however, brevity is the name of the game. Many syllabuses are plain old white, one-page jobs, with a brief intro sentence or two and the schedule of reading topics and corresponding page numbers. That's it.

As you skim your bare-bones syllabus, you notice that you're supposed to cover 20 to 30 pages of reading *per class*. This amount of work may come as a shock to students who are used to covering that many pages *per week* in college. Just keep in mind that you get used to the reading load pretty quickly and soon find out how to keep up with the rapid-fire pace.

Class pace: More like rabbit than hare

You may also find that law school classes move at a quicker pace than what you're used to in college. Each day in class you cover several topics or concepts, and you may find that the professor spends less time on each one than you're comfortable with.

The only way to keep up with class pace is reading your assigned pages on time and trying to keep up with class discussions. You may find that joining study groups (see Chapter 9) comes in handy, especially when you notice that you're missing points made in class or you're not grasping topics.

One exam, one chance

What seems to make new 1Ls the most nervous, however, is the concept of taking only one exam (see Chapter 11 for more on exams). (Upper-class students have a way out of the one exam concept, because they're often able to choose courses that substitute a final paper in lieu of an exam.) When you have only one factor determining your grade (class participation affects it only in extreme circumstances), it's hard not to flip out at the end of the semester when the stress really piles on.

I think the one-exam concept is ridiculous and counterproductive to real learning, because you don't receive any feedback all semester on how you're doing. The one-exam concept doesn't bode well for students who suffer from test anxiety or have more success with intermediate grading opportunities throughout the semester. Additionally, no matter how diligent you've been with your reading or with showing up for class every day, when you blow the exam or you're sick that day, your entire grade for that class is shot. But short of staging a 1L protest, not much can be done about the one-exam phenomenon.

So, try taking comfort in the fact that although the one-exam concept may be a big-time pain in the keister, trying to change that system is fruitless. Just prepare as well as you can. If you need help, Chapter 9 gives you a head start with some great tips for studying for exams.

Lyman Johnson, a professor of corporate and securities law at Washington and Lee School of Law in Lexington, Virginia, says that convenience is one reason for the single-exam concept in many law schools. Using only one evaluation tool can minimize the professor's time. Although Johnson says that some professors believe an exam adequately captures a student's understanding of the material, he advises students who don't like the one-exam concept to look for courses in which class participation or writing projects also factor into the final grade. He believes law professors, in general, don't do as good a job as they can in terms of evaluating a wide range of lawyerly skills. Being quick-witted is only one way of showing your talent, but it's a skill that's heavily rewarded on law school exams. In Johnson's business-planning class, he has students complete four in-depth lawyerly writing assignments, which he thinks is closer than a one-shot test to the real-world reward system that lawyers encounter. Lawyers who've passed the bar exam are not assessed by a one-chance method. It's rare when a lawyer is evaluated for a promotion based on a three-hour performance, and in that sense, the one-exam concept is a disconnect from reality.

Making the Most of Your 450 Classroom Hours Per Year

The American Bar Association (ABA) specifies that law students must attend a certain number of class hours per semester that amount to a total of

450 classroom hours per year. For the most part, that means if you skip too many classes, your grade may be lowered automatically, or you may even be excluded from taking the exam. Because you need to attend the majority of your classes, you may as well find out how to get as much out of them as possible. In-class time is most crucial for finding out what your professor thinks is important, what you need to study for the exam and what you can skip, and what your professor's own special take is on a given subject.

The best way to prepare for class: Read the assignment beforehand, highlight the important areas, and jot down any notes or questions you may have in the margins. Have your case brief ready to go (case briefs are discussed in Chapter 8), and look up unfamiliar terms in your *Black's Law Dictionary* (see Chapter 10).

Arguing with your classmates (in a good way, of course)

A great benefit of going to class is the opportunity it provides for you to publicly argue with and challenge the assertions of your classmates. Saying, "I disagree with Mr. Brown" and then stating your take on an issue is a rush. In fact, classmates often say things that you may find outrageous or just plain wrong. Your time in the classroom is your chance to volunteer and refute their comments. Formally arguing back-and-forth in class is great practice for becoming a trial lawyer, because they not only need to state their cases out loud and succinctly, they also must listen closely to every word their opponents speak and every issue they raise.

Doing extra reading

Some topics you just may not understand, no matter how thoroughly you read about them before class. Don't be a slacker, because you can increase your classroom comprehension by not skipping over these troublesome topics in the casebook.

Whenever you're having trouble with a course topic, ask your professor to recommend a good hornbook. *Hornbooks* differ from study aids in that they cover individual topics in more of a scholarly, in-depth way. Hornbooks include good definitions, background material, and examples. However, because they're usually very expensive, you'll want to check them out from the law library. See Chapter 10 for more information about hornbooks.

Knowing when you absolutely can't miss class

The end of the semester is when you definitely won't want to miss class. Starting about five weeks before the exam, your professors often go into super-speed mode, trying to get through as much material as possible in preparation for crunch time. They may decide at the last minute to cut items that are listed on the syllabus, so you surely don't want to miss out on knowing what you no longer need to study, do you?

Toward the end of the semester also is when professors start dropping hints about what's going to be on the exams. If you hear one say, "Equitable servitudes may show up on the exam," that's a good clue that something is crucial. You don't want to miss any other discussions about exams, either. Professors sometimes explain how they want their particular exams written, and sometimes they may even offer up these explanations unannounced, much to the dismay of students who skip those classes.

Handling Your Professors

Professors, like students, come in all types. For example, even in first-year classes, some may rely more heavily on the Socratic method (see Chapter 8) than others. Some may be more easy-going and conduct their classes in a discussion-type format, where they heavily utilize volunteers, while others may favor a pure lecturing style. Because you'll experience a handful of different professors and teaching styles during your first year, knowing how to deal with them in advance is the best strategy for success.

Staying on your professor's good side

Generally, professors have likes and dislikes that mirror those of the general population. They like it when students come to class, seem interested, are prepared, and participate often. They don't like it when students frequently skip class, come to class late, are unprepared on a regular basis, or are noticeably checking e-mail with their wireless Internet connections.

On the other hand, although professors favor active participators over bumps-on-a-log, there's a definite difference between talking for the sake of hearing your own voice and contributing something meaningful to the discussion. In other words, raising your hand ten times during an hour-long class and offering some mundane or self-serving comment is not the best course of action. Professors, instead, prefer that you think before you speak and try to make your insights thoughtful and relevant.

Figuring out what your professor thinks is important

Professors often have subtle ways of telling you that something is important and thus is likely to appear on the exam. For example, they

- ✔ **Write important concepts on the board.** The general rule is that anything written on the board needs to go into your notes (and needs to be highlighted).

- ✔ **Cross-reference or repeat major concepts.** Professors may refer to something you learned in the beginning or constantly make analogies to a particular discipline. When they do, take note; it'll probably be on the exam.

- ✔ **Put their own unique spin on a topic.** Some professors approach a discipline from a particular angle: an economic or feminist one, for instance. When you figure out that your professor is taking a particular approach to a course, be sure to get a handle on this spin and tailor your exam responses accordingly. Talking to upperclassmen who've taken your course and professor is the best way to figure out your professor's spin, when you're not sure.

Eric Janus, a professor of civil procedure, constitutional law, and mental health law at William Mitchell College of Law in St. Paul, Minnesota, focuses in class on what he thinks is important. He advises students to take copious notes, and then go back, review them, and try to understand why the professor was asking this or that question. He sees his job as taking a spotlight and focusing it on little pieces of a massive contraption called the law. "If students look at what I'm doing in a strategic way, that can help them," he says. "If they ask 'What is he after?' and 'Why is this the answer to the question?' they're on the right path."

Seeking help during office hours

Office hours are lamented by professors as an underutilized phenomenon. Many law school professors have office hours every week; however, they also report that few people ever show up. Why let your professors just sit there, twiddling their thumbs? Think of office hours as your prime chance to get a private one-on-one Q and A session.

Don't go to your professor's office unprepared. Don't say something general like, "So what's this I hear about con law?" Instead, be ready to ask several concrete, specific questions about the reading or class discussion. If you didn't understand a hypothetical (see Chapter 8) in class, now's your chance to rehash it.

The other benefit of office hours is that they give your professor the chance to get to know you. When you're in a class with 100 other students, your professor is likely to remember you more if you've stopped by a few times. Because many summer jobs (and permanent ones, for that matter) require an academic reference (or two), asking for one from a professor you've gotten to know through office hours is a great idea. Of course, you also need to do well on the professor's exams to make good use of that recommendation, but going to office hours is a great first step toward that happy ending.

Yikes! I Was Caught Unprepared

Nothing is quite like the rush of adrenaline you feel the first time you're called on. Your mouth goes dry, your face flushes, and your hands start to shake. Your sense of time becomes distorted, and two minutes of run-of-the-mill questioning feel like two hours of the Inquisition. In fact, even though it happened to me tons of times, I still felt that butterflies-in-the-stomach feeling even as a 3L!

But the feeling is far more sinking when you haven't read the day's assignment. That's when you know you're in real trouble. If you're caught in that most vulnerable of positions — being completely clueless — you may feel as if you're sinking right through the floor. But don't despair — this section takes a look at what you can do to survive this tense situation.

Don't wing it (unless you've at least skimmed the material or you're a pilot)

The only time you should ever attempt to participate when you're called on (and unprepared) is if you can skim the material really fast, right then and there. As a newly minted 1L, you probably haven't gained the (case) reading comprehension techniques that you need to wing it like that. But if skimming comes easily to you, you may be able to get by for a little while, and if you're lucky, your professor will ask volunteers to come to your aid.

If you're not prepared the slightest whit and you get called on, it's best to fess up and admit it by saying "pass." Just make sure to be extra prepared for the next class, because professors love preying on slackers repeatedly. If you feign preparedness when you don't have a clue, your professor and classmates will see your deception immediately. And that's embarrassing.

Most professors (even for upper-class courses) want you to tell them prior to class whether you're unprepared, so the professor knows not to call on you. You generally are allowed a few (two or three) class periods of unprepared-ness before the professor starts getting annoyed with you. If you fail to alert professors to your unpreparedness and they call on you, many professors have been known to express their wrath aloud in class (and some even seem to hold grudges against such students all semester).

Keeping study aids easily accessible

Many wise students bring their study aids (commercial outlines, see Chapter 10; or self-compiled outlines, see Chapter 9) to class, leaving them open to the case they're studying at the moment. This backup method has helped quite a few 1Ls who need extra reassurance survive their Socratic questioning (see Chapter 8). Try keeping the study aid on your lap, out of sight, or hidden by most of your casebook, so your professor doesn't notice you reading out of it, either during class or when you're called on. It isn't that study aids are verboten in class; it's just that professors want to see you really *thinking* in class, rather than getting the material spoon-fed to you out of a study aid. Likewise, some professors are downright hostile to the notion of study aids; you really can't tell which ones, so it's best to keep it out of sight.

Chapter 7

Don't Sweat the Small Stuff: Keeping Academics in Perspective

Some people have an uncanny knack for taking everything in stride. They can tell you that your contracts final is "no big deal," dismiss your concerns about your legal writing assignment with an exasperated sigh, and never look the least bit stressed out, even when they're caught unprepared during class. These same people seem to know the importance of keeping everything in perspective. In other words, they don't sweat the small stuff. After all, is the world really going to end when you get a B instead of a B+ on your civ pro exam or you don't get the exact summer job you wanted?

Probably not. Maintaining this kind of healthy outlook about your law school (and personal) life will go a long way toward keeping you sane (and smiling).

This chapter discusses some simple, painless strategies for better allocating your time between work and play. I explain the importance of maintaining your pre–law school interests and ways that you can develop new hobbies while in law school. By making time each day for the most important person in the law school equation — you — you'll have a much more well-rounded and enjoyable law school experience.

Law School Isn't a 24/7 Affair

Just because you're a law student doesn't mean that law school needs to overwhelm your life. Although being in law school makes you feel as if you're caught in a whirlwind of never-ending responsibilities, you will have *some* free time in your day.

Use your time in-between classes to catch up on your property reading and multi-task during lunch so you can eat *and* read torts. Some law students, especially those with families, like to treat law school like a 9 to 5 job. They come in early in the morning to get their work done, and stay a few hours after their last class to avoid taking too many books home. Of course, if you're a part-time or evening student, time is at a premium, so finishing off a few pages of reading whenever you get the chance can make your life much easier on weekends, when you'll likely be doing the majority of your studying. Whatever your situation, be sure that you take advantage of any priceless downtime whenever you can!

Often the people who are loudest when claiming to be too busy to do anything besides study purposely make their lives that way, because relaxing feels unproductive to them. These same people feel restless during school breaks, believe that doing nothing is slothful, and use "I don't have time" as their favorite catchphrase. The next time your fellow classmates claim to be too busy to have a cup of coffee with you, don't freak out over all the work they seem to be doing that you're not. Their claim of having no time may simply be their own "never-stopping-for-breath" work ethic.

Law students who never take a breather are prone to being so absorbed in the law school scene that they rarely make time for themselves. However, repeatedly sacrificing your own mental and physical health so that you can hit the books soon takes its toll. Falling hopelessly behind because you're so run-down that you miss a week of classes or being sick with the flu during finals is the last thing you want.

That's why the most well-adjusted law students routinely make time for fun. If you plan your day right, you won't feel too crunched to take a long walk, browse in your favorite store, or cook your favorite meal. Part-time and evening law students also need to make time for themselves, even though that's easier said than done, between working a full-time job and going to school part-time. Even the smallest things, like playing with a pet or taking a hot bath before bedtime can make all the difference between stress and success.

Achieving the right balance

In your first year as a law student, balancing work and play may seem difficult. When you're not sure what it takes to prepare adequately for class or do well on exams, justifying a daily two-hour nap or a weekly facial is hard, no matter how much those activities recharge your batteries.

But after your first semester is complete, you're better equipped to know what it takes to do well. That's when you can best decide how to allocate your time. The following list gives you some strategies for striking a healthy balance between work and play.

- ✔ **Keeping a productiveness log.** A *productiveness log* is just a homemade record of what you do every hour of the day. You can use an index card to keep your log handy throughout the day. Simply jot down when you're in class, when you study, when you participate in law school extracurricular activities, and when you eat meals and how long each activity takes. The point of the log is to figure out exactly how and when you spend your time. After seeing that information in black and white, you discover that you actually have an extra few hours left over for recreational activities.

  Part-time and evening law students who try this exercise may find they can squeeze in an hour of reading during the morning commute or wake up a little earlier on the weekends to get extra work done. And students with families to care for may discover they can get more done than they originally thought while watching the kids' Little League game or early in the morning before everyone is awake for the day. Whether your free hours are clumped in a large block of time or spread out in 30-minute increments, the important aspect is that you realize when you can fit in your hobbies and interests.

- ✔ **Figuring out how much you procrastinate when you actually sit down to study and resolving to concentrate better.** For example, on a typical school night, you can do one of the following:

  - Spread your studying over a six-hour period, taking many little procrastinatory coffee, sleep, or Internet breaks (but not really enjoying them because you know you have more studying to do)

  - Bite the bullet and work straight through for three hours, finishing everything and using the remaining time to fully relax and enjoy yourself

  In other words, you'll study far more successfully as a law student if you work productively for shorter periods of time, rather than concentrating half-heartedly and spacing your studying out. Plus, I know from experience that it's easier to read and digest an assignment in its entirety, rather than give it only piecemeal attention, which results in your retaining far less of the material.

Relaxing when you feel like you need to be doing something is difficult, so finishing one thing before you start the next is a great way of getting even more out of your personal time.

✔ **Making a list of your favorite leisure activities and thinking about how many of them you'd like to fit into an average day.** Doing this means that you must classify your favorite activities according to which ones:

- Fit into smaller chunks of time

- Require an afternoon or entire day

- Can be multitasked (such as reading a magazine while eating lunch)

- Require your full attention

When you can see on paper exactly what you need in your life, you're often better able to accommodate your favorite leisure activities. Part-time and evening students will usually have less time than traditional law students to engage in their favorite activities on a daily basis, but fitting in a few pages of reading before bed or drawing in a sketchbook at lunch may be manageable ways to fit leisure into jam-packed days.

Maintaining your previous interests

Some law students believe that the moment they enter law school, they must abandon their love of antiquing, bird watching, or playing canasta. The truth is that law school and your previous interests can peacefully coexist. Treat your previous interests as the precious gems that they are, and never think that you have to postpone your weekly golf game or photography hobby for three long years.

In fact, maintaining your previous interests is a great way of relieving stress. What better way to unwind after a stressful week of studying than a day of skydiving, sketching local wildlife, or simply doing whatever it is that floats your boat? Law students with families and part-time and evening students also need to make time for their previous interests whenever they can. This may mean focusing on interests and hobbies that can readily fit into smaller, more dispersed chunks of time, such as reading or bike riding, as opposed to a major commitment, such as weekly ukulele lessons.

Likewise, maintaining your passions helps you become more than a one-dimensional law student to prospective employers. Employers love to see potential hires doing something they enjoy after logging a day at the office. Here are some specific tactics for ensuring that your previous hobbies remain an active part of your new life:

✔ **Using your favorite hobby as a reward.** For instance, say to yourself, "If I put in five hours studying, I can spend two hours working on my scrapbook." If your hobby is a reward for all your hard work, you can devote time to your interest without feeling guilty.

✔ **Organizing an unofficial law school organization around your hobby.** Posting signs around the school advertising a weekly writing support group, Japanese language conversation gathering, or stamp collecting organization is sure to inspire your classmates to even higher levels of devotion to your hobby.

✔ **When your school is part of a university, finding out how it can strengthen your passion.** Most large universities offer many opportunities in the way of satisfying your interests, regardless of whether it's a course you can audit, a workshop you can attend, or a specialty library you can explore. For example, if art is your thing, many large universities have their own art museums on campus, perhaps even with a fine arts library full of books on your particular interest! Or, if badminton is more your style, many universities offer physical education courses on the topic or have clubs where you can bond with fellow badminton enthusiasts.

Developing new interests

If you arrive at law school without a hobby, you're in luck, because attending law school is the perfect time for developing new interests! After all, when else in your life will you have all the great perks of being at a university or have so much vacation time? If you left college without fully finding yourself, you may want to view law school as your second chance to discover a foreign language, cultivate an interest in the arts, or take in all the free lectures that you can handle.

For example, Jen Weber, a 3L at Indiana University School of Law–Bloomington, saw a flyer advertising classical guitar lessons. Having played the piano, violin, and cello, but never guitar, she jumped at the chance. Weber signed up for once-a-week lessons and soon developed a passionate interest in classical guitar. A diligent one-hour-per-day practicer, she's taken lessons for more than a year and a half, and they've been instrumental in offering a much-needed break from school.

Auditing an undergraduate course for fun

If one of the aspects you loved about college was being able to take a wide range of random courses, you still have that opportunity. Just march right over to the registrar and audit away! Of course, if you're a part-time or night student, you probably don't have the time to audit a class for enjoyment. Instead, you can visit the main university library at your leisure and learn about the history of photography or modern Spanish poetry on your own.

Auditing a course means that you take it for no grade and no credit. The course that you audit may show up on your transcript, but it usually includes the designation of *"NC"* (or no credit) or some other equivalent notation.

Basically, you're just sitting in, listening to the lectures, sometimes participating in the discussion, and reading the assigned books, if you're so inclined. Less commonly, as an auditor, you're allowed to take tests or turn in homework (and have it graded). The great thing about auditing a class is that you can do as much or as little as you want. The focus is on learning for pleasure, which is something that may seem like a foreign concept in law school.

How about sitting in on a Mandarin Chinese or Gothic architecture class? Perhaps the history of film noir or advanced astronomy is more your speed. I audited an undergraduate general chemistry course as a 3L, and got much more out of it that I ever did in high school or college because of the relaxed pace.

At some universities, being able to audit a class means you must register for undergraduate courses with the general (non–law school) registrar, and you may have to pay a small fee. Other schools may allow you to sit in on classes for free. Check with the registrar well in advance of the next semester's registration deadlines to determine your university's policies.

Whatever classes you choose, make sure that they don't add more stress to your already busy life. If you feel compelled to attend every lecture, take volumes of notes, or read every assignment in your audited course, it won't seem as fun anymore.

Checking out adult community education classes

If you prefer a more short-term way of exploring your interests, check out any adult community education center near where your law school is located. Call or check the center's Web site for fees, a schedule of classes, course offerings and other information.

Many centers offer classes in drawing, dancing, acting, and writing in a no-stress, supportive atmosphere. You get to mingle with people of all ages — from teens to retirees — which can be a welcome break from the law school crowd. For example, taking an adult-ed ballet class as a second-semester 1L, enabled me to enjoy the opportunity to be in class with a variety of townspeople.

One benefit of community education is that courses are usually more hands-on than university classes. In other words, you're not learning a ton of theory: You're carving a chair out of wood or learning the movements of jazz dance. They're also shorter in duration — between five and ten weeks — than semesters. A shorter commitment may fit in better with your busy schedule.

Many university student unions also offer community-education-type classes in ceramics, photography, art, foreign languages, and other topics. Prices are usually very reasonable, and because the student union is right on campus, these classes are especially convenient. Stop by your union for the latest brochure of offerings.

Attending a university lecture

During any given week at a large university, you can likely find lectures and talks in everything from contemporary Buddhist philosophy to the inner workings of the brain. If you're in law school at a large university, be sure to take advantage of the myriad lectures and speakers presented at the school each week. Visit your university's main Web site to find out about these lectures, or check in the student newspaper for announcements.

Of course, law schools generally are teeming with weekly and monthly lectures by distinguished visiting judges, professors, and prominent lawyers. Keep your eyes and ears open for dates, checking your law school's Web site, newsletter, or bulletin boards for postings.

Another great way to check for lectures outside the law school is by visiting buildings of any departments on campus that interest you. For example, you can head over to the psychology building and check the walls for flyers or posters announcing lectures of interest or call the departmental secretary and ask to be put on a department e-mail list.

Joining a non–law school club

Although the writing for the law journal and participating in moot court have their own rewards (see Chapter 13 for more information on law school extracurriculars), checking out other clubs and organizations that you can join within the university at large is also a nice change of pace.

At the beginning of the year, most universities sponsor fairs to introduce their clubs and organizations. You can browse the many booths at the fairs in search of clubs for everything from chess to Czechoslovakian, and that's only the Cs.

Joining a non–law school club has a variety of benefits including:

- ✔ **Interacting with new people.** You work or play with freshmen through graduate-level students, so be prepared to make new friends, and be exposed to people with other career interests.

- ✔ **Getting involved in-depth.** Whether you've joined a sports team or a volunteer organization, get ready to be involved. You get the most out of the club when you try to attend most of the meetings and many of the scheduled practices or activities.

- ✔ **Making the time for building a new skill.** If you get involved at the beginning of law school, and really dig the club, you'll have three years to become proficient in your new interest.

Visiting a cultural attraction every month

Making your entire presence on campus revolve around the law school is tempting. You may step outside the law school to eat or shop, but for some law students, that's the extent of their campus exploration.

Ignoring the multitude of educational and entertaining things to do throughout your university's campus, such as attending a dance performance at the auditorium, watching a sporting event, or catching a film at the student union is definitely a mistake. By the time my third year rolled around, I realized that I hadn't made as much use of the rich resources on my campus as I'd have liked. I hadn't explored many of the museums, cultural opportunities, and university events, and graduation was just around the corner!

That's why I decided as a 3L to check out one cultural attraction every month. I found out about these events by perusing the university's main Web site, and looking for any special activities or exhibits. Attending them certainly brought a new dimension to my university experience!

Keeping Active and Healthy

Between classes, law school activities, and all your other hobbies and interests, you may think you have little time left to exercise. Many law students are grateful just to exercise once a month, let alone every other day.

But keeping healthy is as important in law school as it is in everyday life. If you neglect your body, your brain may soon follow. Eating bags full of fast food, cutting corners on your sleep, and feeling constantly sluggish won't help your intellectual stamina. Take the time to devise a good health plan for yourself. Doing so soon pays off, because you need plenty of energy and endurance for the long path ahead of you as a law student

Fitting exercise into your busy day

After making a commitment to stay healthy, you need to take the momentous step of figuring out when you can exercise. Now, I'm the first to admit that exercise is definitely last on my priority list. Normally, I was so tired after a full day of attending class and studying that I could barely make it up the one flight of stairs to my apartment, let alone actually hop on a treadmill or stationary bike. Sound familiar? But many law school students successfully work out a few times a week.

The following are a few good ways of making sure exercise is a priority in your life:

- **Figuring out when you'll do it.** Are you a chipper, sing-in-the-shower sort of morning person? Then hitting the gym early in the a.m. may work better for you. You probably won't be tired that early, and your early morning session leaves you feeling energized for the rest of the day. If, on the other hand, you're the grumpy, "I-hate-the-morning" type like me, then try squeezing in your workout at lunch, right after class, or in the early evening, before you get too tired.

If you're a part-time or evening student, fitting a regular exercise regimen into your already busy day may be tough. Some students with full-time jobs bring their workout clothes to work and use part of their lunch hour for exercise; others use the weekends as their primary workout time. Of course, walking up stairs instead of taking the elevator, and taking frequent walking breaks around the office are good ways to get moving during your workday.

✔ **Keeping your workout clothes at school.** I always found that when I had to go back to my apartment to change into workout clothes, I wouldn't have the energy to go back out to the gym. I discovered, however, that by changing at school and walking over to the campus gym, I dodged the feelings of laziness that set in as soon as I got near my comfy couch.

✔ **Working out with a buddy.** The buddy system really works, because when you know someone's waiting for you at the gym, you're less likely to cop out with a lame excuse like, "Well, I really don't feel like it today." Your buddy helps motivate you, keeps you on track when you feel like giving up, and helps you attain your fitness goals, as long as you do the same for your buddy.

✔ **Setting attainable deadlines for yourself.** Rather than setting a vague fitness goal, such as, "I'll work out every other day for the next year," try setting measurable intermediary goals along the way. These can range from entering a one-mile walk for a breast-cancer benefit with your workout buddy to being in great shape by swimsuit season. Having tangible deadlines like these helps you keep going when the going gets tough.

✔ **Varying your workout routine.** Most people give up their workout ambitions because they grow bored with going to the gym every day and doing the same old routine. That's why varying the types of exercise you do on a regular basis is better for you. For instance, you can go to the gym once a week, swim laps at the pool some days, and jog outside the other days. That way, you won't get bored; moreover, your muscles are constantly challenged in new ways.

Joining a sports team

One way of exercising (that doesn't really seem like exercising) is joining an intramural or university team sport. Many law schools offer either informal or sometimes even formal athletic opportunities, from intramural basketball to pick-up football and softball games. Although part-time and evening law students generally won't have the time to participate in these activities during the week, they may be able to take advantage of any sporting activities offered on the weekend. You may find out information about these opportunities either on signs posted on bulletin boards or by word-of-mouth. Whatever the case, joining an athletic team is a great way to relieve stress, have fun, and relish in the camaraderie of your law school classmates.

Eating well

Although many law students are fond of the traditional student fare of subs, pizza, and beer, adding variety to your diet by cooking (or at least eating) wholesomely some of the time is a good idea.

Eating well gives your brain and body the nutrients they need to operate at peak performance. (Can't you just hear your parents telling you to drink your milk and eat your Brussels sprouts?). This is especially true during finals, when you want your brain fueled by nutritious fare, not greasy fries and empty-calorie sodas. I know that fitting trips to the grocery store into your already jam-packed schedule is hard, but if you go just once a week for an hour, you can buy all you need for a week's worth of meals.

Some law students I knew did all their cooking on Sunday afternoons. They cooked up some substantial dishes like chilies, stews, or lasagnas, and froze them in individual portions. That way, their meals were ready to defrost quickly and eat on the run. You can also make up a huge salad, and voilá — you have a week's worth of great meals at minimal work for you. Sure beats the same old chicken wings and beer, five days in a row.

After two years of doing my own cooking, as a 3L, I discovered that eating out for lunch and dinner every night was actually cheaper than buying groceries and cooking (I skipped breakfast). And restaurant food can be every bit as nutritious (if not more so) than anything you can create yourself. By drinking only water, choosing the cheapest items on the menu, and going to cafeteria-type places (with no wait staff to tip), I dined out for between $4 and $5 dollars per meal. Because my grocery bills were always much higher than what my daily dining-out tab added up to each week, eating out quickly became much more economical than buying groceries. As a bonus, I saved quite a bit of time and energy by not having to cook or clean up. My kitchen was never as spotless as during my third year!

Getting enough shuteye

In the same way some people like to brag about how much work they have to do, in law school, I found that my fellow students enjoyed boasting about how little sleep they got the night before. Getting through a day of classes and schoolwork on two hours sleep or taking a final after pulling an all-nighter became almost heroic achievements.

For me, however, a full night's sleep was number one on my priority list; otherwise, I couldn't function. No matter how many hours of sleep you require, make sure that you establish a routine that works for you. Here are some helpful suggestions:

✔ **Vary your bedtime according to your productivity level.** If you're a morning person, going to bed early so you can wake up early to do your work may be easiest for you. On the other hand, if you're a night owl, you may want to arrange your class schedule so that your first class doesn't start until noon. That way you can stay up late working and then sleep in.

✔ **Prioritize sleep over work.** Whenever the choice comes down to staying up for an hour reading that last case or getting an extra hour of sleep, choose sleep. You can always get to class a few minutes early and skim over that case, or read it during lunch. But a botched night's sleep may affect your ability to concentrate all day long, and with tuition being as expensive as it is, the fewer classes you miss, the better.

✔ **A nap a day keeps dozing off at bay.** When you feel tired, by all means take a power nap. A power nap usually lasts 45 minutes or fewer; any more than that and you may feel more tired than before you fell asleep. Many people find that napping before 6 p.m. doesn't affect their ability to fall asleep later on, but napping any later than 6 inevitably does.

Making Time for Significant Others

Part of achieving the right balance between your studies and your personal life is spending a healthy amount of time with your significant others. Only you and your partner and family can decide how much time feels right. Spend too much time together, and your schoolwork may suffer; spend too little time together, and your relationships may take a nosedive.

Although being with your significant others ideally falls under your *relaxation time,* many law students feel stressed out because their partners want more of their time than they have to spend.

As soon as you decide to apply to law school, or when you're accepted, sit down with your friends and loved ones and talk honestly about how they view the amount of time you're able to spend with them. You may also want to have this talk yearly, so you can gauge how they felt the past year and what you can try differently in the coming school year. Ask them to rate the quality and quantity of your time together, and explain that even if you can't meet the *quantity* they'd like, given the demands of being a law student, you certainly aim to satisfy the *quality* aspect.

Making time for your friends and family need not feel like a chore. When you live together, perhaps spending an uninterrupted hour together works best, enabling each of you to unwind from the day before bedtime. When you live apart, setting aside a few days a week for after-school snacks, drinks, or even dinner may work for you. If you're a part-time or evening law student whose free time is at a premium, you can always ask your friends and family to meet you for an early morning breakfast on campus. Cuddling in a booth or holding hands across the table can help you communicate to your special someone that every bit of time you spend with them is of highest importance to you.

Surveying the Law School Social Scene

Although all law students have their own ideas about recreational fun, from intimate dinner parties with friends to fraternizing at rowdy bars, you're bound to find like-minded people at every school, no matter where your socializing interests lie. Nevertheless, with the amount of partying that frequently goes on at many law schools, J.D. may very well stand for *Joyful Drinker.*

Some law schools are more into the social scene than others. All you have to do to get an idea of how yours measures up is to hang out in the student lounge on Monday mornings. You're sure to get an earful on what parties went on and what crazy antics occurred at them.

No matter what your preference, hanging out with fellow students is a great way to relax, find out about your classmates, and perhaps even discover a golden nugget of law school advice from a seasoned upperclassman (check out Chapter 6 for the lowdown on mining upperclassmen for their time-tested advice).

Part III
Studying Law: Secret Techniques That Really Work

The 5th Wave   By Rich Tennant

All rise!

As your defense attorney I have to say – this doesn't look good, Bobby.

In this part . . .

Being successful in law school is all about preparation — preparing productively for exams by making the best use of your study time. In this part, I show you what steps you need to take to think more like a lawyer, what study aids you need to gather to give you an edge, and what tips you need to know about to do well on exams.

Chapter 8

Thinking and Talking like a Lawyer

*A*lmost everyone has heard the cliché that law school teaches you to think like a lawyer. But what do those thoughts really mean? That after law school you're able to spout off in legalese anytime you get the chance? That you view every new situation as a potential lawsuit? That you completely shed your pre–law school personality and instantly morph into a lawyer-in-training? Not quite.

This chapter demystifies the law school learning process, with an eye on facilitating your shift toward legal thinking as soon as you're ready. It also shows you how to beat the Socratic Method and dazzle professors with your class participation and discusses the most efficient ways to attack your reading assignments and brief cases.

Does Law School Really Change You?

How long does it take to start "thinking like a lawyer?" The first week of law school? The first month? At graduation? Is it definitely guaranteed to happen? These probing questions are foremost on many new law students' minds. Simple though they may sound, these questions are nevertheless hard to answer, because learning the law is such an individualized process. In the same way that children learn to walk and talk when they're ready, law students begin thinking like lawyers at their own pace.

Becoming a lawyer is not as if one day you wake up and suddenly have the word, "lawyer" branded on your forehead for all to see. Instead, you may gradually notice subtle differences in your:

✔ Logical reasoning powers

✔ Ability to see two sides to every issue

✔ Confidence in holding your own in an argument

Additionally, you gain a brand-spanking-new legal vocabulary and a much better understanding of the political and judicial processes than before you began law school. That's right, in addition to your newfound legal mind-set, you also become a more informed and concerned citizen.

One professor I spoke with felt that the transition to thinking like a lawyer tends to happen toward the end of the first semester, or at the latest, by the end of the first year of law school (but certainly not in the first month of school). Professors can tell when the proverbial light bulb goes on for students by comparing the complexity of the arguments they make in class at the end of the 1L fall semester with those toward the beginning. In other words, they can tell that thinking like a lawyer occurs when students start seeing complex *issues* (the conflicts between rules) that they never would have picked up on earlier.

One of the ways *you* can judge whether you're on the right track is how well you understand what's going on in class discussion and in the reading. If you don't feel like you're really getting the material by the end of your first year, it may be a good idea to talk with your dean of students, to identify any problems with your studying or learning and fix them.

In fact, when I think about my own transition to thinking like a lawyer, I'm still not sure when it happened. Because it's such a subtle change, seeing it in yourself is often difficult. Whereas I know that it used to take me several hours to thoroughly read and brief a case, doing so now takes only a few minutes. Whether this is indicative of my thinking like a lawyer is anyone's guess. The best way to figure out whether you've undergone the transformation is to ask around. Your non–law school friends and family may be the best judges.

Introducing a new method of thinking

The way lawyers think is supposedly different from the population at large, and that's because of their role as problem solvers. One way lawyers solve problems is through rational, analytical thinking that tends to disregard their own personal opinions or perspectives in favor of what's objectively fair. Another way is by being able to analyze a problem from different angles — in other words, understanding both sides of a problem. A good lawyer should be able to argue either side of an issue, which is what the Socratic Method (see the "Braving the Socratic Method" section later in this chapter for details) helps teach you.

The best way to demonstrate how lawyers think is to consider the nature of the legal process itself. Society doesn't want judges making decisions about cases based on the way they personally feel about the parties involved. Likewise, rather than hastily coming to a conclusion about a problem, lawyers are taught to coldly analyze a situation. In other words, they try to keep their own personal prejudices, assumptions, and feelings out of the analysis.

For example, Jonathan S. Greene (no relation), a family and immigration lawyer with the Baltimore firm of Howanski & Greene, thought nothing quite prepared him for the reality of thinking like a lawyer. Not until he went through the law school experience did he realize that learning the legal mind-set takes time. He likens gaining this new legal mind-set to flying an airplane; you have to log a certain number of hours with an experienced pilot before you're comfortable being the pilot of your own aircraft. Similarly, in law school, you must read a certain number of cases and attend a certain number of classes before you truly begin to internalize this new way of thinking.

Some people equate legal analytical thinking with a lack of creativity. In fact, lawyers sometimes are stereotyped as less creative and artistic than other professional groups. If you're a creative type who's worried about losing your creativity in law school, hone your creative side as much as possible by engaging in your favorite art, writing, or dramatic activities on a regular basis (see Chapter 7 for ideas about balancing law school with other activities). Doing so can prevent your newfound analytical side from completely taking over.

Seeing the world through a lawyer's eyes

One significant way lawyers differ from the rest of the world is that they see issues better than anyone else. *Seeing the issue* refers to seeing the conflicts between legal rules. More specifically, lawyers want to find what's debatable — the conflicts — and use those to bolster their arguments. One way they accomplish such a refined insight is by separating the wheat from the chaff. In other words, when you walk into a law office and begin telling your lawyer a saga about your car accident, the first thing your lawyer does is determine the real issue of your case by mental filtering, which involves segregating every detail you explain into the factors that are irrelevant and the ones that are essential.

Your lawyer then takes this information, recalls (or looks up) governing laws, and prepares arguments on your behalf, detailing why you should prevail over the other party. Most people look for tough lawyers — notably those who make the most forceful and gutsy arguments, the ones who refuse to back down or be intimidated by the opposite side.

You know that you're internalizing this type of thinking when you see a banana peel lying on the floor of a grocery store and think to yourself, "tort liability," rather than just that "someone should clean this up." When these kinds of thoughts start passing through your mind on a regular basis, you know that you're starting to see the world through a lawyer's eyes.

Speaking your new mother tongue: Legalese

I felt like I'd been immersed into a foreign language course on my first day of law school. Sitting in those first law classes, positively clueless, felt the same as when the professor speaks only Spanish in your Spanish class. In law school you're basically thrown into this new language, legalese, and you're expected to sink or swim on your own.

For example, Shorge Sato, now a commercial and environmental litigation attorney at Latham & Watkins in Chicago, had an amusing mishap with legalese as a 1L. One day in civil procedure class, the professor cold-called him to talk about a case. The case was old (from the 1800s), and the correct cause of action is known as a "trespass on the case." When the professor kindly asked Sato what the action was, he responded confidently — but nevertheless wrongly — that it probably meant that the defendant had somehow interfered with the process of litigation. The professor's bug-eyed reaction immediately told Sato that he was wrong. When the professor asked Sato how he knew his answer, having no better answer than "I guessed," Sato retorted with a Latin phrase: *Res Ipsa Loquitor*, which means "the thing speaks for itself." Although that phrase never is used in civ pro, it was a fitting response for someone who didn't know the correct answer.

Learning *legalese* — that vocabulary unique to lawyers — takes time and patience. Although it may seem like you and your *Black's Law Dictionary* (see Chapter 5) are joined at the hip, as you grow more comfortable with the words and phrases, you'll find yourself growing less and less dependent on it. However, don't even consider tossing your dictionary in a corner where you'll never look at it again. Even as a 2L and 3L, you'll be confronted with new bits of legalese that you'll need to look up, so your trusty dictionary should always stay close by.

One great way to speed up your language comprehension is to read your local legal newspaper or a national legal newspaper or law journal in your spare time. Seeing these words and phrases in other contexts helps cement them in your mind.

One of the reasons that legalese is so hard to learn is that many times the legal words don't suggest their meaning in the least. For instance, in property class, you'll hear the word "fee tail" thrown around quite a bit. At first glance, you may think this has something to do with costs — or furry animals — but alas, the fee tail is an estate inheritable in a particular way. Who would've guessed? That's one of the reasons it took me awhile to catch on to legalese. During my first few weeks of law school, I repeatedly wondered how I was ever going to remember complicated-sounding words such as "tortfeasor" and "summary judgment."

Much to my relief, I learned all these words, and probably 200 more, by the end of my first semester. Flash cards (see Chapter 10) help, but for the most part, I just repeatedly looked up new words whenever I encountered them in my casebook or in class. Don't forget! It gets easier. Little by little you start picking up these new words and even begin using them yourself in your class discussions.

Braving the Socratic Method

Perhaps nothing is quite as hyped in law school as the *Socratic Method*, which is sometimes jokingly known as the sarcastic method. Prelaw and law school students alike generally regard this unique and aggressive teaching style with dread and fear. However, for all the negative publicity surrounding it, the Socratic Method has several positive aspects. If it didn't it wouldn't have lasted this long as an integral part of the legal curriculum.

The Socratic Method is the brainchild of Christopher Columbus Langdell, the Dean of Harvard Law School during the late 1800s. It's based on his opinion that students learn the law best by figuring out legal principles on their own, rather than by being passively taught. Apparently, Socrates created and used the concept of interrogating students back in ancient times, which is the reason it's named after him.

The key to the Socratic Method: Students answer the professor's questions instead of the professor answering questions posed by the students.

Basically, you won't find any lecturing with the Socratic Method. Instead, the professor calls on one or more students during the course of a single class, and intensely questions them. Some professors call on a student to answer only a few questions; others call on someone to grill for the entire hour (or more). I once was questioned alone for nearly two entire class periods! Yikes!

For instance, a typical Socratic dialogue may go something like this: Your professor starts questioning you about a case assigned for class. You're getting the easy questions right, so you're pretty pleased with yourself, that is, until the professor lays a really hard question on you. As soon as your answers become the slightest bit ambiguous, your professor turns into a wolf pouncing on prey, becoming argumentative and all the while attempting to get you to recognize the error on your own by asking you more and more probing questions. Soon, you feel as if you're genuinely being interrogated, because the level of your anxiety is mounting as you have less and less time to think between questions.

Understanding why law classes are taught this way

Although you may think that the Socratic Method sounds a little sadistic, you nonetheless come to appreciate having gone through it by the time you graduate law school. That's because the main difference between the Socratic Method and, say, undergraduate lectures, is akin to the difference between active and passive learning. Many students probably admit to preferring lectures, because you don't really have to prepare on a daily basis and can otherwise just sit there and vegetate. After the lights dim and the overhead projector goes on, no one knows that the professor's voice has lulled you off to sleep, unless, of course, you start snoring.

With the Socratic Method, you don't have a chance to tune out — let alone doze off. That's because you constantly need to be on your toes, waiting for the moment that strikes fear into every law student's heart — when the professor glances down at the seating chart and then up at you. Even as a 3L, my heart raced when I knew I was about to be called on. You must intensely follow the course that the class discussion takes, just in case you're called on to pick up where someone else leaves off. You can see why the Socratic Method is the epitome of active learning.

Learning by the Socratic Method is good practice, because lawyers, particularly trial lawyers, need to be constantly on alert. When you're in a courtroom, the opposing counsel can make a statement that drastically changes the course of your arguments. If you're not paying absolutely rapt attention, you'll be ripped to shreds. You need to know how to think on your feet to be able to dramatically refute your opposition's arguments. The Socratic Method teaches you how to do that. Some other benefits of the Socratic Method are

- ✔ **It kicks your academic rear into gear.** Because you (generally) don't have any quizzes, homework assignments, or midterms in law school, putting off your reading for a few days — or weeks — can be awfully tempting. Without something else to keep you in check, you could go an entire semester without ever cracking a book. Enter the Socratic Method, which forces you to prepare well for each and every class. Otherwise you risk public humiliation when you're called on and can only fumble for words under your professor's steely gaze.

✔ **It helps teach you argumentative techniques.** The reason the Socratic Method helps in this regard is that you're asked questions, the answers to which aren't found in the book. Instead of just lecturing to you (and stating the legal rules directly), your professor gets you to refine your arguments through intense questioning. The process of you arriving at the answers on your own helps train your mind more than plain lecturing ever could.

✔ **It forces you to become more comfortable with public speaking.** Of course, few people enjoy public speaking, especially in the first few weeks of law school, when you need 100 percent of your concentration just to know what's going on. Although many students feel uncomfortable about being put on the spot in front of a hundred of their peers, you soon grow more comfortable with it. In addition, you can derive some comfort from the fact that everyone else is feeling the exact same way you are. In fact, one of the best benefits of the Socratic Method is that it turns you into a relatively relaxed public speaker.

When I first entered law school, I was petrified of public speaking, and my first Socratic questioning was truly frightful. I'd spend hours preparing for each class, dreading the day I'd be called on. And after each class period ended, I'd breathe a sigh of relief that I wasn't the one chosen that particular day. But I survived it, and so will you. By my third year, if I wasn't prepared for class, I'd just read the case a few minutes before it was to be discussed and still be as well prepared as I'd been in my first year after putting in an hour or more on each case.

If you truly despise the Socratic Method, a remedy is in sight. As 2Ls and 3Ls, you find that your professors have eased off the Socratic Method somewhat. The reason they do so is that the first year is when most of the work of teaching law students to think like lawyers is done. Many professors in upper-class courses use purely volunteers, call on one person very informally to get the discussion going for the day, or call on three people at once (so one person isn't put on the spot). When you're a 2L or 3L, you also can choose your classes based on which professors are Socratic and which are not — after you've consulted with upperclassmen on this point, that is. Just find out which classes aren't being taught in the Socratic Method, and register for them.

Because professors ease off the Socratic Method in the second and third years, it's easier to slack off than it was as a first year. Many classes are largely lecture (or discussion), so it's awfully tempting just to let the volunteers raise their hands and contribute. But beware of falling hopelessly behind in your reading. Taking more than a day or two off at a time can put you in a major bind come exam time.

If you absolutely dread public speaking, choose classes in small classrooms as a 2L and 3L, because speaking in front of a small group is much easier, and in my experience, classes in smaller classrooms tend to be more laid-back and discussion-oriented, rather than Socratic. After you become familiar with your law school, when you register for classes, you can remember the size of the classroom based on its classroom number.

Beating Socrates at his own game

The best way to beat the Socratic Method is by preparing well. Preparing well means reading your cases, completing your briefs (see the "Briefing Cases: A Step-by-Step Approach" section later in this chapter), having your materials organized for quick reference, and thinking about or anticipating what the professor may ask. Some other helpful ways to prepare in advance include:

- ✔ **Being extremely comfortable with the facts of the case, such as the identities of the parties, the reason for the dispute, and who initiated it.** Know these facts really well so that you can at least answer the professor's basic questions.

- ✔ **Trying to understand the arguments the judge makes in the opinion.** Then go a step further and try to anticipate the arguments the judge *didn't* make. In the Socratic questioning, your professor may ask how you would have ruled differently. Thinking about what's *not* in the case helps prepare you for these questions.

When you're a 1L, I suggest bringing your *case briefs* (short, well-organized summaries of cases) with you so that you have something to glance at during those first few tense minutes of questioning. Whenever you encounter any ambiguous or confusing facts in the case, make sure that you take special note in your brief, because your professor is sure to zero in on them.

Having a relaxed attitude helps, too. After all, everyone eventually is called on (professors keep track on the seating chart), so you're all in the same boat. Don't sweat it too much, and just ride it out when you're called on. Remembering that your grade is influenced by your classroom participation (only if extremely frequent or infrequent) is comforting (see the section, "Recognizing the Importance of Class Participation" later in the chapter), so just try your best. It gets easier eventually.

Hammering hypotheticals

Hypotheticals, or hypos for short, are one of the main tools of the Socratic Method. *Hypos* are hypothetical situations based on the facts of the case that you're assigned to read. The professor simply takes certain facts from the case, and twists them around, making a slightly different scenario.

Your professor uses hypos to test your understanding of the principles of the case. For example, your professor may ask something like, "Suppose the child who drowned was blind. Would that make a difference?" or "Suppose the fence was high enough, but had just been broken by a rainstorm the night before, how would that be reasoned by the court?"

At that point, your job is

✔ Remembering the facts of the original case

✔ Figuring out whether changing the facts changes the result of the new case scenario

✔ Explaining the logical reasoning behind your answer

As you can see, hypos engage you in active learning, and they help you apply what you've discovered to new situations. That's what attorneys must do every time a new client walks in the door to their offices.

 You can best prepare to respond to hypos by posing a few of your own to yourself when you read about a case. After you finish a case, change the facts slightly, and then defend your arguments for the same or different outcomes. The more you practice successfully answering hypos at home, the more confident you'll feel about answering them in class.

Reading Cases Like a Pro

A large part of what many lawyers — especially litigators (trial lawyers) — do is read cases so they can distill the law and get at the subtleties that enable them to win their clients' cases. Cases are part of the law school curriculum so that students can see a court's reasoning in action. Reading cases isn't like reading a novel or even a textbook. Cases are often dry, difficult, and full of complicated concepts and terminology. But, I always found it helpful to think of each case as an exercise in its own right, which helps you focus on reading it in an active way (by asking yourself frequent questions).

Because reading cases is virtually all law students do (for homework), expect to read about 20 to 30 pages in your *casebook* (a thick book filled with appellate cases) per class per night. This reading will probably take you between four and six hours per night total. At the beginning of your first year, it'll probably take longer, until you get the hang of things.

The first case I ever read for law school — *Garratt v. Dailey* — took me *four* hours to get through, and I still didn't have much of an idea of what I'd just read! Getting the gist of complex cases often requires a few read-throughs, even for seasoned practitioners. As you're reading cases, keep the following strategies in mind:

✔ **Reading each case twice.** The key to reading cases and getting plenty of information out of them, particularly the drier ones, is reading them a few times when you're first starting out. In fact, twice may be only a conservative estimate during your first few weeks of law school but should be adequate thereafter.

Reading a case twice enables you to initially give it a fast, understand-the-big-picture kind of read, and secondly a more thorough, in-depth, comprehensive sort of read. Both reads are important to your overall understanding.

✔ **Color-coding your highlights.** Most people like highlighting the cases as they read them; I certainly found it helpful. But some take the highlighting even further by color-coding what they highlight. You can do this by using pink for the facts, blue for the issue, green for the rationale, and yellow for the court's holding (see the following section for more details on these terms). Highlighting in this manner may help you to keep everything straight as long as you know your color system inside and out.

✔ **Writing in the margins.** Another great way to remember important bits of a case, especially the next day in class when you need to recall information quickly, is writing notes to yourself in the margins of your casebook. I'd often write a brief summary of each important point or significant fact, and make stars next to key points. Serving as an overall means of jogging my memory, at the top of each case, I'd often write a few short phrases about what the case was about and what the court's holding was.

✔ **Taking the material one step further.** After you read your assigned cases for class, you may want to take your preparation one step further. Has the professor recommended any law review articles that you need to check out? Go to the library and look them up. Are any points in the reading unclear to you? Look them up in a study aid or treatise.

If you're already a part of a study group (see Chapter 9), you may want to go over some or all of the assigned reading for the week with your group to clarify any confusing points. Collaborating with your peers and tossing ideas around is one of the best ways of getting the most out of your homework.

Briefing Cases: A Step-by-Step Approach

Most law students have a love-hate relationship with case briefing, mainly because it's important in your legal studies but a big old pain to do. *Briefing* means writing a short, well-organized summary of a case to use during class discussion, personal study, and outline preparation (see Chapter 9). The summary or *brief* (see Figure 8-1 for an example) ideally runs from half a page to two pages; any longer and it grows too unwieldy.

Until you become a well-seasoned law student, case briefing is likely a tiresome activity, ranked right up there with root canals and getting flu shots. But it can help you move closer to your goal of thinking like a lawyer, because it forces you to genuinely consider the legal principles involved in each case.

Vosburg v. Putney, 80 Wis. 523, 50 N.W. 403 (1891)

PROCEDURAL HISTORY:

P filed a complaint in the District Court alleging assault and battery by D. In trial, a finding for P was made, with a verdict for $2800. Judge granted award to P, and D appealed. Judgment was reversed for error, and a new trial was granted. In that trial, a verdict was awarded for P in the amount of $2500. D now appeals from that judgment.

FACTS:

P (Vosburg) is a boy just over fourteen years old. D (Putney) is a boy just under twelve years old.

In January, 1889, P suffered injury to knee that became inflamed and infected. Injury had almost completely healed when, on 20th of February, P was kicked by D on that same leg.

ISSUES:

1. Did the District Court err in allowing P to assert a cause of action against D for assault and battery?
2. Did the District Court err in denying Ds objection to a question upon examination by Ps attorney, ordering the expert witness to respond?
3. Did the District Court err in refusing Ds request to submit questions to jury?

HOLDING AND RULES:

1. Holding: No...
   Rule: In order to be held liable for assault and battery, it must be established that D had either unlawful intent, or was in fault. If action by D is unlawful, than intent is also considered unlawful.
2. Holding: Yes...
   Rule: Opinion of expert witness cannot be rendered until he has all the essential and material facts of the case.
3. Holding: No...
   Rule: D is liable for all injuries to P, whether foreseen or not.

REASONING:

1. D kicked P in a classroom, after class had been called to order. That is a violation of school rules and as such, considered an unlawful act. This being the case, Ds intent must also be considered unlawful, satisfying the requirements for alleging assault and battery.
2. Upon questioning the expert witness, P asks for the doctor's opinion regarding the cause of injury to leg. The doctor is not given the option of considering the first injury and how that may or may not have had implications on the condition of the injury as he saw it upon his first consultation with P. As a result of this fatal error, the jury may have been influenced in their judgment.
3. Although D may not have expected that kicking Ps leg would have resulted in such a severe injury or serious exacerbation of a previous injury, he is still liable.

JUDGMENT/ORDER:

- Reversed and remanded for a new trial.

Figure 8-1:
Typical first-year torts case brief.

Putting the brakes on briefing

Although professors generally don't advise it, many 1Ls stop briefing around the second month of law school, after they think they've gotten the hang of reading cases. Some stop out of laziness (writing those briefs tacks on additional time to your nightly reading assignments); others feel that after a certain point, they get diminishing returns. I, too, stopped briefing around the second month. Other law students keep doing it until the very end; it's totally up to you.

I thought two months was perfectly adequate for me to get the hang of briefing, unless, of course, the case was extremely confusing or I thought I'd be called on. In those circumstances, I'd (briefly) brief. Briefs are downright crucial when you're called on as a first semester 1L. Writing them means less of a chance you'll end up floundering around, trying to hunt down parts of the case when you need to be formulating your argument. In fact, when called on, most first-semester 1Ls just recite directly from their briefs in class, mainly because it's harder when you're just starting out to hold so many facts in your mind.

Case-briefing is a step-by-step process — it works best when you do each step in a particular order, because each new part builds off the previous. Keep in mind that you don't need to write a tome — a few sentences for each of the main briefing steps is perfectly fine.

1. **Identifying parties.**

   Cases don't have names like "The Exploding Fireball Case" or "The Man Who Slipped on the Icy Sidewalk Case." Instead, their official names are the names of parties suing one another. Each case has two parties: the *plaintiff* (the party that is suing) and the *defendant* (the party that is being sued). The parties' names are separated with a "v.," which stands for *versus*. Don't worry that you keep mixing up the definitions of plaintiff and defendant. Keeping the two straight took me the entire first week of law school.

   At the top of the case, beneath the case name, is the name of the court and date. The date is self-explanatory, but figuring out which court the case is originating from is often tricky for a 1L. All the cases in your casebook are (usually) going to be at least *appellate-level cases;* meaning they've already been through the *trial* (lower) court and now one of the parties is appealing that court's ruling.

2. **Discovering procedural posture.**

   The *procedural posture* is a short summary of how the case made its way through the court system to end up where it is today. For example, your procedural posture may state that the case was tried in the lower court and appealed to the appellate court. Although this information isn't usually very important to the facts or the ruling, your professor is nevertheless likely to ask you about it when you're called on, so figuring it out sooner rather than later is best.

3. **Finding the facts.**

   The *facts* are usually described in the first few paragraphs of the case. That's where you find out which party is suing the other, and for what reason or reasons. Basically, the facts are a description of what happened in the case. A broad range of facts is likely to be included in describing the case. Some facts are more important than others to the court's ruling.

   Part of the reason for using the case method is determining which facts are important, so that when exam time comes around and you're given a fact pattern (a set of facts arranged in a similar way to the ones you read in your cases), you know which ones to take a closer look at and which to pass over.

4. **Identifying the issue.**

   The *issue* is anything debatable confronting the court. For instance, if in the case you're reading, a child drowns in a swimming pool, the issue may be whether the pool owner was negligent for not installing a higher fence around the pool. Often, the issue is framed by a "whether" and can be answered "yes" or "no." Spotting or seeing the issue is one of the key elements of lawyering that law school teaches you. In fact, you need to make a point to become good at it, because it's one of the main things you'll do on exams (see Chapter 11 for more information about spotting issues).

5. **Reeling in the rationale.**

   The *rationale* is the reasoning that the court uses in reaching its decision, or *holding* (see the following item in the list). Besides using cases as teaching tools to identify the issues, law schools teach the case method so that you can see and understand the reasoning used by courts in reaching their conclusions. You discover the court's rationale so that you can apply a similar (or dissimilar) one in your own analysis.

6. **Homing in on the holding.**

   Thankfully, courts at least make it easy for law students to find the *holding*. It's most often the last sentence of the case and often is preceded by the words "We hold." The holding describes the court's final decision on a matter, and answers the question raised by the issue. For instance, in the example of a child drowning in a swimming pool, the court might say, "We hold that the homeowner was indeed negligent for not installing a higher fence around the swimming pool."

You also want to read *dissenting* and/or *concurring* opinions, whenever they're included.

- ✔ A *dissent* is written by a judge or judges who do not agree with the majority's holding and want to make their opinions known.
- ✔ A *concurring opinion* is written by a judge or judges who agree with the outcome of the case but don't agree with some or all of the rationale of the majority's opinion and want to explain their views.

Reading these opinions can help point out flaws in the majority's reasoning that you can bring up in class, or later in court. However, briefing dissenting and/or concurring opinions isn't necessary because they do not represent a majority opinion (one agreed to by more than half the judges). It isn't uncommon for a professor to want to home in on the dissenting opinion in class, because she believes the majority opinion is wrong or has serious flaws.

Recognizing the Importance of Class Participation

You can just sit in your classes without uttering a peep and still soak up a great deal of information from them; however, participation obviously gets you even more involved. You tend to listen more and think more deeply about the issues when you're actively participating. Likewise, whenever you volunteer, you show your professor that you care, and show yourself that you understand the material. Many students complain that they'd like to participate in class, but they have a whole slew of reasons why they can't. Sometimes they don't know exactly where professors are going with their lines of questioning, or they feel that the class pace is by far quicker than they're comfortable with.

Most law school classes move much more quickly than the average undergraduate class, but this pace is merely a fact of graduate school life. Keeping up with the pace means that you need to know your material extra well and you must stay tuned in at all times.

How participation (or a lack of it) affects your grade

Although class participation typically won't make or break you, in some rare instances, it can raise or lower your grade a small amount after you've taken the final exam. Generally, you need to have exceptional participation (such as on a daily basis) or exceptional nonparticipation (such as being continually unprepared or never once saying a word) to make a difference. The students who contribute once in awhile usually won't have their grades altered at all.

Most professors adjust grades upward, say from a B to a B+, for exceptional participation or down one notch, from a B to a B–, for missing too many classes, never volunteering, or continually coming to class unprepared. Rarely do professors move grades up or down by an entire letter grade; more often, the adjustment is only one increment. What does that mean for students who want to increase their grades? Participate every day, don't miss many classes (usually four misses per semester is the maximum), and continually ask thought-provoking questions.

Class participation becomes more important, however, when you're applying for a clerkship, you need reference letters, or you want a particular professor to serve as a reference in your job search. When a professor can comment profusely on your excellent participation and reasoning skills, after hearing them firsthand in class discussions, you're likely to benefit.

Most professors want you to tell them at the beginning of class whether you're unprepared, so they won't waste time calling on you. Students usually are more forthcoming about their lack of preparedness later in the semester than during the beginning of class, because professors tend to be more understanding when class work is really piling up (versus during the first week of the semester). Some professors grow annoyed whenever you fail to confess to them and they end up calling on your clueless self. Some of the more blunt ones even comment out loud on this unfortunate circumstance in class.

Anticipating your professor's next move

Another way of gleaning some of those Socratic participation points from class is by guessing your professor's plan of attack. But doing so is tricky. One way I attempted to figure this out was by practicing hypotheticals (see the "Hammering hypotheticals" section earlier in the chapter) as I read my cases each night. I twisted the facts of the case, and then tried to figure out the answers to my own hypos. More often than not, the ones that I practiced were similar to the hypos the professor asked in class the next day. So pondering hypotheticals at home is a great method for students who may need a little extra time — more than the five seconds that you get in class, anyway — to think about their responses.

Another way to anticipate which way your professor is headed is by keeping in mind what material your professor stresses in class. Is policy a main concern with your professor? Then consider how policy impacts the courts' decisions in the cases you read. Does your professor take a feminist spin? Yep — you guessed it, read your cases with an eye toward this approach.

Chapter 9

Romancing the Tome: Making the Most of Your Study Time

In This Chapter

▶ Figuring out when you're most productive

▶ Preparing for exams

▶ Creating outstanding outlines

▶ Discovering the benefits of practice exams

▶ Snagging a study group

Successfully getting through law school is no easy task. It requires plenty of hard work, motivation, and discipline, not to mention first-rate time management and study skills. A healthy sense of humor also helps out tremendously.

Unfortunately, few schools provide 1Ls with fundamental study or time management skills. At some schools, new students are left to flounder, having no idea how to tackle the enormous amount of information they're expected to absorb in a single semester. Because of this lack of traditional instruction, you may feel overwhelmed and frustrated.

In this chapter, I try to ease your fears by helping you get the most out of your study time on a daily basis and while preparing for final exams, so you can manage your coursework with more ease and greater confidence. I discuss exactly what you can do to conquer the immense amount of material and successfully prepare for exams. I also explain how to create an outline that summarizes your entire course in one succinct document, and why taking practice exams is the perfect way to hone your skills for the real thing. Finally, I cover why study groups can make a big difference in your comprehension levels.

Maximizing Your Study Time

People in law school are certainly bright; they're often used to being at the top of their class in college or other graduate study. However, even the brightest student can't get through law school purely on innate ability alone. Without the right work ethic and time management skills, even the most intelligent law students fall flat on their faces come exam time.

That's why the key to success in law school is working *smart* — not necessarily running yourself ragged. You don't have to log 60 hours of studying per week to get top grades, but you must find a productive study system that works for you.

Creating a study schedule

Because most full-time law students take four to five courses per semester and most part-time students take three to four, even if you had no other obligations (such as sleeping, eating, or working out), you'd still be studying most of your waking hours. That's why making a study schedule for yourself, one week at a time, is always a good strategy.

A study schedule differs from the productiveness log I discuss in Chapter 7 in that the latter's purpose is so you can figure out exactly how you spend your time. This involves you keeping track, for a week or so, of everything you do in a particular day so you can see it all on paper (think of it as good training for all those billable hours you'll keep track of as a lawyer in a firm). With your productiveness log, you may find out, for example, that you spend four hours cooking per day or two hours practicing the guitar. This information is valuable for when you sit down each week to compile your study schedule.

Night owl or early bird?

Some people are chipper, wake-up-early-and-watch-the-sunrise types. They sing in the shower, and feel refreshed and energetic when they first wake up. Others, however, are creatures of the night. They stay up until all hours, wake up at noon, and feel most energetic in the late afternoon and evening (that's me). Whatever type you are, don't try to fight Mother Nature. She generally wins. Instead, just plan your study habits around the type of person you are. An early bird won't get much studying done after 10 p.m., and a night owl likewise will probably be too out of it to study well at 7 a.m. Plan your study time for when you feel most awake and ready to go. Otherwise, you're working against your body's natural biorhythms, and you're not likely to do your best.

After you figure out what your time spending habits are by compiling your productiveness log, you're in a better position to make an effective study schedule. Your study schedule, which can be conveniently written into a day planner or on your wall calendar, lets you know exactly when you have carved out time to study. On your schedule, you can note the blocks of time when you're free for studying and then pencil in what you plan to study or accomplish during those times. All this planning helps you avoid wasting time, because you know when you're supposed to study, and nothing else is planned for that time.

The standard ratio of time that you're supposed to spend on each course is three hours out-of-class for every hour in class. In other words, for a three-credit course, you need to spend at least nine hours a week studying. Now, I don't know anyone who actually sticks to this formula, but recognizing it generally helps you remember that you need to spend more time on your five-credit constitutional law course than you do on your three-credit contracts class. Of course, if you have a two or three-credit class that's really kicking your behind, you may want to up the ante on the amount of time you spend on that class, no matter how many credits it carries.

Scheduling ample study time is a great start, but it isn't 100 percent of what you need to do to get the grades you want. The other part of the equation is getting a good handle on what is — and isn't — important. Spending most of your study time learning obscure material the professor doesn't even cover in class isn't productive. Instead, use your class notes as a guide, and put your emphasis on those topics and points the professor stresses in class.

Measuring your overall productivity

How many times have you been studying and looked at a clock or your watch and said to yourself, "Where did all the time go? I didn't get a thing accomplished!" Whenever these thoughts are frequently racing through your mind, you may have a productivity problem.

A *productivity problem* just means that you're not being as productive as you can be when you sit down to study. Everybody's productivity level naturally waxes and wanes (when it's warm and sunny outside it's awfully hard to study for your property final). But for some people, not getting their studying done becomes a chronic issue, and that's when you need to take action. In other words, you know there's a problem when you're frequently not accomplishing as much as you should, taking excessive breaks, or setting study goals so lofty that no mortal could ever accomplish them.

People with productivity problems can't focus easily on the tasks at hand, or sit quietly for a period of time without feeling restless (which leads them to take too many distracting breaks). They usually get up from their study session feeling like they barely accomplished any of their goals. As a result, they often feel frustrated and angry with themselves. Several ways that you can increase your overall productivity include:

- ✔ **Avoiding distractions.** You can do this by:

  - **Finding a quiet nook to work in.** Your apartment, the law library (generally a great place to study but some people find the law library stressful around exam time), or a cozy coffee shop may fit the bill. If you want maximum concentration, head to an under-graduate library on campus where you're unlikely to see law students you know who want to come up and chat. I typically studied at a large bookstore quite a distance from the law school, so I'd rarely run into anyone I knew who wanted to chat up a storm.

  - **Making your study environment conducive to studying.** That means turning off the TV and radio (unless these devices help you focus), shutting off the telephone ringer, and keeping Internet access off limits except for hard-earned breaks. The last point is crucial, because surfing the Web for a short break in-between reading assignments can easily turn into two hours down the drain. I'd actually unplug the phone cord from my computer so I didn't have easy modem access.

  - **Getting a spouse or friend to keep small children occupied for a portion of each night.** Going to law school and taking care of small children isn't easy, particularly when they're not yet school-aged. Finding someone to look after them for a few hours while you get your studying done helps you concentrate. If doing so is impossi-ble, try to arrange your schedule so that you get maximum study-ing done while they're asleep.

  - **Separating work and school.** If you're a part-time or evening law student, putting away work-related concerns when you buckle down to study can be difficult. But doing so is essential, if you're going to give your law school work the undivided attention it requires. Keep a planner with you so you can immediately jot down any work-related meetings or issues that pop up in your mind as you study, and then put it away.

- ✔ **Making a priority list for every study session.** Write down the goals you have for your study time and try to meet them. This simple act helps you subconsciously reinforce your goals. When one of your goals is too lofty, such as reading four chapters of environmental law in an hour, break it up into smaller pieces to work on through the week.

- ✔ **Writing a start and stop time for studying on a piece of paper and keeping it handy.** Sometimes, making a regimented study span for yourself is a great way to make sure you've put in your time for the day without getting sidetracked by other things. Plus, it makes you feel really good when you have "study 4 p.m. to 6 p.m." on your slip of paper and you're actually able to meet that goal, undistracted. As simple as this step sounds, I found it was one of the most important things I did to keep my studying on track all through law school.

✔ **Avoid zoning out (daydreaming).** If you find yourself frequently drifting off into a daydream when you know you need to be studying, resist the urge. Try getting your mind back on track by shutting out all extraneous thoughts and instead focusing your attention like a laser on the task at hand.

If you still find your mind racing with thoughts other than studying, write them down on a piece of paper, so you can schedule time to take care of them later. Then put the paper away. The "out of sight, out of mind" concept really works! (Of course, if you're like me, you may end up with an enormous folder of these papers, but you'll get around to tackling those another time.)

Tackling a Wealth of Information

Although studying a little every day is crucial for keeping pace throughout the semester, your study habits become especially important when exams roll around. (I talk much more about exams in Chapter 11.) In fact, most law students begin feeling the heat of impending finals when they're about a month away. At that point, in spite of all your efforts to stay on top of things, you may feel hopelessly behind after realizing just how much more information you must learn. When the going gets tough (and believe me, it will), keep in mind that generations of law students before you have successfully passed their law school exams, and you can, too. All you need are the following strategies (and a month's supply of caffeinated beverages).

Knowing the value of memorization

Although law school courses aren't like science courses in which you memorize everything, a good deal of memorization nevertheless is involved. You must be familiar enough with the law to spot issues well. (See Chapters 8 and 11 for more on issue-spotting.) You must also know the court holdings of the cases you studied and the legal principles those cases espouse. That's where the bulk of your memorization comes in. You generally won't need to remember specific case names, dates, or party names, though.

But why bother memorizing, you may wonder, when the exam is open book? (Open-book exams tend to be the rule, rather than the exception in law school; see Chapter 11 for the reasons why.) Won't it be enough to just have your notes in front of you? Trust me, you probably won't have time to flip through your books and notes, or even if you do, it slows you down significantly. You need to know the law well enough *before* you set foot in that classroom for an exam so that you don't waste time digging around in your notes. (Notes in open-book exams should be used as a last resort to clarify a particular point or briefly refresh your memory.)

Most of your fellow classmates will know the law (the most basic level of studying), but the students who really distinguish themselves on exams are the ones who are able to work through the reasoning behind the law. In other words, they'll not only be able to distinguish that a tort has occurred, but they'll also be able to analyze the type of tort and show why a given party should or shouldn't prevail on that particular cause of action (see Chapter 11 for more on answering specific exam questions).

Learning small chunks at a time

Of course, leaving all the studying for your exams until the last minute is stressful and unproductive. You have little chance of learning everything you need to know when you start studying only a day or two before the exam. Additionally, as a 1L, you're just discovering the format of a law school exam, and getting into the swing of things takes time. That's why many students say that studying throughout the entire semester is the best approach. Of course, motivating yourself to do just that is difficult, but remember that the rewards are worth it. Studying (especially reviewing after a unit or chapter has ended in class) is a fruitful way of keeping up with your studies and avoiding some of the last-minute panic before an exam.

Attending review sessions

When exams are closing in, nothing sounds better to a law student than the words "review session." *Review sessions* are prime time for:

✔ Asking pertinent questions

✔ Discovering last-minute changes or additions to an exam

✔ Finding out once and for all what your professor wants out of an exam

However, because review sessions in law school are few and far between, you always need to attend any and all of them that your professors decide to conduct.

You'll have the most luck finding review sessions when you're a 1L. Few professors offer them for 2Ls and 3Ls, probably because by that stage they figure you're an old hat at taking exams. When your professor decides against offering one, you have two options:

✔ Petitioning the professor to provide a review session (perhaps by coaxing several people in your class to send e-mail requests)

✔ Staging your own mini-review session by attending your professor's office hours prepared with a list of your own questions. While you're there, ask the professor for thoughts on the ideal way of organizing your exam response. Because each professor has his or her own ideas of how an exam needs to be written, this tactic is guaranteed to put you heads-and-shoulders above the people who never bother to ask.

Instead of a bona fide review session, some professors devote part of a class period toward the end of the semester to a discussion of what they look for in their exams. Perk up your ears while the professor is talking about this information, because you can unveil some valuable insights into your professor's grading persona. A professor's wish list may include:

✔ Writing on every other line

✔ Emphasizing a particular approach to the course (such as economics or political theory)

✔ Organizing an answer in a specific way (such as by party or by cause of action)

Take the most detailed notes of your life during these discussions, because when you follow your professors' desires to a T, you're likely to avoid the pitfalls of ignoring explicit instructions and reap the resulting benefits when they grade your exams.

Some law schools offer general exam-strategy programs for 1Ls (or other interested students). These presentations typically take place in November and feature various professors explaining to the crowd what they generally look for in a law school exam and giving examples of universal do's and don'ts. These seminars are usually very helpful, and I encourage students of all years to attend (even 2Ls and 3Ls, who often forget how to write law school exams after the long summer break).

Posing hypotheticals to boost understanding

When you pay close attention in class, you discover that the use of hypotheticals (or hypos) is one technique your professors rely heavily upon in teaching the law. *Hypos* are bits of facts taken out of the case you're studying and twisted around to illustrate how the same rule of law may apply to a brand-new situation. See Chapter 8 for some specific examples of hypos. Hypotheticals are one of the most valuable ways of learning the law, because no two factual situations are exactly the same. After all, as a practicing attorney, you'll rarely have two clients come to you with the exact same problem.

You can vastly improve your understanding of a concept by using hypos when you study. The best way of incorporating them into your studying repertoire is by posing them to other people in a study group. One person can think up the hypos, and the rest can take turns answering and critiquing them. Another way is by visiting your professor during office hours and requesting a run-through of some of your hypos. Or, you can practice with store-bought (or homemade) flashcards, which have a hypothetical on one side, and answers on the other (see Chapter 10 for more information on flashcards).

Avoiding the law library at all costs

Although the law library may seem like a perfect place to spend all your time studying (and it is, most of the semester), it slowly morphs into a stress haven around exam time. That's when the air is so thick with tension that you can cut it with a knife. People scurry back and forth from their carrels to the vending machine and set up camp in the library conference rooms. Although you'd think that the library would take on an air of, "We're all in this together," more often it feels like, "I'm in this for myself."

That's why my preference favors avoiding the law library like the plague as soon as finals approach and finding alternate places to study. Hearing people talking to each other about how hard their exam will be or how many practice exams they've already taken just distracts me. Plus, you'll have to fend off the people who want to make photocopies of your outline or who want to borrow your notes to add to theirs. And, of course, boasters always are trying to unnerve others by bragging about how many hours they've studied or how long their outlines are.

Who needs all that additional stress? I'd rather go someplace where no one knows my name. If you're looking for a different study setting, try another library at your university or even a public library. Coffee shops and cafes work well, too — any place where you won't run into your law classmates is a good choice.

Getting the Skinny on Outlines

Before you arrived at law school, you probably never heard of the concept of *outlining* for a course. I surely hadn't. However, in law school, many people believe outlining is as essential to success on exams (whether open-book, closed-book or take-home) as air is to breathing. In fact, some law students don't feel completely prepared for exams unless they've created their own outlines. They can go to class and meet with their study groups, but unless they wrestle, grapple, and pin the course material in a half nelson, they never truly know it well.

Outlines are particularly useful for open-book exams. Having the information you need neatly organized in a document you created is much easier than digging through your books and notes for an answer. No materials are allowed in closed-book exams, including outlines. However, making an outline to study for these types of exams is still crucial.

So what exactly is an outline? An *outline* is a compilation of whatever you think can help you understand the rules, case holdings, and principles of law from the course you're taking. An outline usually includes:

- Your class and reading notes
- Study group materials
- Bits and pieces of commercial study aids (see Chapter 10)
- Chunks of upperclassmen's outlines
- Your thoughts and interpretations.
- A table of contents (optional, but may make the outline easier to navigate)

Figure 9-1 shows you the first section of a sample outline.

The point of the outline is to turn the enormous amount of material you absorb in a course into a more palatable and digestible amount (most outlines are anywhere from 20 to 60 pages long). In a typical course, you probably:

- Read close to 500 pages of text
- Sit through approximately 50 hours of the Socratic Method (see Chapter 8 for more on the Socratic Method)
- Debate with your study group for 25 hours
- Read 200 pages of a commercial outline
- Take 150 pages of notes (class and reading)

That's a heck of a lot of information to study buffet-style in preparation for exams. Your new ally, the outline, makes your life a whole bunch easier by condensing all of that material into one (hopefully) coherent document.

Outlining promotes active learning

If outlining takes so much effort, then why bother outlining at all? Can't you study for exams as well — or better — just by rereading your notes and glancing at commercial study aids? Well, maybe, but eons of law students before you were successful when using the outlining method, so you at least need to *consider* outlining as part of your exam preparation.

CIVIL PROCEDURE I
I. Purpose and Due Process

A. Goals:
  1. Show development of lawsuit in federal court to time of trial.
  2. Explore values implicit in procedural choices...purpose of process is to reach correct decisions under substantive law in manner that protects dignity of litigants as well as society's interests in efficient and inexpensive resolution of disputes
  3. Constitution recognizes interest in fair procedures (Due Process cases)
   - Nature of interest
   - Possibility of error
   - Cost of additional procedures
   - Dignity interest of individual/power of government

B. Courts Powers
  1. Injunctions: Court may hold parties in contempt for violating its orders, and it can also hold non-parties in contempt for interfering with the court orders if they are involved with parties. (US v. Hall 5th Cir. 1972). See Rule 65(d) injunctions binding to parties, their agents, officers, servants, attorneys and employees.
       a) Court plays loose with Rule 65, well if our court order doesn't apply to you, then Rule 65 doesn't apply to us.

C. Due Process Rights
  1. Property Interests
       a) Termination of benefits:
         - notice in advance,
         - access to counsel (not pre-termination),
         - opportunity to testify yes, orally, not only by written statement,
         - opportunity to cross examine witnesses: there is a right to confront adverse witnesses and evidence,
         - no requirement of formal written record,
         - requires a statement of reasons for termination of benefits and case/hearing decision.
         - Independent judicial review by impartial decision maker (i.e. not a board composed of the same bureaucrats who cut you off in the first place.)

           i. protected so that people are not put in desperate situations by erroneous benefit termination and government cost cutting. Weighs this issue against maximizing government efficiency.
       b) Termination of Welfare benefits: Goldberg v. Kelly (US Sct. 1970) Welfare is a protected property interest and cannot be taken away w/o due process. Court requires stuff listed above.
       Test: does the person's property interest outweigh the govs interest in efficiency via simple procedures? Is the recipient in an immediate situation that could threaten their survival or subsistence? Yes in Goldberg.
       c) Termination of Disability benefits: Court comes out opposite of Goldberg. They draw a distinction by saying that people on disability have other income, and if they don't, they could just go on to welfare and fix the situation later if a mistake was made in terminating the benefits. (Mathews v. Eldridge US Sct. 1976) H: **No pre-termination hearing is required**.
       d) Seizure of property: constitutional due process rights require state to give notice and an opportunity to be heard before seizing property. See Fuentes v. Shevin (US Sct. 1972), where a person puts down a bond for a writ-of-replevin. Sheriff goes with party and takes the property=unconstitutional.
           i. opposing argument is that people will give themselves the right to do this by including it in contracts for car payments, etc. Creates a repo-man situation that endangers people. Private parties are not restricted by the due process requirements.
  2. Access to the Courts: if a party cannot afford to pay court filing fee to exercise fundamental rights, they can file to have the fee waived. See Boddie v. Connecticut (US Sct. 1971) where welfare recipients sued state to make them waive filing fee to get a divorce court sided with them, marriage (and dissolution of one) are fundamental rights.
       a) To waive filing fee: Use 28 USC / 1915(c&d) which requires you to make a motion and affidavit stating why you cannot pay and that you have nothing to give for security. See Rule 7(b) and 10 for info on basic motions.
  3. Access to a lawyer: indigents right to counsel exists only where the litigant may lose his physical liberty if he loses the litigation.
       a) No right to counsel in a hearing for termination of parental rights. (Lassiter v. Dept. Soc. Serv. NC (US Sct. 1981). State courts should determine this in a case by case basis. Ironic that one is entitled to counsel for a two-day marijuana prison term, but not for a hearing where gov seeks to take ones child away. Court basically said that if you have a bad case, you don't need a lawyer anyway waste of state $.

Figure 9-1:
Sample
outline.

Here's why. Reading your notes, commercial study guides, or other people's outlines, in general, is *passive studying,* which means that you sit there with the book and try to absorb the material without doing much else in the way of reinforcing your efforts. Passive learning is okay, but many people believe that it isn't quite as effective as active learning.

Outlining, on the other hand, is 110 percent active learning. Proponents of outlining argue that it enables you to actually organize the material in your own way and in a format that makes sense to you. Instead of reading what someone else writes about your course, you actually roll up your sleeves and dig into the material yourself. In other words, when outlining, you're engaging in a *synthesis,* pulling all the material together, drawing connections between concepts, and highlighting those connections. You're also linking cases together, forming conclusions, and seeing the big picture. Most law students say that synthesizing the material makes all the difference between a high exam grade and an average one.

If making an outline doesn't help you learn, you don't have to do it; outlining isn't required. But, trying the outlining approach at least *one* semester is a good idea so you can determine that it really doesn't work for you.

Finding a workable outline format

If you've never seen a law school outline, you may wonder how to structure such a document. Because outlines are so named for a specific reason, they're usually constructed in the way an undergraduate or law school syllabus is — with roman numerals and sub-letters denoting each topic and subtopic.

For example, you start with a main heading under a roman numeral, then list subheadings 1 and 2 under that, and so on. However, if the traditional outline format turns you off, feel free to experiment with whatever format works for you. Some people make straight lists; others write up their thoughts in paragraph form. The traditional outline format never worked for me, so I always constructed my outlines in paragraph form with bullets to highlight the most salient points.

If you're having trouble with the outline format concept, try using your law school course syllabus or the table of contents of your casebook as a starting point. That way, you'll be able to see exactly how your professor or the casebook author outlined a topic — perfect for tailoring your own outline.

Above all, keep in mind that no one lays eyes on your outline except you. Your outline needn't be fit to publish in a law review. All it needs to be is something that you can use to study the material and/or help you during an open-book exam.

Deciding What to Put in Your Outline

Most outlines total between 20 and 60 pages, but they can be as short as five pages or as long as 120. The key word to remember in outlining is summary. You don't want to write a tome; you just want to condense the immense load of information into more manageable chunks. In other words, the catchphrase, "everything but the kitchen sink" definitely doesn't apply to your outline.

Good outlines need to sport a rundown of all of the following items:

✔ Every important principle or rule you studied

✔ A short summary of the relevant cases

✔ Any tests (specific conditions when a rule applies) that courts have devised to explain a principle or rule

✔ Any exceptions to the rules

✔ Any policy issues that are brought up in your course

Your outline needs to be tailored to your particular professor's approach, as gleaned from class discussions and study-group consultations. For example, when your professor is economics oriented and mentions economics policy preferences in class, you want to develop your outline with this tendency in mind. Glancing over some past exams on file in the library may further help you tailor your outline to your specific professor's approach.

Many law students puzzle about what's important enough to address or include in their outlines and what isn't. This quandary is often tough to sort through, and most students seem to err on the side of including too much rather than too little. I, too, fell victim to the problem of including too much the times I made my own outlines; they routinely topped 100 pages. The dilemma is that you don't want to exclude something important that can potentially appear on the exam, but 100 pages is by far too much to be useful.

The solution to figuring out what to put in and what to leave out is remembering that exams can test only so much. (After I internalized this guideline, my outlines returned to a much more manageable length.) All professors cover the main points. That, after all, is all they have time to assess during a three- to four-hour exam. Because most professors test major rather than minor, ancillary concepts, you don't need to waste your time focusing on the latter to the exclusion of material that's more likely to be tested. So when you're in conflict about whether to include several piddily concepts that were discussed for five minutes in one class period, remember the wise saying, "When it doubt, leave it out."

Condensing your outline even further

Some people firmly believe in the benefits of whittling a big, unwieldy, 20- to 60-page outline into something more compact. In fact, many law students aren't content with leaving things as they are when they finish their main outlines. Instead, they condense their original outlines into one-third of their original size and may even create *checklists* (three- to five-page summaries of the most important points).

A checklist can take the form of a flow chart (or a simple list with no particular order) of the most important issues your professor is likely to test and information that you shouldn't leave out in your essay answers. Instead of flipping through an immense outline and hunting down a particular point, the key issues are boiled down to fit within your three- to five-page checklist.

Some students find condensing all that information an integral part of the studying process. After mastering the material in their original outlines, they feel like such an enormous document has become like excess baggage. So, they pare it down to the bare bones to make it more user-friendly during an open-book exam or just to study from for a closed-book exam.

One way that you can keep your outline focused on the main points is by selecting the three most important concepts from each class session to include in your outline. Three points per class is plenty, and when you figure about a third of a page devoted to one point, your outline will run about 50 pages total, a more manageable size.

Members of many study groups find much success by working together on a group outline. Doing so enables them to debate with their fellow study group members about what they think is essential and what can be left out. Each member of the group is assigned a chunk of the course to outline, and when complete, the individual outlines are combined and distributed to each member. However, the outline that the group produces may be lacking in some areas, and you may think that updating these areas on your own time is a necessity.

Determining When to Start Your Outline

How much time do you need for making your outline before the start of finals? Some law students say that you need to begin creating your outline about four weeks before the start of finals. Others, however, prefer waiting until the last minute (the week — or night — before) to begin. As in life, being the early bird and/or the last-minute Charlie has its pros and cons. I know, because I've been both.

By starting early, you feel less harried, and you can work on your outline in easily digestible nuggets instead of writing it up in a few frenzied all-nighters the week before the exam. However, waiting also has its benefits: At the last minute you may finally grasp the big picture. That's because many 1Ls don't grasp the overall concept of their courses until the last two weeks or so, after they've dug into their study aids and worked in study groups. Sometimes this clarity may not come until the night before the exam! That happened once to me, but hey, at least I didn't have to wait until during the exam for it to happen!

One caveat against waiting until the last minute: You may not actually have time to study your outline. Sure, the process of constructing your outline is valuable, but studying it is the other *crucial* part of the exam preparation equation. Make sure that you have enough time to read it over, from beginning to end, at least a few times (five is ideal). I always read my outlines with a highlighter and colored adhesive tabs in hand, so I could mark it up and tab the most important parts. If you finish your outline but don't have time to read it over even once, you won't know how to find anything in it and thus won't be able to make the best use of it during open-book exams.

The bottom line is that when you begin your outline is completely up to you. No professor is going to question you about the status of your outline. Heck, no professor will ever know whether you even make one.

Adding to your outline each day

When you decide to bring your laptop to class each day, you're far ahead of your computerless peers, because typing class notes each day can lay the foundation for your outline with minimal effort. Because you're already typing your class notes, all that you need to do to create a gourmet, full-length outline by the end of the semester is add in your reading notes a little at a time, each day. You can begin synthesizing the material immediately, or you can wait until after each main section or chapter if that feels more natural for you.

Even if you don't bring a laptop to class, you still can work on your outline every day from the beginning of the semester. All it takes to stay on track is a good dose of motivation.

Getting back on track if you fall behind

When exams are looming and you've finished only the first page of your outline, should you try to catch up and finish it in a whirlwind — or forget it entirely? I'd advise you to catch up and finish it, even if it's only a bare-bones model. Mustering only a one-sentence summary of each case, all in chronological order, is far better than nothing. When your exam is open book, having some semblance of an outline is especially important.

Getting a Little (Outline) Help from Your Friends

If you've never seen an outline before, you're probably going to want to check one out before trying to create one of your own. So, where can you find a repository of upperclassmen's outlines? If you're a first-year student, try hitting up your new-student-week/peer-group leaders for their old outlines. Because all 1L courses are the same, they probably have a plethora of them to offer you. If your peer group leaders are duds (or overly cutthroat), cozy up to upperclassmen in general. When you start searching early, you make use of most of the semester for finding friends and allies among the 2Ls and 3Ls who can shower you with outlines.

You can also gain access to outlines by joining a club or student organization (see Chapter 13 for more about various clubs and organizations). Many clubs offer their members access to a special club outline file, which usually can be accessed with a password on the club's Web site or checked out at the reserves desk in the library only to members on the official club list. Serving on moot court or a journal (also covered in Chapter 13) may have similar benefits. These groups are known to offer only their members access to their private outline files.

Putting Your Outline to Work for You

Your outline finally is finished — hooray! Now, take a step back and admire all your hard work. Now that you have your completed outline, you can

- **Study it.** Cross out parts that no longer seem relevant, and highlight the ones that seem especially relevant. Make notes in the margins regarding any additional points you may have left out. Meet with your study group to talk over your completed outlines and note any issues that come up in these discussions.

- **Read it over many times.** Five is great, ten is better, and even more is best. You want to become as intimately familiar with your outline as you are with your diary. I found that in all my classes how well I did on the exam correlated precisely with the level of mastery I had of my outline. In other words, the more time I actually had to study it, the better I performed. Try to memorize it, and sear the concepts into your brain cells. After you're familiar with it, close your eyes and try to see it in your mind's eye. More often than not, after reaching this level of mastery, you start having dreams about your outline.

✔ **Compare it with classmates' outlines.** One good way of knowing whether your outline measures up to the ones prepared by others in your class is to get together with a friend in your class or your study group partners and compare. Find out whether you phrase case holdings and legal principles similarly, what your friends emphasized and deemphasized in their outlines, and what particular approaches of the professor everyone incorporated in their outlines?

Comparing outlines is also a great way to work out any unresolved issues that you still have about the class. Some of my best grades in law school occurred after I engaged in this process with a classmate, because making comparisons enabled me to find weaknesses in my outline and fix them before the exam.

✔ **Sleep with it under your pillow.** Hey, it can't hurt, right? Maybe you'll be the first to learn law by osmosis.

One of the best students I ever met in law school told me his secret over lunch one day: He prepared his outline early enough to read it almost 15 times in the *reading days* (the few days before exams start when you don't have any class). This person emphasized that doing well meant knowing the material cold, and for him, that meant reading his outline until it was completely committed to memory. It took him about 15 times to do that; but your mileage may vary.

Taking (Many) Practice Exams

Practice exams are to studying what yeast is to baking. If you leave out this crucial step, your grades won't rise.

The purpose of taking (or at least reviewing) practice exams is to find out what kinds of questions your professor has asked in the past. Professors don't often dramatically revamp their exams every year. Instead, they're far more likely to stick to a tried-and-true method. Their predictability works in your favor. If you have a good grasp of what they've done in the past, predicting what your own exam will be like becomes easier.

Finding practice exams is a snap. You usually can find them either on reserve at the library under your professor's name, on your course Web site, or on your law library's Web page, which often is accessed under a special password that you can get from your law librarian. After you print or photocopy as many practice exams as you can, lay them side by side. What do you see in common? Do fact patterns highlight the same issues year after year? Are some course topics emphasized in every exam? What do the policy questions have in common? See Chapter 11 for more about fact patterns and policy questions.

Some, but not all, practice exams include model sample answers. When they do, that's a big bonus, so you need to study the answers as thoroughly as you do the questions. One of my hardest law school professors made practice exams and answers available. I spent more time extensively studying those answers than doing any of the practice exams, and it paid off. By critiquing each answer, I found *buzzwords* that my professor liked to use, and saw that he wanted his answers structured in a particular way. If your professors don't provide answers, see whether your study group can get together to puzzle them together. Answers show you things like:

- ✔ How in-depth your professor wants you to go
- ✔ How your professor wants certain issues treated
- ✔ How you need to structure and organize your answer

When time allows, you can actually sit down and take as many full-length practice exams as you can, rather than merely reading through the questions. Although actually taking a practice exam takes a great deal of motivation, it enables you to find out whether you can answer the questions in the allotted time and how fast you're able to spot issues (see Chapter 11 for more about issue-spotting).

Don't worry that the practice exams seem much too hard when you first sit down with them, because it's all a matter of perception. The difference in your level of concentration while casually taking practice exams during your study time versus taking the actual exam is a big one. Likewise, unless you're taking your practice exam the day before the real final, you're likely going to have much more time to study. So be sure to give yourself a break when you're feeling in over your head. It's perfectly normal.

Ellen Deason, a professor who's taught civil procedure and dispute resolution who is now at The Ohio State University Moritz College of Law, believes that taking practice exams is extremely helpful. She recommends that her students work through practice exams, if they have the time, as the final stage of their course studies. Deason says the main benefit of practice exams is that they help put students into an exam mind-set and are a way to build confidence. Doing an outline integrates the material, but then students have to apply the material to hypotheticals on an exam. Practice exams help make that transition. However, she warns that using old practice exams is dangerous, because they may include issues that your current class hasn't covered, and you don't want to stress yourself out unnecessarily. If students haven't finished the outlining process, Deason thinks they need to scratch practice exams in favor of focusing on pulling everything together and understanding it.

Discovering the Joy (or Pain) of Study Groups

Even when you're a lone eagle type, you may find that participating in a study group improves your course comprehension more than anything else you try. Although you probably never encountered many study groups in college, in law school, they're a mainstay. A *study group* is essentially a group of any size (two to eight people are more common) that forms either to study regularly throughout the semester, to cover one, some, or all courses, or to study together at the very end of the semester in preparation for exams.

No one is in charge of study groups in law school; they're arranged informally by the students themselves. Each study group decides on its own what it wants to accomplish. Some groups assign each member a portion of the course to present. After these presentations all members discuss them. Other groups review practice exams or pose hypotheticals to each other. Although most students form groups with people in their same classes, you can join or form study groups with anyone.

Study groups run the gamut from the ultradisciplined to more laid-back and casual. In fact, I knew of one law school study group that sponsored potluck dinners at every meeting. Regardless of the atmosphere your study group provides, make sure the people in it can get the job done. When your group tends to gab about the latest law school gossip, instead of focusing on criminal procedure, you may want to consider finding a new group.

Not everyone is comfortable studying and talking in a group setting, but because so many people consider these groups essential to law school success, you may consider trying it at least once. Here's a list of questions you can ask yourself to find out whether a study group is for you.

✔ **Do you mind studying with others in a group?** Would you rather go over your materials alone, without the distraction of a group, or do you like tossing around ideas with a few people? Although some people grow nervous speaking in front of people they don't know, after you become better acquainted with your group, that feeling generally wears off.

✔ **Is your study group more businesslike than social?** The success of a study group depends in large part on the ability of its members to stay on track. If your group meetings veer from discussing constitutional law to what happened over the weekend, then you may not get as much out of your study group as you need.

> ✔ **Are you able to prepare regularly for study group meetings?** With all your course reading, you may feel like you have no time left to prepare for your study group. However, the most productive and effective sessions occur when members come equally prepared. They've read the assignments, done any agreed-upon practice exams or hypotheticals, and are ready to discuss. If you can't shoulder these additional responsibilities, your fellow members may see you as "the weakest link."

Forming groups with strangers and friends

As a new 1L, you may not know anyone well enough to feel like you can simply join their existing study group. That's why biting the bullet and forming your own study group is a great idea. Round up a few of your classmates. So, you don't know any of them? Great! They probably don't know many people either. Some of the closest friends I made during my first year were people I met as study-group partners, people I didn't know until the group formed. When you're meeting on a regular basis and discussing such difficult issues, you can't help but get to know people well.

Another approach is starting a study group with your friends; however, you need to bear in mind one caveat: Study groups consisting of friends can often get off track and conversation can quickly move to more fun topics. Although chatting with your friends is enjoyable, you won't get much studying accomplished when it's a regular occurrence. You may find that you're more productive in a group with strangers.

The joy of study groups can quickly turn to pain when feelings are hurt. This happens more frequently when you discover your friends (or last semester's study group) formed a new study group without you. Remember they may have perfectly good explanations for such occurrences (such as you're no longer in their same course section or they know your schedule isn't compatible with theirs). However, they may simply be trying to tell you something — that you're not a good study-group member or student. They may have felt that you didn't "hold your own weight" in the previous study group because you came continually unprepared or couldn't discuss the issues at the level the rest of the group wanted. You have two options: confront them or ignore it. I advise the first option, because you don't want a simple misunderstanding to ruin your friendships. However, be prepared to hear the unflattering truth.

If you and just one other person want to form a group, that's great, too. More is not necessarily merrier. A group of two often is more productive than a larger one, because you work more intimately with each other, can more easily tailor your discussions to each other's strengths and weaknesses, and smaller group meetings are easier to schedule than larger ones.

LEGAL EAGLE

An über law student:
The true story of Kellianne Chancey

Kellianne Chancey always wanted to attend law school, but her problem was timing. She didn't feel ready for law school when she graduated from college, so she decided to work on her master's degree. The master's program was designed for working students, so Chancey worked full time. Although balancing school and work was difficult, she was able to manage it, and completed her degree in 1999. Finding success working full time and going to school part time, Kellianne decided that maybe the time was right for law school. However, she didn't want to leave the workforce for three years while attending law school. So that she'd be able to work and go to school, she decided to focus on schools with evening programs. She decided on Brooklyn Law School's evening program, because it offers plenty of flexibility and provides the opportunities she was looking for.

Like most 1Ls, Chancey was a little overwhelmed during her first semester and her focus throughout her first year was on survival. Chancey's typical day began at 6:15 a.m., when she'd get to work by 8:30 a.m. She'd work until 5 p.m. and then headed directly to class, which usually ran from 6 to 8 p.m., or sometimes until 10 p.m. On a late night, she was home by 10:30 or 11 p.m. Her weekends weren't much easier. She tried to wake up early to spend a few hours relaxing in the morning before working on homework and other assignments the rest of the weekend. During the beginning of the semester she sometimes found time to visit with friends and family, but by the end of the semester she was much too busy for that. That's when she spent all her free time preparing for finals.

In addition to acing her classes, this superwoman competed on the moot court team (see Chapter 13 for more about moot court), which required plenty of weekend time to prepare for competition. If all that wasn't enough, she also was active on campus, having cofounded a student organization for evening students. She also tailored her course schedule according to the skills in legal drafting and negotiations that she wanted to develop. During some of her law school career, Chancey worked as a legal assistant with a litigation law firm. She felt that the environment was very supportive and flexible, because attorneys at the firm all have been in her shoes. Her career goal was focused on becoming a litigator in the corporate/securities field, thus her job enabled her to gain hands-on experience, which helped put what she learned in the classroom into context.

As is obvious even to full-time law students, balancing everything at once can be tricky. Chancey believes this balancing act requires the ability to think of and do more than one thing at a time. One of the secrets to her success was being as productive as possible and utilizing downtime effectively, regardless of whether it's only five minutes or an entire weekend. For instance, Chancey read on the subway ride to work and on her lunch breaks and went to work a few minutes early to have time to write quick e-mails to friends and family or look up something for class.

Today, Chancey is well on her way to achieving her career goals and expects to graduate in May 2004. Looking back at how far she's progressed, she doesn't think that working full-time and going to law school requires any extraordinary personal characteristics. She firmly believes that any person willing to work hard and make some sacrifices can succeed. As Chancey's amazing tenacity shows, staying motivated is easy when you love what you do.

Ousting unproductive people

You may find that someone in your group is dragging you and the others down, someone who continually shows up unprepared, never contributes to the discussion, or asks far too many elementary questions. Of course, when it's one of your friends, it's difficult to find a nice way to get rid of someone who's already been a part of your group. A few blunt suggestions to shape up (or else) may be in order.

When the unproductive member is merely some random person in your group, the rest of you may decide that person just isn't working out. Perhaps at your next meeting you can say something like, "Everyone in our group is putting in a great deal of time and effort, but we feel you aren't always as prepared. If you're not willing to put in the necessary work, maybe you need to try another group." This ultimatum either makes that person reform or voluntarily leave.

Laying down the ground rules at the outset is one way of avoiding this type of uncomfortable confrontation. Your group's ground rules can include every member always coming on time, being ready to deeply discuss the material, and taking turns presenting the material. That way, everyone knows what's expected of him or her.

Chapter 10

Assembling Your Personal Study Aid Arsenal

. . . .

In This Chapter

▶ Deciding which study aids are right for you

▶ Determining when and how to obtain study aids

▶ Making use of other valuable study resources

▶ Using the law library to its best advantage

. . . .

Despite all the hard work that you do in your classes, sometimes you just don't get certain parts of a course. And when that happens, you're not in the mood to grapple further with legal concepts on your own; you just want to be *told* the law, plain and simple. Don't slap yourself upside the head because you don't understand a particular concept; instead, turn to the myriad study aids that are available.

This chapter helps you sift through the myths and realities of study aid use, so you can determine which of them are right for you. Besides traditional study aids, plenty of other tools — from flashcards to online legal databases — can help you pull together everything that you're studying. And don't forget the law library, which can make your life loads easier by providing you with study aids on reserve, legal encyclopedias, and law review articles to boost and speed understanding.

Improving Your Comprehension with Study Aids

Study aids (otherwise known as commercial outlines or summaries) are any items outside your assigned course books that help explain legal concepts. (See Chapter 9 for more information on self-compiled outlines, which are not considered commercial study aids but are nonetheless a helpful tool when studying for exams.) More specifically, a study aid ideally takes everything you learn in a single course, explains it in plain English, condenses it, and organizes it in a user-friendly way.

Study aids are thought by many to be essential to law school success because they help you become familiar with unfamiliar language, fill in gaps in your knowledge, and take the mystery out of case briefing (see Chapter 8 for detailed information on case briefing). Students appreciate the ease of navigating study aids because they don't "hide the ball" as casebooks do. In other words, study aids summarize the cases for you and explicitly tell you each case's rules or principles (holdings).

Study aids are most helpful to get an overview or some background information on a topic when your casebook or class notes are unclear or vague. When you're just starting out, you'll find many times when your class notes (or class discussion) won't make one iota of sense. So as you're trying to figure out how a particular concept fits in with the unit you're studying, or what the holding of a particular case is, just whip out your good friend the study aid. Everything you need to know will be in there.

You have countless study aids from which to choose, but there are several series that are very popular with law students and are especially known for high-quality content and presentation. They include:

- ✔ Emanuel Law Outlines
- ✔ Gilbert Law Summaries
- ✔ Aspen Publishing Examples & Explanations Series
- ✔ West Nutshell (Law in a Nutshell) Series
- ✔ Legalines Series

 Keep in mind that each series has titles for individual courses. For instance, Gilbert Law Summaries is the series name, but Gilbert's has separate books for each course — property, torts, and so forth.

All first-year, and many 2L and 3L courses are covered by commercial study aids, but some of the more focused 2L and 3L courses, such as HIV and the law or law and biomedical advance, are not. Because you're unlikely to find any study aids for these types of specific courses, you're better off compiling your own outline or finding an upperclassman's to use as a model (see Chapter 9 for more information on compiling outlines).

 The use of study aids needn't be limited to last-minute studying for finals, though that's what many students end up using them for. In fact, consistent use of them throughout the semester can help you stay on top of your coursework, get a better grasp of class discussion, and develop questions for further study.

Boxers or (canned) briefs?

Canned briefs are a subgroup of commercial outlines. Canned briefs are commercial study aids dedicated to summarizing case facts, rationales, and holdings and providing you with *black letter law* (well-settled law). Books with canned briefs are often keyed to your casebook (author and edition), so the material will be presented in the same order you read it in your casebook. Canned brief books give you a short overview of every major case in your course, however, many times, not every case that you study is included. Many 1L students like to keep their canned briefs open to the right pages during class, in case they're called on and need to recite the facts quickly. Professors, as you can imagine, don't like students using canned briefs, because you end up reading someone else's brief rather than writing and digesting your own.

Determining whether one series is better than another

With so many study aids to choose from, how do you know which of them are of higher quality than others? Do you rely on word of mouth? Or do you personally inspect each one? Although all study aids aren't considered equal in terms of how well they treat particular courses, no hard-and-fast rules exist governing whether one series is better than the others for a particular course. Instead, as is true of most people's tastes in movies or music, preferences are highly individualized.

The main consideration for determining whether a study aid is right for you is how well you like its format. For example, you may prefer one study aid's outline format or another's practice questions. Some study aids offer more in the way of practice tests, answers to practice tests, quizzes, and easy-to-digest summaries. Still others are more problem- or hypothetical-based. You may also find that you like using study aids that are written by the author(s) of your casebook. Although you can't find this arrangement for every course you take, the fact that your casebook and study aid are on the same wavelength, so to speak, may appeal to you.

The best way to find out which study aids are better than others is to ask around. Find out from upperclassmen what worked for them and why when they took your particular course. Ask about what perks the study aid offers, such as practice problems and self-tests. Because they've already taken the course, they may even offer to lend you their copy. One way I compared series was to get one different series of study aid per course during my first semester as a 1L. For instance, if you choose this method, you can select Gilbert's for torts, Emanuel's for property, and so on. Trying it this way may be the best way to really figure out what features of a particular series appeal to you (in ways briefly flipping through it in the bookstore or library can't).

If you're considering law school, or have yet to begin your first year, it may be educational to browse in a law school bookstore or peruse the study aid section of a law school's library to get a feel for what study aids are all about. It probably wouldn't be productive to actually purchase a study aid at this point, but by looking through a couple, you can get an idea about what the content of your first-year courses will be like.

Deciding when to procure study aids

Many law students probably agree that you need to wait a few weeks before plunking down money or searching the library for study aids. (I debate whether to buy or borrow study aids in the section, "Figuring out where to find study aids" later in the chapter.) The following are a few good reasons for waiting a little while.

✔ **You need time to decide where and how you need help.** Take a few moments to write down problem areas you face in each of your classes. For instance, you may not have enough examples or hypotheticals (see Chapter 8) to work from; you may not be able to write fast enough in class to take down all the hypotheticals, or your particular casebook may not provide any at the end of particular sections. If that's true, you want to look for a commercial study aid that emphasizes what you're missing. Or, say that your weakness is that you don't know how to organize your notes into a coherent outline. In that case, you want to look for an outline-format study aid, one with similar emphasis on topics mirroring the course you're taking, so that you can use it as a model for your own outline (see Chapter 9 for more on preparing outlines).

✔ **You want to be able to make an informed decision.** Consult with a few upperclassmen who've had your particular set of professors to determine which study aids can benefit you the most. For instance, your upper-class buddies may inform you that Gilbert's is great for one of your courses, but that Emanuel's is far better for another. Instead of going out and buying or searching the library for a bunch of different outlines, you'll have first-hand advice from students who've been in your professor's class.

When you're feeling brave, you may even ask your professors for their opinions. If you talk to them about the problems you're having in their courses, some professors won't hesitate to recommend a particular study aid or hornbook (see the section, "Comparing hornbooks and commercial study aids" later in the chapter). Professors of 2L and 3L courses seem more open to offering recommendations than do the 1L profs, but you never know until you try. Another great reason for getting direct recommendations from professors is that they may recommend a particular study aid because it stresses the same topics they focus on in the class, which you otherwise may not pick up on if you were to select them on your own.

✔ **You don't want to risk information overload.** You don't need to buy or check out of the library one of every study aid available. Trust me, one study aid per course suits you perfectly well. If you have several study aids for one course, you may never get around to using them all, given the risk of information overload. In other words, too many study aids per course can often hurt more than help because there's too much information there for you to digest.

Here's an example of the pointlessness of stocking up on too many study aids. For my corporations course, which I was highly worried about as a 2L, I bought and/or borrowed five study aids. Doing so was a mistake because study aids contain so much material that I'd never get my money's worth out of all five. I ended up using only one; the other four grew mold in my locker. At least I was able to sell them back to the law school bookstore. Of course, I received only a fraction of what I paid for them.

✔ **You don't want to drain your life savings.** Because study aids aren't cheap (they average between $20 and $40 each; hornbooks are often around $50), saving your money for when you really need them is your best bet.

Figuring out where to find study aids

The decision about whether to buy or borrow study aids depends in large part on what you plan to do with them. For instance, buying study aids is useful if you're looking to take the study aid to class with you each day, highlight it, or incorporate your class notes into it. But if you just want to read a study aid for background information, or if you need a little extra help in one or two areas of a particular course, purchasing study aids may not be your best option.

Also keep in mind that the full-price law school bookstore isn't your only option for *purchasing* study aids. Many law schools feature student-run used bookstores, where you can pick up used study aids at discounted prices. If you do enough digging, you'll probably be able to get two or three used study aids for the price of one new one. Alternatively, you can post a want ad on your law school miscellaneous bulletin board; upperclassmen will line up in droves to sell you their used study aids.

If you don't have the inclination or the cash to buy study aids, you can often find some of them behind the reserve desk at the law library, just waiting to be checked out. (Some libraries may also keep study aids in the stacks.) Although it differs between law libraries, at many, study aids are available for nearly every course the law school offers. However, many libraries offer only one to a few series of study aids. For example, your library may only offer the Nutshell series and the Hornbook series, but no others.

Just remember that if you get study aids from behind the reserve desk, you can probably check them out for only a limited amount of time — usually between 24 and 48 hours. Additionally, around exam time, you may be able to borrow study aids for a limited amount of time, such as a two-hour block. Plan accordingly, so you're not desperate for a study aid only to find that the waiting list is a mile long.

The Internet is another extremely valuable resource when it comes to finding study aids. Although you won't find commercial study aids reproduced in their entirety online, you can find some great Web sites that offer

- ✔ Study tips for particular courses
- ✔ Overviews of particular subject areas
- ✔ Links to individual students' outlines for specific courses from other law schools

Understanding why some professors discourage the use of study aids

Professors' reactions to study aids range from enthusiastic encouragement to tolerance to adamant discouragement. Although most professors generally think study aids are helpful, they champion their use only as long as they're used appropriately. To many professors, *appropriate use* means when study aids are used for background reading about a subject or to help illustrate how a particular case or topic fits into a course's overall picture. Professors want you to first learn the law on your own; not by reading how someone else analyzed the law. In other words, study aids should be a supplement to your casebook — not a substitute.

At the beginning of the semester (particularly in your first year), your professors are likely to give your class a brief talking to about the evils of study aids. They caution you about how study aids do law students a disservice and how, if you rely on them, you won't learn to think like a lawyer. Basically, professors regard study aids as crutches — they're there for you in the tough times but really don't help you learn the material on your own.

Many professors also advise against using them because they believe that you won't learn the course the way they teach it when you use study aids. Professors have a good point when they say that any kind of commercial study aid needs to be used only *in addition* to whatever outline you make or notes you take for yourself. The reason: Each professor's course is unique to that professor, and commercial outlines, by their broad nature, are meant to be applicable on topic to as many professors' courses as possible. Your professor may teach criminal law differently than the study aid outlines it by emphasizing or deemphasizing certain parts. Or, your torts professor may emphasize an economic perspective that your study aid doesn't. However, as long as you have your course syllabus, you can easily figure out which sections of the study aid you can use, and which ones to ignore.

As long as you know what topics your own course covers and doesn't cover, and as long as you have a firm understanding of your professor's approach to the course, overreliance on a commercial outline needn't present the kind of catastrophic problems that many professors want students to believe.

Comparing hornbooks and commercial study aids

Commercial study aids are materials outside your assigned coursebooks that are sold commercially and aimed at giving you maximum information in minimal time. *Hornbooks* (also called treatises), on the other hand, are more scholarly treatments of a particular course topic. They even look serious, having hardbound covers and resembling your casebook in weight and size. Similar in content to a textbook, hornbooks aim to provide an in-depth, heavily footnoted discussion of your course.

Although commercial study aids are often more user-friendly (with their outline formats) than hornbooks, you may find that hornbooks cover your course topic more thoroughly. You can find hornbooks at the bookstore, but they're quite expensive. They're also available at the law library (usually on reserve); many commercial outlines are not.

The good, the bad, and the ugly of study aids

Ellen Deason, a professor of civil procedure and dispute resolution who's now at The Ohio State University's Moritz College of Law, thinks study aids have their pros and cons. She says they're fine when you're trying to pull material together for an outline, and you've really tried organizing the material on your own. That's when study aids help you develop a structure for the material you've been reading and then fit it together with your class notes and other material you've gathered into a big picture view. They can also be helpful for students who tend to panic and lose confidence heading into exams. Deason says that students who make the effort to compile an outline, can then turn to a study aid to find out whether they're on the right track. If they are, they can go into the exam with a more confident state of mind.

On the flip side, Deason believes that using study aids for classes only hurts students. She says you won't get the practice that you need in reading cases and good class performance isn't worth that risk. Moreover, when you get out into your practice, you won't have study aids around, so you need to get into the habit now of reading and interpreting cases on your own.

Loading Your Study Arsenal with Other Essential Tools

Besides your hornbooks and commercial study aids, several other important study resources shouldn't be overlooked, because they can make your life as a law student much easier, provide you with additional practice, and guide you to resources for your legal research and beyond. Among them are

- *Black's Law Dictionary.* *Black's Law Dictionary* is an important resource for all those new words you'll be looking up on a daily basis. Get a pocket-sized one to carry with you at all times during the school day; you'll find it especially helpful for looking up foreign-sounding tidbits of legalese (see Chapter 8 for a discussion of legalese) in the nick of time during class.

- **Lexis and Westlaw ID cards.** Lexis and Westlaw are competing online databases that attorneys and law students use to conduct legal research. A few weeks into your first year, you receive free subscriptions to these services that last until you graduate. You get ID cards with ID numbers on them, which you'll need for logging on to both systems (you'll come to have these numbers memorized soon enough!). These free subscriptions provide you with unlimited use of their respective databases but only for educational (not on-the-job) use.

  You use them most heavily during your legal research and writing course during your first year, but don't overlook their usefulness for studying other courses. For instance, when you're assigned to read a particular case for class, you can look it up on the Lexis or Westlaw database, and when you have the case in front of you, click on links to other cases that may help put the one at hand in better context. Other links to law review and other articles discussing your case also are accessible with the click of a mouse.

- **Flashcards.** Flashcards present short hypotheticals (similar to the type you get in class) and are handy for reviewing legal concepts in preparation for exams. Grab a friend or study-group partner, sit down with a stack of these premade cards (like the *Law in a Flash* series), and start quizzing each other. Because flashcards generally have a hypothetical on one side, and possible answer choices on the other, you have plenty of fodder to discuss and debate with your partner for hours! You can buy these cards in your law school bookstore; you won't find them in the library.

- **Upperclassmen's outlines.** No law student's study aid arsenal is complete without a bevy of outlines from 2Ls and 3Ls. These outlines are invaluable because students who actually took your course wrote them.

If you're lucky enough to score several, you can lay them out side-by-side and compare them. Which one seems the best? Which has the tightest organization? Which is most complete? Which has the most helpful table of contents? Which is most oriented to your professor's particular leanings?

You can use outlines of upperclassmen exclusively as your study aids, or you can consult them when you're making your own outline (see Chapter 9), just to double-check any concepts or principles that you're unsure about. So find yourself an upper-class buddy, and start soliciting for outlines. Your grades — and sanity — will be enough thanks for doing so.

Taking Advantage of the Law Library

Many law students sadly don't take advantage of the vast resources available through their law libraries. They use the library only as a place to study, snooze, and check e-mail, but in reality, the law library is waiting for you to step inside its doors and discover all it has to offer.

Making friends with your law librarian

Meander over to the reference area, and make a point of meeting and greeting your friendly law librarians. These folks have master's degrees in library science and want to help you get the most out of the law library. They can point you to resources you never knew existed, give you a head start on your legal research, and show you how to use the many online databases to which *your* library subscribes.

At many schools, you can even make personalized appointments to sit down with the librarians for help devising a research strategy for a paper or brief. The librarians can help you expand your search terms and lead you to obscure sources on microform or microfiche, or they can at least show you how to use these complicated-looking devices.

My school offers a legal research skills refresher course that's taught by the law librarians in the late spring before school ends. The purpose of the course is to reacquaint students with how to use online databases, how to look up cases and statutes, and where everything is located, all in time to dazzle legal employers. At many schools, the law librarians even are available all summer to answer any research quandaries that arise while working at summer jobs! Now that's dedication!

Networking with upper-class students

The library is a great place to get the latest scoop on the law school scene. People tend to congregate in the lobby area to check e-mail, and the library lounge is probably one of the better places to rub shoulders with upperclassmen, and get the 411 (the scoop) on everything from which professors are the hardest to what the most popular electives are. So, grab one of the comfy lounge seats, kick up your feet, and chat with passers-by. Soon, you'll know so much about the ins and outs of studying for law school that you'll be advising newbie 1Ls next year.

Whatever you do, don't pass through your three years of schooling without becoming intimately familiar with everything the law library can do to help you. You'll make considerable use of the library during your 1L legal research course, but as 2Ls and 3Ls, you may have less need to venture into the stacks for your coursework (except for research paper courses). Practicing for when you have to use your firm's or a county's law library is good preparation for life as a practicing attorney.

Chapter 11

The Longest Three Hours of Your Life: Acing Your Law School Exams

. . . .

In This Chapter

▶ Understanding the most common exam formats

▶ Getting used to law school exam protocol

▶ Ensuring peak exam-day performance

. . . .

*Y*ou've taken copious notes, attended class (most of the time), and met with your study group religiously. Now, the heat is on, and it's time to show what you know! Of course, no one particularly enjoys the stress, nail-biting, and all-nighters that inevitably surround law school finals, especially when they're all one-shot deals. But if you follow the tips and advice in this chapter, you can pass your finals with flying colors. So, whip out that blue book and sharpen your No. 2 pencils, because Dean's List here you come!

Mastering the Most Common Exam Types

After the Socratic Method, the second most universally feared aspect of the law school experience is the final exam, one three- to four-hour test given at the end of all 1L (and most 2L and 3L) courses. Although the likelihood is great that you experienced essay, multiple-choice, and short-answer exams in college, you probably never had anything quite like the tests given in law school.

That's because law school exams are a unique breed. Their uniqueness lies in the fact that instead of merely asking you to regurgitate information, they test your ability to *issue-spot,* which refers to identifying the conflicts between rules of law. Issue-spotting is hardly an innate skill, but rather, it's what you've been exposed to in class and in your own studying throughout the semester. See the "Issue-spotting is the name of the game" section later in the chapter for more information.

Regardless of which exam format (I describe each of them in the coming sections) ultimately confronts you, keep in mind that you need to approach all your studying in the same way, by creating an outline and doing practice exams (see Chapter 9 for details on both). You also need to divvy up your time to accommodate exams that weigh more heavily into your grade-point average (GPA). The general rule at most schools is that you have one hour worth of exam per credit hour of the course. For example, if your civ pro class is three credit hours, you'll have a three-hour final exam.

Essays

Essays are by far the most common type of law school exam, which is comforting in one respect. Unlike all-or-nothing multiple-choice tests, essays at least give you the chance to earn partial credit. On the other hand, the sheer amount of writing that you do in a semester's worth of essay finals isn't so comforting. I hope you came to law school liking to write, because you do a heck of a lot of it.

A typical three-hour essay exam usually consists of three essays. You write all the essays in a *blue* (test-taking) *book*. Remember blue books from college? (Why they're blue is something I've never figured out.) Most professors don't give you a page or blue-book limit; however, I've never needed to use more than four blue books for a single exam. Professors also vary on whether they want you to use a fresh blue book for each essay.

Introducing the fact pattern

Describing these tests as essay exams is kind of misleading. You certainly won't see the typical essays that you had in college, such as "compare and contrast the Civil War with the French Revolution." After you set eyes on your first law school exam, you know you're not in Kansas anymore. That's because rather than a normal essay you have what's called a fact pattern.

Fact patterns are best thought of as a variation on the story problem (like the kind you had to solve in high school algebra). Basically, your professor takes a bunch of (sometimes outrageous) facts and puts them into a hypothetical story format (the *pattern*). Think back to the types of facts you've read in cases all semester. When you weave six or seven of those fact patterns into a story (liberally embedded with issues), you come up with something that resembles a law school exam. Take a look at Figure 11-1 to get a better idea of what I mean by fact pattern. The purpose of this traditional law school exam approach is to highlight the overlapping subtleties of various legal principles.

Question 1

Joann Farmer owns and operates a 600-acre farm near Smallville, West Dakota. One Saturday morning, Farmer has to make a trip into Smallville to get some supplies and she asks her hired hand, Hired Mann, to saddle up "Black Beauty (BB)", a horse that she had recently bought for recreational riding, so that it would be ready when she got back in about an hour.

Since Mann knew that it would only take him about 20 minutes to prepare the horse, he went inside his living quarters to finish watching one of his favorite Saturday morning TV programs, "Mutant Ninja Law Professors." Unknown to Mann, the gate on Black Beauty's stall was open. The horse escaped from the stall, jumped the fence on Farmer's property, and entered the property of one of Farmer's neighbors, Fred Rancher.

Rancher's 12-year-old daughter, Kari, was playing in the yard when Black Beauty jumped the fence. When Kari approached the Black Beauty, the horse bit her on the arm. Hearing Kari's scream, Fred Rancher ran outside and saw the horse near his daughter. Rancher grabbed his rifle from the porch, aimed at the horse, and fired. The bullet missed the horse and hits Farmer's dog, Lassie, who was sleeping under a tree next to Farmer's house.

At the sound of the gunshot, Hired Mann runs out of his quarters, sees Lassie bleeding and Rancher holding a gun. "If you ever get near this farm again, I promise that you'll be the one who gets shot!" said Mann.

At that moment, Black Beauty bolts away and runs toward the two-lane county blacktop road that runs along the property owned by Farmer and by Rancher. The horse ran onto the middle of the road just as E.Z. Ryder, a motorcyclist, was approaching at a reasonable rate of speed. Ryder swerved to avoid the horse, fell off his motorcycle and broke his collarbone. The motorcycle continued to skid across the road, where it hit an oncoming pesticide truck operated by Crops, Inc. On impact, the gas tank on the motorcycle exploded and set the fertilizer truck on fire. The driver of the truck escaped unharmed, but the burning pesticide created a toxic cloud that drifted away from the land owned by Rancher and Farmer but did drift onto several nearby farms, causing crop damages and severe personal injury to several residents.

Discuss the legal issues raised by this set of facts.

Figure 11-1: Sample essay exam question for first-year torts course.

Fact patterns run quite long. In a three-hour essay exam, they're each generally a page to two pages in length. But despite their length, not every fact in the fact pattern is important in your answer. Keep in mind that your professor purposely inserts a few red herring (extraneous) facts to throw you off track. Top students can spot these red herrings, briefly identify them as irrelevant in their answer, and move on with the rest of their discussion.

Issue-spotting is the name of the game

The point of having a fact pattern as an exam is to test your skills at issue-spotting. Issue-spotting is exactly what it sounds like: identifying an *issue* (identifying the conflicts between rules of law) in a fact pattern. You've had plenty of practice spotting issues in fact patterns all semester, because that's what your professors help you discover when giving you hypotheticals (see Chapter 8) in class.

What do you do when you spot an issue in your fact pattern? At that point, you want to

- ✔ State the issue
- ✔ Specify the relevant rule(s)
- ✔ Apply the law to the facts and analyze why or why not (arguments for and against) the rule should be applied to those facts
- ✔ Provide a conclusion (take a stand) on how the issue should be resolved

Professors allot points based on how many issues you spot. In a typical one-hour single fact pattern, you can find as many as 10 to 20 separate issues. Professors also award points for how well you discuss the issues, and how well you view the complexities (such as subissues and exceptions) that are involved.

Most essay exams are structured so that almost all students can spot basic issues. From there, however, your professor inserts subtler issues. Students who score high grades successfully spot more of these subissues than their peers.

As you're working through a fact pattern, you may find that physically crossing out issues that you've already spotted and discussed is helpful. I found this method really helped me stay on track and avoid redundancy. Another helpful tactic is having a *checklist* handy (a checklist is an extensively whittled-down outline). Your checklist can list, in abbreviated form, all the possible issues for the course. When you're taking the exam, you run down your checklist and ask yourself, "Does this question touch on any of these issues?" See Chapter 9 for more details about outlines and checklists.

Watching out for the policy question

Many law school essay exams sport a policy question in addition to two or three fact patterns. Nearly all my law school essay exams (and most take-homes) had them. A *policy question* asks you to evaluate a particular court's stance on an issue, discuss a legal idea or theory, or comment on a recurring theme of the course.

A typical policy question could be something like: "Choose three cases we read over the semester and discuss how you'd rule differently." On some of my law school exams, professors would take a quote that we'd never talked about and make it the policy question, by saying, "Discuss how this quote applies in the context of this course." In other words, it's more like a typical college essay question.

Policy questions may cause you to breathe a huge sigh of relief, because it's an area on the exam where poor issue-spotters can redeem themselves. Because your answer can be more touchy-feely than a typical fact pattern answer, you may think you have more freedom to experiment; however, don't make the mistake of thinking that you don't need to study for the policy question. After all, in a three-hour exam, a policy question usually counts as one-third of your grade. So, when you want to earn maximum points (and who doesn't?), giving some serious thought to what your professor may ask actually pays off.

Predicting the policy question needn't be a daunting task. Just think back to what your professor stressed during the semester. Did your professor stress feminist or economic theories? If so, make sure that you review your notes about these areas thoroughly. Did the professor assign outside articles on a particular topic? Find those articles and reread them before the exam. If you need help brainstorming possible policy question topics, get together with a classmate or your study group (see Chapter 9 for more about study groups) and start throwing around possibilities.

In writing your response to the policy question, you depart from the traditional law school exam writing approach (see the following section, "Writing the essay answer"). Instead, try writing it the way you'd respond to a college essay. Concentrate on making as many points as possible and tying different aspects of your course together. Organization is key; sketching out a rough mini-outline of the points you'd like to make is always a good bet.

Policy questions are usually the last question on a three-question test. That usually means you'll be down to the wire by the time you get to it. (I always ended up spending more time on the fact patterns, because they were usually the first and second questions on the exam, and I just did the questions in order.) If you're only halfway through your response to the policy question and you realize there's only 10 minutes left in the exam, sketch out your remaining points in outline form. That way, you'll at least get some partial credit.

Writing the essay answer

Simply knowing the material cold isn't enough to score a top mark in law school. In addition, you must master the *art* of writing the law school exam. The majority of law school professors are quite particular about how they want their exams written. Here are some key factors to keep in mind as you write your answers.

- **Organize, organize, organize.** Your professor doesn't want to wade through a hodgepodge of random thoughts and observations; instead, you need to state each issue in a topic sentence and then arrange your discussion of that particular issue underneath. In other words, if stream of consciousness is your trademark writing style, you need to find a new style during exam season. One of the best ways to ensure top-notch organization is to sketch a rough outline of the issues and subissues that you want to cover, in order, in a "scratch" blue book or inside your exam itself. This way, you can continually check against your outline that you're heading in the right direction. The reason that professors stress good organization is because they don't want to see anyone changing gears mid-paragraph or switching their stand on an issue halfway through the discussion. That signals to them that you don't have a clue what you're talking about. And on an exam, being perceived as incompetent is the last thing you want.

- **Write clearly and plainly.** This isn't a literature exam; you aren't being graded on your literary skills or your grasp of difficult nonlegal vocabulary. In fact, the simpler and more pared-down your writing style, the better. Get to the point in as few words as possible, and leave the flowery language for your career as a novelist.

- **Do a thorough analysis.** Lawyers are precise; they don't make blanket statements without explaining them. Thoroughly explore each assertion you make, by applying the law to the facts. If you merely state the relevant law without explaining how that law applies to your particular situation, your analysis is incomplete, and you'll be docked major points.

A good analysis always includes *counterarguments* — arguments that are in opposition to your main argument. Incorporating all counterarguments shows your professor that you can anticipate what the opposing side will do next, an impressive skill.

At the end of your analysis, always make sure to formulate a conclusion, such as "the situation suggests there was a battery." However, don't use definitive language in your conclusory statement, such as, "this definitely was a battery." Nothing in law is black and white, and your professor appreciates that you're comfortable with uncertainty when you suggest rather than assert.

Multiple-choice

If you're like me, you view multiple-choice exams as a mixed blessing. Sure, you don't have to do any writing, but unfortunately there's only one right (or "best") answer. In general, you won't see many multiple-choice exams in law school; they're far less common than essay exams. Out of all my exams in law school, for example, only three were multiple-choice. Some professors, however, give you half and half — half multiple-choice and half essay.

Multiple-choice exams tend to fall into three camps:

✔ Those consisting of mini–fact patterns (see the "Introducing the fact pattern" section earlier in the chapter)

✔ Those consisting of short questions about *black letter law* (well-established legal rules)

✔ Those consisting of mini-fact patterns and short black letter law questions

The frustrating thing about multiple-choice exams is that two of the answer choices often can be hair-splittingly close. Agonizing over which of the two answers is the right one can take a lot of time, and time is always at a premium on multiple-choice exams. In fact, on many law school multiple-choice exams, your time allotment averages out to between two and three minutes per question.

The trick to multiple-choice exams is understanding the format ahead of time. The best way to do this is by getting a hold of the professor's previous exams (like other types of exams, they're usually on reserve in the library under your professor's name or on the course's or your law library's Web site) to see what the questions were like, and to practice with them.

Short-answer

Short-answer exams give you either a mini–fact pattern to answer, as in a regular essay exam, or questions about black letter law. They differ from multiple-choice exams in that you're writing out the answer in (short) essay form in a blue book or right on the exam itself. Sometimes these exams involve one to two sentence answers; other times, you'll write a few paragraphs. They're relatively uncommon in law school. During my entire law school career, I had only one, and it was actually part multiple-choice and part short-answer. Prepare for short-answer exams the way you would for the other two types of exams — by creating outlines (see Chapter 9) and by finding past exams to look over.

Take-home exams

Yet another type of exam you may encounter at law school is the take-home. *Take-home exams* are a cross between an exam and a paper, and are quite common (I tended to have at least one per semester as a 2L and 3L). You probably won't get any as a 1L, however, because 1L professors tend to stick with essay or multiple-choice exams.

You probably remember your old friend the take-home from college. Unlike papers, with a take-home you generally won't be required to use footnotes or endnotes and proper *Blue Book* style (a citation manual for the legal profession) or write in an overly scholarly way. But unlike in-class exams, you usually get a more generous time limit of 48 hours to a week for your take-homes. Take-homes often require very lengthy answers. Having to type up 5 to 8 pages per question is not uncommon. How many questions appear on your take-home varies, but three-credit courses usually feature three questions.

In my opinion, take-home exams are the worst possible type, because they're long, drawn-out ordeals, rather than quick and painless three-hour jobs. In fact, I avoid any classes that are known to have a take-home for the final, because I tend to lose momentum whenever I have an entire weekend or week to complete an exam. If you're anything like me, you may want to also steer clear of classes featuring take-homes. But if you enjoy the flexibility and the lack of time pressure they offer, you'll want to register for as many classes with take-home exams as you can.

Open versus closed book

One aspect of law school that genuinely surprised me is how many exams are open book/open note. That's because in college, I don't remember ever taking a single open-book exam. But of all my law school exams, only four were closed book. One of the rationales for open-book exams in law school is that lawyers always keep their own books around so they can look things up. When a client walks into your office, you obviously need to have a certain level of legal mastery, but beyond that, you can always look up anything that you don't know about in the case law or statutes. Open-book exams validate the idea that lawyers don't need to memorize everything.

Even though you'll have your notes and books around for open-book exams, don't think you'll be able to find everything you need to know while you're actually taking the exam. Most professors write their questions so that you won't be able to find any "easy" answers in your books or notes. Many students taking open-book exams find that they don't even have time to peruse their materials. Only diligent preparation beforehand can adequately prepare you for these exams.

Regardless of the philosophy behind open- and closed-book exams, most students simply want to know which type is harder. Here is a rundown of their differences, so you can judge for yourself:

- ✔ **Some people find that open-book exams are more stressful.** Between your books, notes, and outline, you have plenty of material to sift through to find the answers in a short time period. However, psychologically, you may feel like you don't need to study that much before your open-book exam, because you have everything right there. The presence of their notes and books makes some people overconfident, because they think they'll have ample time to dig around for what they don't know. This rationalization may backfire, especially when you're confronted with questions that you didn't adequately prepare for (or your outline is a disorganized mess).

- ✔ **Closed-book exams often don't go as deep.** Professors are only human; they know you can recall only so much from memory. In my experience, questions on closed-book exams tended not to probe at the same level of difficulty as the ones on open-book exams. Students who are good at memorization usually excel on closed-book exams.

- ✔ **Some students "freeze" on closed-book exams.** They see a blank blue book and suddenly can't remember a thing they studied. It's fairly common to tense up when you don't have your notes or books around as a comfort, but I always found that re-reading the questions got me to relax and allowed me to look for even the smallest issues I recognized. Doing a "brain dump"— where you use the first ten minutes of the exam to write all the important things you can remember on the first few pages of a scratch blue book — always helped me immensely on closed-book exams.

- ✔ **In open-book exams, many students find the presence of their notes, books, and outlines immensely comforting.** For these students, the presence of these items helps them relax and perform better, because they know their safety net is right in front of them. Additionally, when your outline is outstanding, you can easily find what you need.

Lyman Johnson, professor of corporate and securities law at Washington and Lee School of Law in Lexington, Virginia, believes students like open-book exams because they think they're not going to be as stressed when they take one. Johnson generally doesn't offer open-book exams in his courses, however, because he thinks they often make for inferior testing experiences. His reasoning: When the notes are in front of you, you may avoid thinking deeply about the question being asked and, instead, simply start canvassing the materials for the answers. Besides, he says, the answer is not likely to be in your notes or the book. As a result, he thinks that open-book exams present an ironic situation, one where although students feel better about them, the testing experience turns out to be less helpful to professors and students.

One of the more important resources that you have at your disposal is other students. The ones who have taken your course in the past can give you the lowdown on the exam (whether closed or open and the difficulty level), tell you what sort of questions your professor favors, and explain how your professor wants the exam written.

Understanding Your School's Exam System

Law schools across the country differ about their rules and regulations for exam taking. Your professor usually informs you about the school's policies, but when you're in doubt, see the dean of students.

Getting used to being anonymous

Most law schools use the anonymous exam system. The way the *anonymous exam system* works is that the registrar assigns each student an exam number that is randomly generated only for you and changed every semester. The *exam number* is your test identification. Instead of writing your name on the exam and/or blue book, you write only your exam number. That way, the professor has no idea who wrote what until after they submit the exam grades to the registrar. At that point, many registrars provide faculty a class list with the grades matched up with the names, thus enabling faculty members to adjust the grade up or down one notch to account for extraordinary class participation or lack thereof (or bad attendance).

Dealing with only one exam per course

Almost all law schools universally have just one exam that determines your entire grade in a course. Many law students find this one-exam concept nerve-wracking. After all, one bad exam day and your GPA can be irrevocably damaged. You may, as a 2L and 3L, be able to find classes (such as a seminar; see Chapter 12) that offer a paper (see the following section) in place of an exam as the sole form of evaluation or a class that offers a paper and a final. But be advised: The majority of law school classes follow the one-exam format. See Chapter 6 for more on the one-exam format.

Preferring a paper to an exam

The one-exam format is the gold standard and papers are more of an exception to the rule, but you'll still find options for "paper" classes as a 2L and 3L (legal research and writing is usually the only paper class for 1Ls). Third-year seminars, for instance, have a research paper (and usually presentation) as their forms of evaluation (see Chapter 12 for more on seminars). Many schools offer advanced legal writing and other classes that offer multiple short papers that make up your grade.

Although it's unlikely that your school offers enough paper classes to take three or four each upper-class semester during law school, do peruse your registration packet if this option interests you. Realistically, you'll be able to find one or two paper courses per semester at most law schools.

The following are some reasons that you may prefer having a paper as your final evaluation:

- **A paper enables you to work at your own pace.** You can work on it throughout the semester without any stress from cramming at the last minute. You don't need to methodically spill the contents of your brain onto the pages of a blue book during a three-hour time period; instead, you can refine your thoughts more or less at your leisure. The only due dates for papers tend to be those of turning in the topic selections, outline, and rough draft.

- **A paper is more collaborative.** When writing a paper, you can usually discuss your thesis and argument development with your professor, but when taking an exam, you're completely on your own. In addition, when writing a paper, you can sometimes talk with other students and practitioners about the key issues. But different professors have different rules on the allowance or extent of collaboration; check with your individual professor for guidelines.

- **A paper allows you to conduct a more in-depth exploration of a subject.** Although you may yearn to cover all of trademark law in a three-hour exam, it's unlikely that you'll even scratch the surface. In a paper, on the other hand, you usually have as many pages as you need to discuss the issues.

Coasting on the curve

Although all professors grade differently, almost all of them use some sort of curve. Unlike in college, where you were graded on how you performed independent of your peers in most classes, the law school curve pits you and your classmates against each other. For that reason (among others), law school sometimes has a cutthroat reputation.

Exam Day Survival Strategies

The day you've been waiting for is finally here! You're prepared, and you know what's expected of you. Now, all you need to do is spill the contents of your brain down onto paper. Knowing the material is only part of the battle. The rest depends on how well you present your answers, follow your professor's instructions, and manage stress.

Knowing what's allowed

Before the day of the exam, make sure you know exactly what you're allowed to take into the exam. You don't want to make the horrific mistake of bringing in your books, only to find out at the last minute that the test is closed book. Similarly, your professor may specify that bringing in one book, but not another, is okay. For instance, your statutory book may be okay, but your casebook may not. Or, any outlines you prepare yourself may be okay, but commercial study aids aren't (see Chapter 10 for more on commercial study aids). Make sure to clarify any confusion beforehand; otherwise, you're bound for disaster.

Getting a full-night's shuteye

Although it sounds elementary, getting a good night's sleep is essential if you're to have enough steam to plow through your exam. Law school exam lengths are between three and four hours, and even the most well rested student is going to feel a drop in energy somewhere toward the end. If you've gotten only three hours of sleep the night before you'll barely make it past the first question without your thoughts turning from criminal law to your comfy bed.

Staying up until the wee hours the night before can only be counterproductive. If you don't know your stuff by the evening before the exam, you're never going to.

Revealing what professors love to see in an exam

Ask any professor what makes up a good exam, and you're likely to hear similar answers. I asked a bunch of professors what qualities they always find in A exams. Here's what I found, straight from the horses' mouths (so to speak). Professors suggest that you always

✔ **Read the instructions.** Many professors lament that they read exams marred by one fatal flaw: Students fail to answer the question that is asked. Sure, you may write an A answer, but if you answer a different question (perhaps the one you *wished* your professor had asked), you're not going to score many points. Another costly mistake students make is that they write their answers from viewpoints other than the ones professors specify at the end of the question.

For example, a typical exam question might ask how you'd respond to the fact pattern as counsel for the defendant. Even if you write a great response as plaintiff's counsel, if you're being asked to represent the defendant, you'll be docked major points. Similarly, if the instructions tell you to assume certain facts or limit the scope of your answer, you're wise not to deviate from your professor's wishes.

✔ **Heed time limits.** Many professors do you the favor of specifying how long you need to spend on each exam question. If the instructions say spend 30 minutes on the first, an hour on the second, and an hour and a half on the third, you'll do yourself a major injustice by spending 20 minutes on the first two questions combined and two hours and 40 minutes on the last. Make sure you stick to prescribed time limits.

✔ **Answer questions in the order they're presented.** On my survey of environmental law exam, I answered the questions in reverse order (for no particular reason), and guess what happened: I was docked points because the second question built off the first. I missed some key issues that I otherwise would have seen had I answered them in the correct order. The moral of the story: The professor probably put the questions in a specific order for a reason, and when you answer them *out of order* you risk missing a part of the exam that's cumulative.

✔ **When you're running out of time, outline the remainder of your answer in your blue book.** Professors understand that students sometimes run out of time on exams. When that happens (particularly on the last question of the exam), just write the remaining part of your answer in outline form. Although you will probably receive only partial credit, you can at least receive some credit by letting the professor know that you knew the right answer.

Typing versus writing

Some schools permit students to bring in laptops, but you need to check with your dean of students about the policies. Typically, laptops aren't allowed, however, so students must print out any versions of their notes (or outlines) to use during open-book exams.

If laptops are allowed, depending on the school, laptop students may or may not be separated from their writing peers (for noise reasons). Most schools send test-takers who plan to type to special rooms, but most schools also require you to bring your own equipment, even if it's a typewriter. If you can manage to scrounge up a typewriter, some people find they can type faster than they can write — and so they're able to say more in less time. Your professor won't know who's typing and who's writing, because of your anonymous exam number (see the "Getting used to being anonymous" section earlier in this chapter). So don't be deterred from typing just because you think you'll stick out in a class full of writers.

Writing legibly

Illegible exams are law school professors' biggest and most universal pet peeve. Although the quality of your analysis is how you score the most exam points, professors subconsciously or even consciously dock points when they can't make out your writing.

Why is good handwriting such a big deal? Imagine yourself as a professor, reading the 50th student exam. You can barely decipher a single word of the chicken-scratch handwriting in front of you. It's not hard to see why professors facing illegible exams are less likely to give you credit when your answer is almost right and may even subconsciously mark your answer more harshly in a fit of annoyance.

Putting forth a little extra effort to write neatly can help you avoid any problems in this area. If you somehow cannot find a way to improve your penmanship, you may want to try writing in all capital letters, writing on every other line, or simply printing. I always printed on exams, and although doing so is a bit slower than writing in cursive, my exams were much easier to read. If that doesn't improve your situation, perhaps you need to consider typing.

During the course of writing an answer, everyone occasionally needs to cross out passages or make additions. Whenever you cross something out make sure you're thorough so your professor knows not to read it. Likewise, when you need to add something, make a star or carrot symbol, and write your addition neatly in the margin or on the line above or below. Just make it clear where exactly the additions need to go. The last thing you want is your professor having to decipher a mess of arrows pointing every which way. Furthermore, although many professors don't specify, they generally like it when you write on every other line and on only one side of a page. Doing so makes reading your handwriting easier for them and prevents your ink from bleeding through to the other side of those thin blue book pages.

Eric Janus, a professor of civil procedure, constitutional law, and mental health law at William Mitchell College of Law, in St. Paul, Minnesota, believes that when professors can't read what you've said on your exam, they subconsciously or even consciously tend to grow very frustrated. Janus warns that when reading an exam response is hard for professors, they may assume that it isn't correct, instead of giving the student the benefit of the doubt. In his experience, students who type tend to do better because they see what they're writing, and that makes reading those exams much simpler for the professors. He adds that students need to bear in mind that professors read many exams, and any difficulty that gets in the way can affect their evaluations. Janus also recommends that students with bad handwriting figure out what key words and phrases they're using in their essays and then be especially careful about writing them.

Answering nature's call

Lasting three to four hours without a bathroom break — especially when you've consumed a lot of caffeine — is definitely difficult. Instead of writhing around in an uncomfortable state, sometimes you just need to give in to the urge. But, you may ask, is this idea a good one given that you're flushing precious time down the toilet? A typical bathroom break costs you between five and eight minutes of exam time. So, the best approach is eliminating any possibility of having to use the facilities, perhaps by avoiding any pre-exam beverages. Similarly, because getting up and leaving the room may break your concentration, you may want to wait until the exam is over. If you simply can't wait, make it quick, and lay off the liquids before taking exams in the future.

Bringing a snack

Most law schools allow students to bring drinks, candy bars, or other small snacks with them to exams as long as they don't make noise. Crackers and carrot sticks are probably bad ideas; a favorite candy bar or cream-filled spongecake is perfectly fine.

In fact, bringing a small snack is a good idea because doing so can raise your blood sugar level at this crucial time and that can improve your focus. I often brought a plastic sandwich bag full of miniature candy bars. They're easy to unwrap and eat without looking, and the small bursts of sugar kept me feeling energized and ready to go throughout the entire exam. Plus I could hand them out to friends before the exam started for good luck.

Managing stress

Exams are stressful for everyone, across the board. But it's important not to allow stress to interfere with your exam performance. The last thing you want is to draw a mental blank, freeze up on a question, or get so frustrated that you can't proceed with the exam. Some simple techniques that you can use for easing stress when you're waiting for the exam to start and while you're taking it include

- **Taking deep breaths and visualizing a happier place.** Whenever you feel overwhelmed, close your eyes for a minute and think about being in the warmest, most comforting place, like at the beach or in bed. Inhale deeply (just not so deeply that you nod off). After several deep breaths, you should feel less overwhelmed and ready to dig into the question.

- **Avoiding the panic when confronted with a question you have no idea about.** This happens to most law students at least once or twice during their careers; the important point is to stay cool. Reread the question several times. Doing so may calm you down and alert you to issues you didn't see the first time you read it. If it's an essay exam, start outlining an answer (see the "Writing the essay answer" section earlier in the chapter), and be confident that whatever you're not seeing soon will come to you. Whatever you do, don't panic. When all else fails, remember it's just one question and you'll be able to make up for it on the others. When every question stumps you, well, you have a small problem. But, hey, in the grand scheme of things, it's only one exam, and there's always next semester to turn things around.

- **Not freaking out when you're running out of time on a question.** Simply decide how much more time you want to spend on that question, and then move onto the next. If you can't adequately conclude your answer in the remaining time, just outline the rest of your answer (on essay exams). You (usually) get partial credit for the outlined portion. One question isn't going to make or break your entire grade, and spreading your time more or less evenly according to your professor's directions is important. For more on time limits for questions and following your professor's specific directions, see the section, "Revealing what professors love to see in an exam" earlier in the chapter.

- **Doing some easy stretching exercises whenever your hand starts to cramp up.** Massage your writing hand with the other hand, especially working the thumb muscles. With your free hand, try bending the writing hand back, stretching the tendons in the wrist. Move your fingers in a circular motion to loosen up tight muscles. Take momentary writing breaks to ease out the kinks.

Keeping an eye on time

Keeping track of time during your exam is as important as having pens that work. The last thing you want to hear your test proctor saying is, "Okay, time's up," especially when you've just started on the second question. That's why you need to watch the clock at all times. Making sure that you have a watch with you during the exam is important in case you're not in direct line of sight with the classroom clock.

One way to ensure that time's on your side is by heeding the suggestions your professor's makes regarding the amount of time to devote to each question (see the "Revealing what professors love to see in an exam" section earlier in the chapter). I kept track of the time by writing my starting and ending times for each question at the top of each page. That way, I knew exactly when to start and stop.

Similarly, whenever you finish your exam early, don't be one of those triumphant people marching up to the front of the room and smugly depositing their exams in the box with an hour to spare. By all means go back and look over your answers. What else are you going to do with that extra hour, anyway?

Use the remaining time to check your grammar, punctuation, and overall clarity. In fact, you can always go back and add something to your answers or cross out irrelevant passages, because doing so may make a noticeable difference in your grade.

Putting it out of your mind

Your exam's finally over; vacation (or next exam), here you come! As tempting as rehashing every question and discussing details of your exam with your friends afterward may be, try to avoid giving in to this temptation. That sort of rehashing only makes you nervous. When you ask your friends whether they spotted a particular issue, and none of them did, you'll spend the night tossing and turning over what else you missed. After all, the last thing you want is to be so distracted by today's exam that you can't perform at 100 percent on tomorrow's exam. The best thing to do is let bygones be bygones.

Part IV

You're Halfway There (2Ls and 3Ls)

The 5th Wave   By Rich Tennant

©RICHTENNANT

"I'm glad your second year in law school has you
thinking like an attorney, but you've got to stop
submitting a bill with your homework."

In this part . . .

You've made it halfway, and now you can claim the title of upperclassman. In this part, I share my battle-tested approach for choosing the best electives and give you the lowdown on pursuing a bevy of extracurricular interests.

Chapter 12

One from Column A: Choosing Your Courses

*Y*ou've made it through torts, crushed your legal research and writing assignments, and aced your 1L exams. Now that you're officially an upperclassman, you'll probably wonder whether there's any truth to that oft-quoted law school saying: "The second year they work you to death; the third they bore you to death." Guess what! You're going to find out. However, these unflattering views of *your* upper-class years needn't hold true to that saying when you choose your courses wisely.

As a 2L and 3L, you're in complete control of your schedule. With the possible exception of a few graduation requirements, you therefore have the freedom to mix and match your courses at will. Finally, you can focus in on feminist jurisprudence or Internet law rather than the standard 1L fare.

So what are the *best* courses to take? That's the subject of this chapter. I walk you through the most important criteria to consider when devising your schedule and introduce you to time-honored strategies for choosing your electives. I also cover the frequently overlooked option of taking courses outside the law school and how to decide whether an adventure awaits you via study-abroad options. With the right combination of advance planning and self-assessment, you'll remember your upper-class years as an intellectual smorgasbord for years to come.

Choosing a Successful Course Load

All law students choose classes in their own unique ways. Some students choose them based on what tickles their fancy that semester; others strategize based on an ideal exam schedule. And still others focus on packing in all the *bar courses* — courses that are highly recommended in preparation for the bar exam (see Chapter 18 for detailed information about the bar exam). A few try a different approach every semester of law school. The decision is all yours.

Because 2Ls and 3Ls take their classes together, you may find that some of the less-popular courses are offered only every other year. For optimal planning, consult your most recent law school registration booklet, which usually notes which courses aren't offered the following year.

Second-year law students may want to consider a lighter course load during the fall semester, when their time is nearly monopolized by interviewing (see Chapters 14 and 15), cite-checking for journals, and the moot court competition (see Chapter 13 for more about journals and moot court). I took the fewest number of credits during my 2L fall semester, and I'm glad I did, because extracurriculars and the summer job search often seem like classes of their own.

During the third year, academics notoriously take a back seat to job searching, studying for the bar, or sometimes just having a good time. Additionally, some 3Ls contract *senioritis* the day they accept a job offer and slack off the rest of the semester (or year). Professors tend to expect this reaction, but keeping up with your courses and putting in as much effort as you can is still a good idea. After all, you are paying good money for a legal education. However, after you have a job, you're in the clear (no one will ever see or take much notice of your remaining semester's grades), so you can sign up for advanced secured transactions or international tax law without worrying about ruining your grade-point average (GPA) too much.

Satisfying graduation requirements

For better or worse, satisfying graduation requirements is the most important aspect of choosing a good course load, because not doing so means you won't graduate. Before throwing down your registration packet in frustration, bear in mind that many law schools allow you to satisfy their graduation requirements with courses of your own choosing.

Many schools have from one to several graduation requirements, more often involving a professional responsibility ethics course, a writing course, and a research paper seminar course. Some schools also require a course that meets a *perspectives requirement* — in other words, a class that emphasizes a nonlegal perspective on legal problems, such as law and literature, psychology and the law, or economics and the law.

Many schools don't mandate that you take these required courses at any specific time during your upper-class years; but some, for instance, require you to take the writing course during the second year and the research paper seminar course during the third. Knowing that you often have a wide variety of courses from which to choose to satisfy any writing or perspectives requirements is exciting.

Focusing on courses tested on the bar exam

Some courses come highly recommended as great preparation for students who plan on taking the bar exam (see Chapter 18 for more information on the bar exam). A list of them may include:

- Corporations
- Evidence
- Family law
- Wills and trusts
- Sales
- Secured transactions
- Criminal process

Check with your state to find out exactly what will appear on its bar exam; specific requirements vary from state to state.

Although taking these courses is not a requirement for taking the bar exam (you'll learn everything you need to know about these courses later in your bar exam prep course), many law students end up taking these courses in law school because of the extra confidence that doing so gives them heading into the bar exam. Some of the courses, such as corporations and secured transactions, tend to be very hard, and some people believe they need the extra reinforcement that taking them provides before the bar.

At most schools, none of these bar courses are required for graduation; so they're pretty much always optional. Even if you plan on taking the bar exam, you don't have to take one or any of these courses; it's just highly recommended that you take a few to get a solid foundation in preparation for that almighty exam.

If you decide that taking the bar exam isn't the right choice for you, you can still take any of the bar courses just for personal knowledge and/or a well-rounded legal education. If you don't take the bar exam, you still emerge from law school a J.D., like everyone else, but you won't be a practicing lawyer.

Discovering the value of practice-related courses

Because law school students don't have formalized majors, the curricula that define what classes are most beneficial for you to take in given areas of specialization rarely are spelled out. Beyond basics such as introduction to environmental law (if you're wanting to become an environmental attorney), you're on your own when figuring out what you can take now to benefit your career later.

I consulted with a range of J.D.s in their respective fields to get the inside scoop on what law school classes helped them the most. Their fields, names, and commentary follow:

✔ **Litigation — K. Bartlett Durand, Jr., a complex litigation lawyer at Bickerton Saunders & Dang in Honolulu:**

"I'm working at a firm that deals with very complex litigation — foreign tort law, malpractice work (plaintiff and defense, legal and medical), business torts, environmental/social justice causes, and bad faith. The single most helpful class for this type of work was *contracts,* followed by secured transactions, civil procedure, and my writing classes. After you've learned to

research, you can learn any area of the law, but these classes really focused on the language of the laws/agreements, and that is a common thread throughout all of the work we do. Learning to focus in on the key problems to be solved, to research quickly yet thoroughly, and to write clearly and cleanly are the primary abilities you develop in law school in preparation for a successful practice."

✔ **Teaching — Eric Janus, professor of civil procedure, constitutional law, and mental health law at William Mitchell College of Law in St. Paul, Minnesota:**

"Civil procedure, contracts, and property courses were three that heavily influenced my future career. It was in civil procedure, particularly, where I enjoyed the type of questioning that got me to understand the need to read the rules and see how they relate to each other. My federal courts class was also very influential, and I've taught that course myself. I think it's one of the most difficult and interesting areas of the law."

✔ **Intellectual property law — Harold Davis, Jr., an intellectual property lawyer at Katten, Muchin, Zavis, Rosenman, in Chicago:**

"One of the classes that best served me was accounting for lawyers, because with intellectual property litigation, one of the hardest issues is how do you value an idea. Learning standard methods of valuation is invaluable background for dealing with the numerous issues that arise in intellectual property transactions. The other class that's helpful from an intellectual property stand-point is a property class, because many of the fundamental concepts of intellectual property come from the background of jurisprudence revolving around real and personal property. And finally, a civil proce-dure class is indispensable to any litigator."

✔ **Environmental law — Leverett Nelson, an environmental lawyer with the Office of Regional Counsel at the Environmental Protection Agency in Chicago:**

"Because I knew upon entering law school that I wanted to focus on environmental law, I took almost every course I could (at the University of Colorado–Boulder) that was related to the environment. This helped me stay sane and helped me better define my interest. Although it all was interesting, I may have overdone it. For example, I seldom run across water law issues or oil and gas law issues, although this may be because of the fact that I wound up prac-ticing in the Midwest. In retrospect, besides the usual survey course covering the basic environmental statutes and an advanced seminar or independent study, I'd strongly recommend a course in corporations/agency/partnership (identifying the right corporate entity to name in an enforcement action is obviously essential), bankruptcy (this area is unfortunately a more and more common aspect of environmental practice), administrative law (this area is a constant on the sides of rulemaking/permitting and enforcement), and advanced criminal pro-cedure (to cover civil warrants under the Fourth Amendment).

Making room for courses that interest you

After the graduation requirements are out of the way, you can really roll up your sleeves and dig into the fun stuff: whatever interests you. No longer lim-ited to torts, contracts, and civil procedure as you were as a 1L, you can now try your hand at estate planning, trial process, environmental law, or health law. Your law school registration packet is bursting with thought-provoking courses, such as land-use controls and negotiable instruments. By your upper-class years, you've learned most of the basics; now you can find your true calling, if you haven't already.

Some people know right away what they're interested in; others, particularly students with minimal pre–law school exposure to the law, don't have a clue. Your second and third years are the perfect times to take a wide assortment of random courses. Try real estate finance, international human rights, and federal criminal law all in one semester. A diverse schedule is the best way to dabble in different subject areas.

My strategy was to take as many *survey courses* (those that introduce the student to a broad overview of the subject matter, such as introduction to environmental law versus public natural resources law) as I could as a 2L; then, as a 3L, I went in-depth into some of the areas that I enjoyed most the year before. Doing so enabled me first to understand the foundations and later to augment them with more focused courses.

Although finding courses that you're interested in as a 2L is pretty easy, during the second semester the third year, you may find that you've already taken all the courses you're interested in, and as a result, you're forced to register for the leftovers. Yet even in that situation, be bold and experiment. You may find yourself loving advanced corporate taxation law far more than you ever dreamed.

Don't rely too heavily on courses that your law school lists in its glossy promotional brochure in place of the ones listed in the registration packet. Some courses mentioned in the promotional material may be taught only during alternate years (or even less frequently), so don't set your heart on taking torts in literature only to discover that it won't be taught in the years you're at the law school.

Working toward a comfortable exam schedule

Your exam schedule can make or break you. Whenever you have two exams scheduled on a single day, have two or more slated on consecutive days, or have all your exams squeezed in one week, you risk getting burned out faster than if your exams are scheduled at a more leisurely pace.

That's why some law students choose their classes based primarily on the exam schedule. I tried this approach during the fall semester of my third year by choosing only classes whose exams fell during the last week of the *exam period* (the two weeks or so at the end of each semester that law schools have designated for exams.) Doing so meant that I'd have an entire extra week to study for them, uninterrupted. Of course, this approach limited my course choices, but I think the extra week made a big difference in my end-of-semester stress level.

Revealing Strategies for Selecting the Best Electives

After you form an idea of what goes into a solid schedule, bear in mind that many factors come into play when choosing individual electives. For example, you may hear rave reviews about a particular professor and want to take his or her class no matter what the subject matter. Or, you may hear that a particular course is a killer and want to stay away from anything that may destroy your GPA.

Casting a wide knowledge net versus concentrating in one area

Although no majors are awarded in law school, some students choose to focus on particular areas, such as intellectual property, environmental law, or criminal law, and as such, take multiple courses within those areas. Few schools have formal specialty tracks, so students simply decide on their own to take a bunch of classes in a particular area. The main benefits of this strategy are getting the best professional preparation for your chosen area of practice and convincing employers that you're serious about a particular field.

On the other hand, some students prefer taking a generalist's approach, getting the broadest education possible. If your aim is to be a general practitioner, this approach can work well for you. But if you're looking to specialize (which isn't required, see Chapter 16 for more information on choosing practice areas), you probably want to take at least two or three classes in your area to make sure it fits your personality and temperament.

A third approach, which can be mixed in with the other two, is gaining as many practical skills for your professional plans as possible (see the "Getting hands-on experience at law clinics" section later in this chapter). Your specific career goals dictate how you decide to structure your course load. For instance, if you want to be a litigator, focus on trial process and advocacy courses, and courses where you can work on your persuasive writing. If you're going to be a *transactional* (deal-making) lawyer, you'll want to try your hand at negotiations, mediation, or arbitration.

 Michael Pastor, a clerk for a federal judge in the District of Maryland, chose his law school courses based on variety. He wanted a good mix of classes. So, whenever he chose one large lecture course with a famous professor, he'd then mix it up with a smaller seminar. He also didn't want to specialize in any particular area in law school, because he thought that he'd glean that kind of specialized knowledge on the job. As a result, Pastor always ended up with a diverse schedule.

Mixing case law and code courses

Some people flat out hate reading cases; they'd rather pour over statutes any day. If that describes you, try to avoid the *common-law* (judge-made law) *courses* such as contracts, torts, and property, and aim for *code* (statutory) *courses,* such as sales, tax, or secured transactions. Although many law school courses generally require you to read cases and look over statutes, avoiding one or the other isn't terribly difficult.

Knowing what courses can make or break you (and your GPA)

Every school has its legendary professors; you know, the ones that you just have to take. They're the ones who captivate you with their dynamic presence, dazzle you with their grasp of the subject matter, and astound you by making even the driest of subjects come alive. At the same time, every school has tough and boring professors, who are infamous for giving plenty of Cs, failing students, or being generally dull presenters. They're the ones who have the uncanny knack for making a fascinating topic fall flat.

Of course, you need take courses with as many of the truly amazing professors as you can, while avoiding the dull ones at all costs. Sometimes, you encounter both types of professors purely by chance and not by word of mouth. For instance, during the fall semester of my third year, I took all my classes based on the convenience of their exam schedules. I'd never previously heard about two of my professors that semester, but they turned out to be the best I'd experienced in all of law school. I'd never have encountered them had I not randomly chosen their courses. The funny thing is that I have to admit that I had absolutely zero interest in the subject matter before starting their courses.

When your GPA is sagging, a good option may be finding the easy professors. Present at most law schools, they're the ones who give a disproportionate share of A's. If you're hoping to land a job at a large firm or a prestigious clerkship (see Chapters 14 and 15 for detailed information on these options), taking an easy professor may factor heavily into your course-selection decisions. Find out about these gems through the law school grapevine (see Chapter 6 for more information on using upper-class students to get the lowdown on professors).

Choosing responsive faculty in your field of interest

Some students, particularly the ones in their second year, often choose courses based on their perception of how good of a reference the professor will be. If you've heard that a particular professor is best buddies with the judge for whom you want to clerk, or used to work at a firm where you'd be interested in working, obtaining a reference from that professor is key.

Other students in need of reference letters for jobs or clerkships choose courses where they know they can excel. That way, they're virtually guaranteed a sparkling reference from that faculty member.

If you're going into tax law, for instance, you may want a strong letter of reference from a tax law professor who's particularly well known within the field. That letter may open doors for you, so doing well in the class and continually showing up for office hours (so the professor knows you) is wise.

Students who want to go into law school teaching also need dynamic references from faculty; such students are especially advised to enroll in seminars where you get more one-on-one interaction with professors. Having a professor who can eloquently speak to your academic gifts is crucial when applying for teaching positions (see Chapter 17 for more information on law school teaching jobs).

Another great path leading to a strong reference is to serve as a research assistant (see Chapter 13 for more information on landing these positions). This position enables you to delve into the professor's area of expertise, thus getting the inside scoop on a field and emerging from the experience with fodder for a sterling reference and a golden entry on your résumé.

Finding out what's expected of you

Before you sign up for Professor Smith's international securities regulation course, you may want to find out exactly what's expected of you. You can discover these juicy tidbits by reading the course registration packet, which alerts you to whether the class is primarily a paper or exam class, the form of instruction (Socratic versus lecture or discussion), and whether any short exercises or presentations are required. (The next section tells you more about how to judge the various forms of instruction.)

Part IV: You're Halfway There (2Ls and 3Ls)

If you're the type of person who has a less-is-more mind-set, then avoid classes that require anything more than a final exam. On the other hand, when you feel more at ease with a class that offers multiple grading opportunities, you may opt for taking one with more than just a final.

Many law schools offer *seminars* for 2Ls and 3Ls. Seminars are usually the same number of credits as regular courses, and usually involve one long research paper and a class presentation element. At many schools, taking one research paper seminar course in your third year is a graduation requirement. Many schools allow students to sign up for multiple seminars, so if papers are your thing, this approach may appeal to you. Of course, your school may offer nonseminar classes that also have more grading opportunities than one final exam, such as advanced legal writing. Peruse your registration packet for more details. See the "Surveying spectacular seminars" section later in this chapter for additional information.

Besides papers and exams, some courses, such as negotiations, mediation, or a clinic (such as the child advocacy clinic or community legal clinic) may involve an end-of-class simulation or oral argument rather than an exam or paper. The focus of clinics varies from school to school, so see your dean of students to find out which ones yours offers. These *skills courses* interest students who want more of a hands-on approach to legal problems, including the way they're graded at the end of the semester. See the "Getting hands-on experience at law clinics" section later in this chapter for more information.

Weighing lecture versus Socratic Method

Although professors generally tend to ease off on the Socratic Method somewhat during the second and third years, some courses remain decidedly more Socratic than others. Relax, you have plenty of options if you're not a Socratic fan. See Chapter 8 for a complete explanation of the Socratic Method.

Consulting the course registration packets and upperclassmen gets you the lowdown on which courses are Socratic versus lecture or discussion. The packet normally indicates the style of the presentation; however, you can also double-check during the *shopping period,* which is usually during the first week of the new semester (the number of days varies by school). During the shopping period, (otherwise known as *drop/add* at many schools), students can drop and add courses without penalty.

One caveat regarding pure lecture courses, which I call the *slacking-off factor:* You can go weeks, if not months, without reading, and no one will ever know when you're taking a lecture course. Contrasting that idea, the Socratic Method entails daily public and often humiliating interrogation when you're caught unprepared. If you need a kick in the seat of the pants to get your reading done, either find a friend who can be your taskmaster or stick with the Socratic Method. Otherwise, you'll be cramming a semester's worth of toxic and hazardous substance control the night before the exam. I actually took that course, and trust me, it's hard enough.

Discussion courses are a nice compromise. Unlike in lecture courses, you're actively participating, and yet unlike in Socratic Method courses, you're not being interrogated. Think of discussion courses as the friendly seminars you had in college, where everyone is encouraged to *share*, which in law schools may seem like a fresh breeze compared with your 1L boot camp days.

As an upperclassman, I avoided any classes that had Socratic-style teaching whenever possible. One of the ways I was able to do so was by checking on the size of the room where the course was being taught, based on the information in the registration packet. The smaller the room, (I found) the less likely that the course is taught using the Socratic Method. Smaller rooms tend to facilitate more of a discussion format.

Surveying spectacular seminars

Many schools offer 3Ls the opportunity to satisfy their research paper requirement by taking a seminar. Or, they (and 2Ls if permitted) can take one just for the interest. Seminars are intimate courses, usually with fewer than 15 students, that are set up in a discussion format.

Seminars are a refreshing change of pace because they usually don't utilize casebooks. On the contrary, they mainly use law review and other scholarly articles, individual cases, and books, and they're graded on the basis of a final research paper and accompanying student presentation. However, some seminars require multiple short papers in addition to the long paper, which can become tedious. Others require selected students to present the day's reading during each class meeting.

You may be temped to load up on a semester's worth of seminars, because they:

- ✔ Tend to have light reading
- ✔ Often meet only once a week for two to three hours
- ✔ Often end early in the semester (or have a lengthy break for students to work on research papers)

However, bear in mind that most seminars require a lengthy 25- to 35-page research paper, which in my opinion is much more work than studying for a single exam. That's because the research paper needs to include *primary* (cases and statutes) and *secondary* (scholarly articles and books) sources, and finding all that information is extremely time-consuming. For example, the research paper I wrote took around 80 hours to complete.

The seminars at many schools often are tailored to the particular research interests of their professors; therefore, you may find detailed and finely tuned topics such as law, morality, and community; law and society of Japan; and children and the law in modern America. For my 3L seminar, I took a course called intellectual property in the European Union and United States, and wrote my 35-page research paper on biotechnology patent protection in the EU and U.S. I enjoyed the relaxed pace of the seminar, the discussion format, and the emphasis on policy rather than pure case law. But you'll have to decide whether these qualities sound appealing to you.

Delving into directed reading

Most law schools offer students an opportunity to take one or two credits as *directed reading*. In other words, you find a professor in an area of the law in which you're interested, compile a reading list of cases, scholarly articles, and books, and create a syllabus. You read the materials on your own and meet with your professor once a week or so to discuss them.

Directed readings are a great way of satisfying a credit or two that you need to graduate, especially as a second semester 3L. They can help you build a strong foundation in a particular area of the law in which you're interested and help you form a mentoring relationship with your professor. As an added bonus, they're normally graded pass/fail, so they should give you minimal stress.

Introducing independent research

In a similar vein, some schools allow you to undertake an independent research project for course credit. Similar to a seminar's research paper requirement, you're responsible for:

- ✔ Coming up with an idea or topic
- ✔ Approaching the relevant and appropriate faculty member
- ✔ Writing up an outline and rough draft
- ✔ Turning in a research paper similar to the one required for a more structured class.

Many students favor this option when they have specific research interests that aren't met by existing courses. Whenever your area of interest is somewhat obscure, corral the appropriate faculty member and propose your idea. You never know when you'll be able to parlay your research paper into a writing competition entry or publishable note (see Chapter 13 for more information on these opportunities).

Bear in mind, when you're signing up for independent research, no one's there to egg you on when you don't feel like researching. At least during a seminar, you have other students to interact with and carved-in-stone due dates for each stage of your paper: topic selection, outline, rough draft, and completed version. Without a professor breathing down your neck (they're related to dragons, you know) to submit these documents on time, you may find yourself in over your head with a semester's worth of research to do during finals week. Whenever you choose this option, make certain that you're a self-starter, because you're largely left to your own devices.

Deciding whether to take morning, afternoon, or night classes

If you're a night owl, an 8 a.m. administrative law class is going to drive you crazy all semester. Similarly, if you're at your best in the morning, late afternoon classes probably find you dozing off.

Whenever possible, take your own sleep/awake patterns into account when planning your schedule. After all, when you feel awful during class because all you can think about is taking a nap, you're not going to get much out of it.

As a night owl, I tried to take as many late-morning and afternoon classes as possible. In fact, during one well-planned semester, I managed not to have a single class before 11 a.m.

Gaining Credit for Real-World Experience Outside the Classroom

Many law schools offer the unparalleled opportunity to gain credit, work on real cases and get hands-on experience doing legal research and writing out in the field. You can take advantage of these real-world experiences through participation in either clinical opportunities and/or independent clinical projects (externships). These are generally open only to 2Ls and 3Ls, though many schools will allow 1Ls to do externships in the summer after their first year.

These options especially appeal to law students who are tired of learning only about theory and policy in the classroom; in clinics and externships, you get to really show what you know by

 ✔ Writing memos and briefs

 ✔ Assisting attorneys with interviewing clients

 ✔ Preparing for trial

But you won't be on your own entirely; in both opportunities, you work under the supervision of faculty, practicing attorneys, and/or judges.

Getting hands-on experience at law clinics

Clinical programs (where people from the community come for free legal advice) in law schools have increased in numbers through the years. They've become more popular as law schools realize that pure theory doesn't resonate with every student. Many students want more of a hands-on experience in practical lawyering that's similar to the kind of schooling that medical students receive in their clinics.

Your law school may have from as few as one (or none) to as many as several clinics, all specializing in differing subject matters. Clinics are often located on the university campus, often near the law school. Other times, they're out in the community, and in this instance are usually called *external clinics.* My school offers students the opportunity to work in the Child Advocacy Clinic and the Community Legal Clinic; other schools offer everything from environmental law to poverty law and landlord-tenant law clinics.

The main activity that students do at law clinics is work on real cases. You interview clients, manage intake files, write briefs and memos, and even represent clients in court (under a professor's supervision, of course). In fact, you are supervised every step of the way. Many students say that working in a law clinic is one of the more satisfying achievements of their law school careers, because it's one of the few times they actually get to apply what they've learned.

Most schools require a course in conjunction with the clinic in which you find out how to interview clients, take depositions, practice your oral arguments, and discuss issues that come up in the course of your clinical work with the other students.

You sign up for clinics and receive academic credit for them in the same way you do for any other course. Clinics usually carry the same amount of credit as regular courses. Many, however, have extreme space limitations, often for only ten students or fewer, so check well in advance to find out what you need to do to secure a spot. Remember that law clinics generally are open only to upper-class students.

Taking externships for credit

Another opportunity that many schools offer is work at a public-interest organization, courthouse, or governmental organization for credit but no pay. You can often take these independent clinical project or *externship courses* during the summer and during the school year.

Like clinics, externships are excellent for getting hands-on experience in a new legal environment. You'll be around many other attorneys or judges, so you can gain valuable information about a particular area of the law. The only downside is that unlike a clinic, you'll probably have little, if any, client contact. Instead, you'll likely be doing plenty of desk work, such as legal research and memo and brief writing.

Generally, you arrange for an externship on your own and secure a faculty advisor in the relevant subject area. Your school's career services office may be able to help you with placement (see Chapter 14 for more information on how career services can help with general job searching). Because you'll be free labor, not too much arm-twisting is necessary to convince an organization to take you on. However, you need to figure out transportation, which can become expensive.

Depending on how many credits you want out of your experience, you can attend your externship from one day a week to all five. When you want maximum credit hours, you probably need to work three full days a week all semester. If you opt for a summer externship, you may need to work every day for six to eight weeks for maximum credit. Externships are often graded pass/fail. Many require you to keep a journal of your daily work experiences and turn this in along with a portfolio of written work you completed, such as memos or briefs.

During the summer before my third year, I worked at the Environmental Protection Agency, Office of Regional Counsel, in Chicago, for my externship. Not only did I get to write memos and conduct loads of legal research, but I also experienced what working at a governmental agency is like and interacted with practicing environmental attorneys on a daily basis. In addition, the four credits I earned enabled me to take one less course as a 3L, which made my third year much less stressful. All in all, I highly recommend externships, because I got much more out of my externship than I did out of an average law school course.

Taking Courses Outside the Law School

Many law schools provide you with the option of taking a few classes outside the law school for course credit. Taking a course outside the law school can be a great change of pace. For example, taking a course about women in art can help refresh your spirit during a semester filled with antitrust, bankruptcy, and real estate finance law. An outside course also can help you gain a new perspective on the law — from a sociological, psychological, or anthropological perspective, to name a few.

Many schools limit this option to one course per semester, for a maximum of two or three total outside courses. Furthermore, you want to check with your school regarding its policy about whether the courses must to be strictly graduate-level classes and whether some departments or schools are excluded.

One of the more popular places for law students to take outside classes for credit is within the business school, especially for students planning to go into corporate law or solo practice. Taking a few courses at the business school, such as accounting, finance, or tax, can compliment your legal skills well. Other popular schools or departments include social work, political science, women's studies, sociology, creative writing, and foreign languages.

Of course, you can always audit a course outside the law school for fun (see Chapter 7), regardless of whether it's at the graduate or undergraduate level. Because law school may likely be your last foray into academia, I suggest you live it up and sample something entirely new.

Getting a Global Perspective from Study Abroad

As the legal profession becomes more global in nature, understanding other legal systems and their approaches to legal problems grows ever more important. In response to this increasing need for global legal understanding, many law schools offer an array of study-abroad courses.

When you're interested in international law, for example, studying abroad can be an especially great opportunity to experience other legal systems first-hand. Many study-abroad programs include an *internship component,* which is an unparalleled opportunity to gain experience by working in a foreign court, nonprofit, or governmental organization.

Some schools set limits on when you can study abroad; they may permit summer study abroad, but forbid it during the academic year. Full-year study-abroad programs are rare in law schools; spending a semester or summer studying abroad is much more common. Whenever you have your eye on a particular program with which your school has no affiliation, don't hesitate to petition your dean for permission to enroll in such programs.

Make sure that studying abroad won't affect your graduating on time, because you'll still need to meet your school's graduation requirements. However, studying abroad during the summer may give you additional credits that may enable you to graduate early, if that's an option at your school.

Hitting the road for a semester or summer

If you've never studied abroad in college, you're in for a real treat. The main benefit of studying abroad is gaining an understanding of a new culture, whether it's India, China, or England. You're immersed in an entirely new culture and environment, which can do wonders for reawakening long-dormant law school enthusiasm. Likewise, you'll grow in ways you didn't think imaginable while traveling on your own, discovering your way around a new city (or country), and interacting with the locals.

Although you learn plenty academically, because you take a course load similar to a normal law school semester back home, some students let school-work take a back seat to experiential learning. That's because you may soon forget some of the semester's worth of international communications law that you've taken overseas, but you won't forget about taking the train cross-country by yourself, climbing to the top of Mount Kilimanjaro, or haggling with merchants in their native tongue.

Choosing a program that fits you and your budget

Many law schools offer students an array of programs from which to choose. Some law schools have their own programs, which feature their own professors overseas. Other schools participate in programs formed by agreements they've reached with other schools that meet their academic standards and direct enrollment from agreements they've reached with foreign law schools. Other schools offer only a few options. Check with your school's international programs office, or look on its Web site to determine your options.

The cost of studying abroad obviously is prohibitive for some students, because on top of paying tuition, you may be required to pay special program fees that can run into thousands of dollars. Add to that, the amount of money you need to take with you for housing, food, and entertainment, and you can see that expenses can quickly get out of hand, especially in Europe or Japan. That's why when you're planning to study abroad, you need to plan early and responsibly.

Taking out extra loans in anticipation of these added costs is an option for some people. Other students, however, know in advance that they'll be studying abroad and save up money from their summer jobs or work part-time to accumulate enough cash during the school year. One hassle when you study abroad during the school year is finding someone to sublet your apartment. Some study-abroad students arrange to live with a friend for the remaining semester.

Although studying abroad takes some advance effort for smooth planning, it's by far worth it, especially after you acclimate to your host country and begin having the time of your life!

Chapter 13

Not a Moot Point: Getting Involved in Law School

....

In This Chapter

▶ Discovering your extracurricular choices
▶ Differentiating between top contenders
▶ Finding ways to get involved outside the law school

....

Talk to any law student and you'll be hard-pressed to find one whose mantra is "Law school is all work and no play." Getting involved in extracurricular activities provides a refreshing break from your academic load, a great way to beef up your résumé, and an opportunity to develop your interest in a particular area of practice. For example, you can captivate an audience as a moot court competitor, dazzle your professor as a diligent research assistant, or join the world of legal scholarship by working on a journal. With so many options available, I'm sure you're wondering how you can *best* become involved. And that's exactly what this chapter is for.

In this chapter, I examine why law reviews are the most coveted of all law school activities and show you how to land your spot. I cover the ins and outs of the moot court competition, and tell you how to come out a winner. Further whetting your extracurricular appetite, I discuss other ways to make your mark in law school through participation in clubs, part-time jobs, research assistantships, and academic writing contests.

The extracurricular activities that I discuss here needn't be done all at once. In fact, you're better able to fully devote your energies when you limit yourself to two or three per year. You have three (or four) years of law school and that's plenty of time to sample all the activities you can fit into your free time.

When you're a part-time or evening law student, your extracurricular participation may be significantly diminished because of your full-time work commitments. If you have time for only one activity during your entire law school career, I recommend making it either the moot court competition or a law journal or law review. These activities pack the biggest punch in terms of giving you valuable lawyerly skills and wowing employers.

Benefiting from Extracurriculars

When you think about law school, you probably think about studying for endless hours per week and dragging around those huge casebooks (see Chapter 5). However, law school has more to it than keeping your nose buried in books; it has a wealth of activities for you to explore. Getting involved in extracurricular activities provides numerous benefits that help you feel more in touch with your law school experience. Participating helps you

- Meet people you wouldn't ordinarily mingle with and interact with different groups of students, which is especially crucial when you're a 1L

- Build your professional skills by taking an active role in deciding the mission and purpose of the organization with which you're involved

- Find out more about what you want from the legal profession

- Discover opportunities to get out into the community, regardless of whether you're volunteering at a homeless shelter, interviewing clients, or visiting prison inmates

The most satisfied students say that law school is an experience that can educate you in many ways inside and outside the classroom and provide you with leadership and professional skills that make you stand out from the crowd and put some shine on your résumé.

At many schools, the law review, law journal, and moot court are called *cocurriculars,* because they're viewed as an academic complement to the curriculum, not as *extra,* more recreational activities. But other activities, such as clubs or writing contests, still fall under the extracurricular heading.

As a first-year student, you're probably bound and determined to try out as many new extracurriculars as possible. Take it from me, however, that going overboard before finding out what you're capable of handling, timewise, just isn't a good idea. After you've successfully conquered your first semester, you'll be better suited for determining how much time you can productively spend on outside activities.

Besides, when you're a 1L, some of the activities in this chapter probably won't be open to you, such as all law journals and law reviews, (sometimes) moot court, and (usually) working part time outside the law school. However, finding out about these extracurriculars now puts you in a better position for deciding whether they're right for you when it comes time to apply.

Introducing you to various areas of practice

Clubs such as the Environmental Law Society, the International Law Association, or the Business and Law Society, focus on areas of legal practice. Joining clubs like these provides you with:

- Access to practitioners within the particular field the club represents (through speakers and presentations at the law school)

- Information about the area of practice represented

- Experiences that are relevant to the particular area of practice you prefer, such as drafting a will for an elderly community member or performing environmental research for a nonprofit organization.

Another fabulous benefit of getting involved is finding out early on whether you're well suited for a particular kind of practice (see Chapter 16 for more on practice areas). For example, if you think employment law would be fun, join the Employment Law Society and offer to provide research for a project during the school year. Without spending the summer at an employment law job, your extracurricular involvement can quickly tell you whether the work fits with your personality.

An important thing to remember about law school extracurriculars is that many are geared toward enhancing your professional competence and knowledge. Depending on the club or activity, you can improve your legal-research, client-interview, and brief- and memo-writing skills.

Strengthening your résumé

Although the state of your résumé need never be your *sole* motivating force for becoming involved with anything, I'd be neglecting my authorly duties if I didn't point out that employers love seeing résumés that are well endowed with extracurriculars. If you were on the other side of the table, which would you rather see: a student with a naked résumé, or one who joined two or three activities, held leadership positions, and gained useful legal skills in the process? The latter, without question, of course. Employers are only human. They want multidimensional students who have something more to contribute to the firm or organization.

Ever heard the saying, "Everything in moderation?" Well, that statement applies especially well to overloading on extracurriculars. Extracurriculars are bound to impress as long as you don't list five or six without any evidence that you served in leadership roles or gained any concrete skills. Employers know when someone's a token member of the Public-Interest Law

Foundation, so don't show up for the first meeting just so you can jot it down on your résumé. Roll up your sleeves and dig in to that activity!

Explaining Law Reviews and Law Journals

Of all extracurricular activities in law school, working on the law review is by far the most prestigious, followed closely by working on a law journal. What's so unique about these kinds of publications, when compared with other student publications around the world, is that they're entirely student operated and managed. They may have faculty advisors, but their roles are minimal.

The mere mention of the words "law review" to anyone, regardless of whether they're in the legal community, evokes an immediate across-the-board recognition of this hallowed tome as a symbol of honor and integrity. *Law reviews* are scholarly publications aimed at a readership of practicing attorneys, judges, and legal scholars that primarily are *generalist* in nature, meaning they cover wide ranges of legal topics, from employment to family law and everything in between. Inside, you find heavily footnoted articles, notes (student-written articles), and case comments (analyses of court rulings). Almost every law school has one law review (but not more than one), which usually is known as the *(Name of the College or University) Law Review.* Law reviews typically are published between three and six times per year.

Law reviews are usually considered the most prestigious of all the law journals and most practitioners aspire to being published in them. Not that your school's regular journals are dog food, but landing a membership on a law review generally is more difficult than on a regular journal. Not only are the standards of law reviews higher, but also more people usually are competing for positions.

Law journals, on the other hand, are specialist publications that are read mostly by practitioners and scholars interested in the particular subject areas or fields upon which they are focused. Their topics span diverse ranges — from Oklahoma's *American Indian Law Review* to Tulane's *Tulane Maritime Law Journal* to Maryland's *Journal of Health Care Law and Policy,* and on and on. Individual law schools may not sponsor any journals, or they may have many. My school, for example, has two law journals and one law review.

The terms law review and law journal are often generically and collectively referred to simply as *journals*. However, remembering that they're two different species is extremely important.

Deciding whether journals are worth the massive time commitment

No one disputes that law reviews and law journals are hands-down the single most time-consuming law school extracurricular activities you can do. If you thought studying a few hours a night was rough, try spending between 10 and 25 hours on a single cite-checking assignment, and you'll probably be assigned between three and six of these tedious tasks as a 2L journal staff member). See the "Cite-checking and note-writing: The work of the 2Ls" section later in the chapter for more details.

As a 3L editor (only 3Ls can hold editorial positions), your time commitment skyrockets even more; however, many schools provide academic credit to editorial staff members. If you're an editor-in-chief, well, you can forget about your social life. Students in that position regularly spend between 30 and 40 hours per week on their journal duties — the equivalent to a full-time job! Yikes!

Several variables go into deciding whether this gargantuan time commitment is right for you. Consider the following questions.

- ✔ **Are you secure enough in your studies that you have time to spare?** If your grades are low, you may want to avoid any time-consuming extracurriculars so you can spend extra time plumping up your grade-point average (GPA). In the long run, employers are more likely to prefer an upward trend in your GPA to extracurricular work with a journal.

- ✔ **Do your career plans mandate journal membership?** Are you entering a work environment where journal membership is encouraged or required, such as big-firm jobs, law school teaching, or prestigious judicial clerkships (especially at the federal level)?

  If you're entering solo practice, journal membership is completely irrelevant. The same is true for many nonprofit and governmental positions and other outside-the-box jobs (see Chapter 17), where your time is better spent networking and building practice-specific skills. Be sure to consider the opportunity costs associated with journal membership, and decide whether your time and efforts may be better spent elsewhere.

- ✔ **Do you have any other significant time obligations that can interfere with journal membership, particularly unpredictable ones?** If you're a parent, a part-time or evening law student, or have a time-consuming hobby, you may want to think twice about whether you can *really* spare the time.

When you're still straddling the fence, several other ways you can find out what journal membership *really* entails include:

✔ **Talking to a journal's editor-in-chief or a 3L staff member.** Ask all your brutally honest questions of someone who has experienced the work. I did this as soon as I received my journal invitation, so I could get down to the nitty-gritty about exactly how many hours I'd be working on the journal.

✔ **Hanging around the journal offices, particularly at production time.** Witness the frenzy. Chat with staffers who actually put the journal together. Ask them what they like and don't like about the experience. After all, you serve on a journal for two years, because you can't quit halfway through without serious repercussions that may include having a letter placed in your law school file by the dean stating that you withdrew. Employers who inquire may thus find out that you reneged on your responsibilities.

✔ **Talking to some of the employers you're interested in, and finding out what they think about journal membership.** By doing so, you're getting advice straight-from-the-horse's mouth about whether they highly value work on a journal.

David M. Marquez, a 3L at Northwestern University School of Law in Chicago, counts his participation in a journal as his only regret about law school. "In retrospect," Marquez says, "my real motivation for entering the journal competition was the thought that I wouldn't be seen as a successful law student if I wasn't a member of a journal." During Marquez's first year on the journal, he found that his duties, such as checking citations in submitted articles, bore little relation to the skills he thought were essential to his future success as a lawyer — skills relating to interpersonal communication, creativity, and persuasive writing. He admires the students who made a deliberate decision early on to avoid journal participation and, instead, pursue activities and experiences with more personal relevance, such as volunteering at a legal-aid clinic or conducting independent research.

Becoming a member of a journal is not for everyone. If you aren't going to enjoy it and reap the career-enhancing benefits, it isn't worth doing. Plenty of options to distinguish yourself as a law student are available, and journals are not the be-all, end-all of those options. In other words, journal membership isn't the only key to law school success or happiness. When you don't make it, or don't want to join, you still can become a great lawyer.

Landing a spot on a journal

You need to follow your school's particular entrance procedures to land a position on either type of journal. In general, however, here's how it works.

✔ The whole process begins during the spring semester of your first year, when all the journals schedule an information session at which the editors-in-chief describe the mission and content of their respective journals and their particular entrance requirements.

✔ At that point, you receive a *preference sheet,* on which you mark which of the journals you're most interested in, on a scale of 1 to 5 (or however many journals your school has). At many schools, after you fill out this form, you can't change your mind. So, if you're offered admission to your first choice journal, you either must accept the offer to join that journal or you won't be on any journal.

When your school has more than one journal, how do you choose which one to rank highest? Most students choose journals based on how much they enjoy the journal's subject matter and how much work is involved. I decided to rank my journal, the *Federal Communications Law Journal,* highest because I genuinely wanted to know more about the subject matter. Because journals are published in varying amounts per year, how much work is involved is directly related to how many cite-checking and proofreading assignments you'll have to do. Similarly some students choose their journals based on whether it makes note-writing mandatory. Students who don't want to write the note choose a journal that makes it optional. (For more on note-writing and cite-checking, see the section, "Cite-checking and note-writing: The work of the 2Ls" later in the chapter.)

✔ You then return the completed preference sheet to the journals, which alerts them to how many people are entering their competitions. After that, you bide your time until after spring exams, when the fun of your writing competition begins!

Grading-on versus writing-on

In times of yore, you were appointed to a journal solely on the basis of your 1L grades. Today, however, many law schools take a more egalitarian approach, with grades being only a part of the selection process — if that much. Most schools hold a *writing-on competition* in lieu of considering grades for membership. That's where 1Ls are given a packet of cases, statutes, and law review articles at the end of spring semester exams and expected to write a journal article based on those materials and the particular topic they're assigned (within a certain timeframe).

Some schools also make an editing component part of the writing-on competition, meaning that students are also given an article full of typos to mark up, and the students who are more successful editors are awarded high scores. Although rare, a few schools have been known to conduct personal interviews in addition to or instead of the editing competition. My journal, the

Federal Communications Law Journal, conducted a writing competition without any editing component. All I had to do was write the article based on the material in the packet. All in all, I had a two-week timeframe, but I probably spent less than 10 hours doing it.

So which is better — writing-on, or grading-on? Writing-on competitions are usually favored by students because they're seen as fairer to those who may be excellent writers and editors, but not *magna cum laude* students. In a grading-on competition, you walk onto a journal based on your 1L grades. When your grades put you in some top echelon, such as the top 10 percent, you're automatically awarded a spot. Many schools have completely done away with their grading-on competitions in favor of the writing-on approach, and other schools employ a mix of both. The best way to find out how your school makes its journal selections is by asking around the journal offices or asking an upperclassman.

Acing the writing-on competition

You need at least a day or two of rest after your 1L exams before starting to research and write your entry in the writing-on competition. I had two weeks to complete my entry in the writing competition, but I gave myself a full week's break to recuperate from my 1L finals.

When you're staring down a huge packet full of scholarly materials for your article, knowing where to begin is hard. Not only do you have to come up with a cohesive argument, but you also must add in case law to support your argument, refer to statutes as necessary, and supplement the discussion with references from law journal articles. Although everything that you need is conveniently included in the packet, the work nevertheless seems awfully daunting. That's why I advocate the start-out-strong (take-the-break-first) approach.

Expect to spend anywhere between 10 and 30 hours on your writing competition piece. Sure, articles have been written the night before they're due, but with such an important position at stake, do you really want to leave it up to chance like that?

After you finish writing your article, don't neglect to put the footnotes in proper *Bluebook* form, because the editors are also looking to see how good you are at citation. *The Bluebook: A Uniform System of Citation* (Harvard University Law Review Association, Gannett House) is one of the most universally used citing systems in the legal profession. You find out about *Bluebook* form as a 1L in your legal research class, so putting those skills to the test shouldn't be too much work (and a good review).

When you're done with your writing competition entry, put it in an envelope and mail it off to whatever address (often the dean of students) is indicated on your information sheets. When it reaches its destination, the 3L editors start to work. When you're off having fun in the sun or at the daily grind at your summer job, they sift through a large volume of entries, reading through them all and deciding which contestants are worthy of issuing invitations.

You'll probably hear the results of the competition in late July, when students selected for journal membership are notified by an invitation letter. This letter tells you what you need to do to accept, and when to show up for orientation, which is usually the week before school starts.

Working on Law Review and Law Journal

What you do when working for a law journal depends on your year in school. First-year students aren't allowed to participate, so 2Ls are the lowest on the totem pole. They serve as cite-checkers and proofreaders. Second-year students' other main activity is writing a *student note* (or student-written scholarly article) on a topic of their choosing. If the note is good enough, it is published in the journal. Some journals make note-writing mandatory; with others, it's optional. As a 3L, you move up in the world, no longer relegated to cite-checking and proofreading grunt work. Instead, you serve mainly in editorial capacities, such as managing editor, executive editor, or editor-in-chief.

The next few sections take a closer look at the specific duties of 2Ls and 3Ls.

Cite-checking and note-writing: The work of the 2Ls

When you're working for a journal as a 2L, most of your duties are associated with what's affectionately known as grunt work.

The lowdown on cite-checking

The brunt of grunt work involves *cite-checking* journal articles. Generally, for each issue that your journal publishes, you do one cite-checking assignment. For each assignment, you verify that each footnoted item actually stands for the proposition stated by looking up the propositions in books, articles, and cases. Although grunt work is almost universally disliked for its extremely boring nature, some law journal staffers derive some satisfaction from doing it.

Some of the benefits you can get from journal cite-checking are

- **Becoming extremely detail-oriented, a skill that lawyers need every day on the job.** When you're poring through a book or article, looking for one sentence cited in the article you're working on, and painstakingly checking to make sure it's correct, you gain an understanding for the attention that practicing lawyers must pay to detail and discipline in their work.

- **Becoming familiar with the law library (see Chapter 10), which is essential for many lawyers.** Some firms or organizations don't offer online legal research, so you need to know how to do your own work in a law library. After hunting for so many obscure citations, you gain a command of the premises that most of your peers won't have.

- **Becoming well-versed in *Bluebook* style.** Lawyers generally use *Bluebook* style every time they write a brief or law journal article, so it's best to have a good command of it.

- **Reading interesting articles (while cite-checking and proofreading) that expose you to areas of the law you otherwise may not encounter.**

In addition to cite-checking, most journals require 2Ls to work during several proofreading sessions per semester, reading parts of journal articles with a partner to double-check punctuation, grammar, and spelling.

The 3L editorial board members generally don't do much grunt work. Instead, they serve as managing editor, senior articles editor, or senior production editor. If you decide that you don't want many journal responsibilities as a 3L, however, you're relegated to staff editor positions, in which you'll continue doing 2L-type grunt work. I knew I wouldn't have much time to devote to the journal in an editorial capacity during my third year, so I elected to be a staffer. As a result, I completed several super cite-checking (advanced cite-checking) and proofreading assignments each semester, and that was the extent of my journal duties.

Introducing the note-writing process

Second-year law students often are required (although on some journals it's optional) to write a note as part of their journal membership. Students working for journals where note-writing is optional can elect *not* to write a note for many reasons. Those students often:

- Don't want to put in the time (which can be 5 to 10 hours per week)
- Don't like to write or can't think of a good topic
- Don't care about being published

Although the journal that I worked for made note-writing optional, I decided to write the note. I enjoyed some parts about researching and writing on my topic, but on hindsight, I realized that those long hours spent in the library could've been better spent discovering information about different areas of practice or informational interviewing. Talking to 3Ls who've completed the note-writing process on your journal and finding out how they regarded the experience can help you decide whether note-writing is the right choice for you.

Writing the note is often the highlight of many students' law school careers, because they choose a topic they're interested in, work closely with a faculty mentor, and turn in a publishable product. Other students elect to write the note because they want to sharpen their writing skills, and a massive research and writing assignment like note-writing provides the perfect opportunity. Although only a small minority of all notes end up being published (because of journals' extremely high quality standards), many journals offer students a second chance to refine their note after it's declined the first time. Keep in mind that having a published student note in any journal is considered a prestigious honor, one that employers also view with interest.

Now, don't kid yourself. Writing the note is a huge time commitment. Think of it as a research paper — only harder, in my opinion, because you must find a topic that no one has ever done before — or find a more common topic with your own unique twist. The real bummer: Even if you choose this unique topic, if another practitioner publishes an article on your topic before yours is published, your topic becomes *preempted*, dimming that bright publishing career you'd hoped for. Another reason that note-writing is so difficult is that you must consult so many different and complex sources — cases, statutes, other law journal articles, popular articles, and books.

Generally, notes are due during the second semester of your second year, and you pretty much have all of the first semester to write them (some journals impose due dates along the way for your topic selection, outline, and rough draft). Some procrastinators end up writing their notes the night before they're due, but most students put in as much time and effort into their notes as possible, because being published is a much sought-after honor.

If you're on a law review, which is a generalist publication, you can write your note on any topic. If you're on a journal, however, the topic of your note must fall within the journal's recognized subject matter. For instance, I couldn't have written about tax law (unless it somehow related to communications) as a member of the *Federal Communications Law Journal*. Instead, I was largely limited to communications and intellectual property–related topics.

Considering an editorial board position as a 3L

Most 3Ls elect to apply for *editorial board positions,* which are pretty much the same across all journals. Specific titles, however, may differ. These titles include managing editor, notes editor, and executive editor, among others. For students whose talents lie in areas besides editing, Web site editor and senior business manager positions also are available.

You can apply for one or more of these positions around February of your second year. That gives departing 3L staff plenty of time to interview candidates.

Arguing for Fun and Profit: Moot Court

Moot court is basically an *appellate* (after a decision has been made in a lower court and is appealed) *court simulation.* In other words, you go through the motions but no *real* cases are being decided.

Familiarizing yourself with the different levels of competition

Moot court competition is waged on many levels both within your law school (intramural) and on the national level.

On the national level

You can participate on the national level in several ways. One common way is to join your school's mock trial team (if one's available), which competes in moot court competitions (usually once a year) in a variety of different subject areas, such as intellectual property, health, and international law. Competing on a mock trial team usually requires a tryout, which usually takes place at the beginning of the school year.

Another way you can participate in national moot court competitions is through extracurricular clubs (and some journals) at your school, which often send some of their members to national competitions relating to their fields of interest. All you need to do to be considered is be a member of the particular club (or journal) and show an interest and dedication in preparing for the particular moot court competition.

Alternatively, some law schools have specialized moot court teams dedicated to a particular subject area, such as the environmental law moot court team, which sends its team members to the corresponding annual national moot court competition. Sometimes, members of these moot court teams are chosen from the most outstanding students of the previous year's school intramural competition (see the next section for more about intramural competitions).

Regardless of how you end up participating in a national competition, you need to know that most teams consist of only a few people — usually three to eight — so they can intimately work together and be coached by fellow students or faculty in the extensive preparation required to succeed at these competitions. In addition, many different schools participate in these national competitions, which are sponsored at law schools around the country.

On the intramural level

Within your school, members of the moot court board (or moot court honor society), who are students with stellar moot court credentials from the previous year, are invited to organize and coordinate the intramural competition. The board chooses one topic (scenario) for the competition to be based on, and it can be in any area of the law. You don't need to try out for moot court at the intramural level; it's open to anyone (usually only 1Ls and 2Ls participate) with an interest.

At some law schools, 1Ls participate in moot court as part of their legal research and writing course obligations. At other schools, moot court is only open to 2Ls. Check with your school's moot court board or check its students activities Web site for guidelines.

Intramural moot court essentially involves teaming up with a partner of your choice, getting a packet of cases, law review articles, and statutes based on the two-issue assigned problem, with each member writing about one of the two issues (their choice). Each team of two students is assigned to take the same side — either plaintiff or defendant, and each team of two students argues against another team of two students assigned the opposite side during each round.

Next, each team writes a combined appellate brief consisting of both of their assigned issues. After the brief is written, you and your partner practice oral arguments with each other for several weeks, asking each other difficult questions and playing devil's advocate. You help each other hone your arguments and counterarguments. You normally have about a month or six weeks between receiving the assigned materials and the first round of arguments.

Then the real fun begins. Moot court competitions generally are conducted in rounds that open with all competitors and then whittle away the field during the coming weeks until only two competitors remain and are declared Moot Court Champions. During the first of (usually) three preliminary rounds, each team argues their respective issues against one other team. During the second round, they argue the opposite side of the same issue (if they were plaintiffs in the first round they become defendants). During the third round, they're notified shortly before the competition begins which of the two sides (plaintiff or defendant) they'll be arguing. But during all three rounds they keep their same issues.

After the preliminary rounds, the moot court board tallies up the contestants' scores on their briefs and oral arguments, and the best individuals advance on to later rounds. The semifinal and final rounds often are suspenseful events that are well attended by law students and faculty.

Besides the two champions, winners also are declared for the best brief and best oral argument.

One reason moot court is especially fun: The panel of judges for the competition often is made up of attorneys and judges from the community. Thus, you present your arguments in a somewhat realistic setting. Moot court also is considered somewhat of an entertainment event for the entire law school. As the championship rounds draw near, more and more spectators gather to watch the proceedings. Auditoriums sometimes are packed, especially when the two remaining moot court champions are about to be chosen.

Reaping the benefits of moot court

Moot court is an especially valuable tool for students who want to become litigators (trial lawyers), because of the great experiences it provides you for working on your oral argument and advocacy skills. Part of being an advocate is knowing how to be persuasive. After all, you're trying to persuade members of the panel that your side should win.

The other main benefit of moot court is that it provides you with another chance to work on your overall legal writing skills. Aside from their legal research and writing classes, many law students won't get another chance in law school to work on brief-writing, which, if you plan to be a litigator, is one of the main activities you'll be doing.

A third good reason to participate in moot court is to improve your ability to maintain your poise while answering pointed rapid-fire questions from your panel. If you're not too swift at thinking on your feet, moot court may be a good opportunity to change that.

Considering Clubs

When the two most visible law school activities, law journals and moot court, don't tickle your fancy (or even if they do), try joining a club or organization. Every law school has a wide variety of interesting clubs, from the Health Law Society to the Evening Students' Association and the Jewish Law Students Organization. You can even find clubs focusing on older students, volunteer-minded students, or even students with significant others!

Most law schools stage an organizations fair at the beginning of the school year to enable 1Ls, 2Ls, and 3Ls alike to find out what clubs their school offers. Sign up for as many clubs as you can. Attend their introductory meetings so you can find out what they're all about before deciding which ones you want to focus on. Throughout my law school career, I participated actively in three clubs, and found them to be a fun way to meet new friends, learn more about different specialty areas, and network with practitioners in a field.

Taking a peek at what's available

With so many clubs to choose from, knowing where to start is tough. You may want to try a different club each year of law school, or choose one in which to participate actively for all three years. The following list describes some of the types of clubs available to you.

- ✔ **Advocacy clubs:** Your law school is likely to have several clubs that focus on advocacy, such as the Protective Order Project, Inmate Legal Assistance Clinic, or Street Law Society. These clubs are an excellent way to become involved in a cause that you're passionate about. They're also useful for gaining relevant experience in preparation for summer or permanent work at nonprofit organizations. Nonprofits are notorious for requiring evidence of strong commitment to their causes, so if this is an area you're looking toward, getting solid work experience is the best approach.

- ✔ **Student government:** Just like in high school and college, each law school has its own form of student government. At many schools, the government is called the Student Bar Association (SBA) or Student Law Association (SLA). When your school has a Barrister's Ball, annual Halloween party, and other social events and parties, chances are that your friendly SBA planned it. The representatives on the SBA generally select students to serve on various committees (such as educational and special activities) that organize these types of events.

The SBA also

- Schedules town meetings at which students and the dean of students (or other faculty and staff) can air their grievances. If problems are occurring at the law school, such as bad chairs in the classrooms, a lack of adequate snack machines, or inadequate library closing times, town meetings can be a good way to get different perspectives on the situation.

- Participates in the search for new deans and faculty. If your school is conducting dean or faculty searches, student input often is requested. Members of student government may have first dibs on serving on related steering committees.

- Often operates the used law school bookstore. Some law schools operate a student government-run (used) law school bookstore, where students can drop off their old books to sell and browse through other used ones to purchase. This is a great place to get hugely discounted books and study aids.

How do you participate in student government? Generally, each year, students seek office during an election for an SBA or SLA representative. These representatives are elected based on the votes of their classmates. Joining student government is a great way to practice good leadership skills and to be in the know at all times about what's going on in the law school.

✔ **Special-interest organizations:** The Women in Law, Black Law Students Association, and Christian Legal Society are among several examples of clubs that serve the interests of their members. You may also be interested in joining clubs for older students (often titled OWLS — Older and Wiser Law Students), for law student parents, and for law students with significant others.

Joining one or more clubs is a good way to meet students with similar interests and situations, who you otherwise may not meet up with in other law school settings. If you're a minority or nontraditional student, you may find that these organizations offer a sense of comfort and community in which you can socialize with other students about issues of mutual concern and interest.

But bear in mind that student organizations vary greatly in their usefulness from year to year depending on the leadership and membership. Some clubs put on a variety of events one year, and don't offer much the next, depending on the effectiveness and enthusiasm of their leaders. That's why joining a club and getting elected to a leadership role is a great experience — *you* get to be in charge of that club's future.

✔ **Activity clubs:** Some law school clubs are quasi-involved with law, such as the drama club, which puts on plays with legal themes, or a club where you teach legal concepts in middle and high schools. If you're looking for a fun environment where you can meet new people and work on new skills, these clubs may pique your interest.

Striking out on your own

Whatever your interest or hobby, you can probably find at least a few other like-minded students who'd love to share their experiences with you! If you're itching to start up a knitting or restaurant-reviewing club, go to your dean of students office and find out what you need to do to get the wheels turning. Whether it's starting a law school literary magazine or a wine-tasting or ski club, all you need are a few others who are interested.

Jumping on the Research Assistant Bandwagon

Being a *research assistant* is exactly what it sounds like — you work one-on-one with professors on their research. Your duties depend on the particular professor, but most often they include:

- ✔ Performing legal research online or in the library
- ✔ Proofreading articles or book chapters
- ✔ Giving feedback on writing projects

Finding an opening

Finding a research assistantship isn't difficult. Professors usually advertise openings on the career services Web site, put a notice in the law school newsletter, or post flyers in hallways. They may ask for a résumé and references when they advertise, because a bunch of students usually apply. At other times, they announce an opening in class or may even ask you directly (if you've done well in their classes or are a particularly vocal participator).

Choosing a professor in your specialty area of interest is usually the best way to go, but you can find out about your school's heavyweights by perusing the faculty section on your law school's Web site for the credentials of various professors. If you find someone whose courses and research interests match yours, then you can drop him or her a line. Another approach is to type the names of faculty members at your school into an Internet search engine or in a Lexis or Westlaw search. Read whatever comes up, and decide whether working for that professor can help you in your career plans.

A third way is to ask around. Find out from upperclassmen which professors worked at what firms and which professors clerked for which judges after law school. Find out who has ties to the particular organizations or firms you want to work for. Then, be aggressive as you follow up!

When you're absolutely chomping at the bit to work for a particular professor who hasn't advertised with the career services office (or in the hallways), approach her or him directly and ask whether any help is needed. You never know when the professor may say something like, "Come to think of it, I could use somebody right now!" And you'll be first in line!

I was a research assistant for an intellectual property professor during the fall semester of my second year. I thought the opportunity was invaluable in terms of gaining more legal research and proofreading experiences, and I loved the chance to learn more about my favorite specialty area.

Because research assistantships usually are paid positions, you need to set up your paperwork with the law school's payroll department. The pay is generally low (often between $5 and $8 per hour), but your hours are usually flexible, and much of the work usually can be done at home.

Revealing the advantages of an assistantship

One big advantage of being a research assistant is that such positions are considered prestigious because the professors handpick you to work closely with them on their research. You may even get an acknowledgment in their book or article for all your efforts.

The following list details some of the other important benefits you'll gain.

- ✔ **You get hands-on experience doing legal research and writing in your chosen field.** This is a prime opportunity to figure out whether the field is, indeed, for you.

- ✔ **You have access to an expert in the field.** What better way to get all your nitty-gritty questions about health or corporate law answered?

- ✔ **From working so closely with your professor, you're bound to get a personalized, stellar reference from a well-known authority in the field.** This benefit can give you an "in" in ways you can't begin to imagine, whether you're interviewing with a firm, for a clerkship, or for a law school teaching position, especially when your professor worked or clerked at the firm or court you're considering.

The really neat thing about the job is that you'll be the first to know about your professors' new scholarly pursuits, and you'll be offering your advice and input, which can make you feel like an integral part of their projects.

Getting Involved Outside of Law School

In the same way that you can become involved with extracurricular activities within the law school, you can also become involved with real practitioners outside of law school. Doing so is something that many law students don't think about, because it's not often touted as an alternative — or in addition to — the usual law school extracurriculars. One of the best parts about getting involved outside of law school is that you don't necessarily need to be a 2L or 3L to take advantage of these opportunities (except for part-time jobs)! Getting involved right away ensures that you get a head start on exploring your career path.

Joining your city, state, or national bar association as a student member

If learning more about your desired areas of practice, mingling with attorneys in your city of choice, and attending continuing legal education seminars isn't fun, then I don't know what is. Joining your city, state, or national bar association as a law student is a much-overlooked opportunity.

If you're really serious about networking and learning more about a field, joining the association in your hometown, or the town where you hope to work, is one of the best investments you can make, especially when you want to practice in a city other than where your law school is located. You can join another city's bar association and just attend functions whenever you're in town. No set requirements are in place for the number of functions you must attend as a student member, which is one of the great benefits of joining. Simply do as much or as little as you want. This fact is particularly relevant to part-time and evening law students, who may have time to attend these functions only on weekends or during school breaks.

Using academic writing contests to garner fame and fortune (well, almost)

Okay, just admit it . . . you have a writing genius inside you that just wasn't satisfied by your journal note or moot court brief (see the earlier "Introducing the note-writing process" and "Arguing for Fun and Profit: Moot Court" sections). When you're hankering to crank out another 20- to 35-page paper, look no further than the myriad writing contests open to law students of all years and areas of interest.

The best way to find out about contests is from flyers that are usually posted on bulletin boards around the law school campus or building. Some contests that pertain to subject matter of particular interest to journal members are also posted inside the respective journal offices.

Sure, writing a submission takes plenty of time and effort, unless, of course, you happen to use something you've already worked on, which, in most cases, already is in the format of a law review article (approximately 25- to 50-pages long). In any case, putting forth the effort is worth it when you're truly interested in the topic and eager to have another writing sample that you can show to potential employers. Besides, some of the contest awards are pretty hefty. They can range anywhere from a hundred to thousands of dollars! And at least three cash prizes usually are given out, so you have a decent shot at getting some sort of monetary prize.

If you're serious about winning some cash, try pursuing some of the more obscure contests, the ones where you think fewer people will show an interest in submitting. You never know which contest will be the one in which yours is the only submission!

Working part time during the school year

Many full-time law students opt to work part time, either to gain skills in a practice setting or make some extra cash to float them through law school. Some 2Ls and 3Ls are able to arrange their schedules so they're taking classes at the law school only three days a week, meaning they can work the other two. Or, some students choose only morning classes so they can work during the afternoons, or vice versa.

In essence, you have time for a part-time job if you so choose. After all, you're in the classroom for only about 15 hours a week, tops. That leaves plenty of time for studying and a part-time job.

Recycling your work

So, you've put hours worth of blood, sweat, and tears into your journal note, only to have it denied publication. Or maybe you wrote one heck of a seminar paper, and want to put your crowning glory to another use. Sound familiar? Then look no further than your writing contest bulletin board, because there's bound to be one that's a the match made in heaven for your paper. Believe me, the best part about this kind of recycling is that you've already done the hard work. You need only to tweak your submission a bit or adapt it to the specific subject matter, mail it off, and voilà — your paper can be on its way to stardom.

Part-time and evening students, of course, won't have time for additional work *on top* of their full-time jobs. But full-time law students with spouses or children may have time for a part-time position that requires only a few hours a week. Contact the firm, court, or organization for which you'd like to work and explain your family responsibilities and how much time you're able to devote to part-time work. It's likely that you'll be able to work something out, particularly in big cities where the opportunities are numerous and varied.

The American Bar Association discourages 1Ls from working at all, and its standards mandate that all law students work no more than 20 hours a week in any semester in which they're taking more than 12 credit hours. Besides, employers within the legal field are less likely to hire 1Ls, because they're generally not considered quite as efficient as upperclassmen (with good reason — 1Ls still are heavily involved in the learning process at that point).

Some of the most common part-time school-year legal jobs include working at private law firms, clerking for judges, or working at nonprofit or governmental organizations. Generally, your expected pay depends on:

- ✔ The size of the city you're in (larger ones pay more than smaller)
- ✔ Your year in school
- ✔ The type of organization you're working for (firms tend to pay the most; nonprofits the least)

You'll generally find the most opportunities at firms, because they're especially plentiful in big and small cities, and many of them are interested in having part-time law students do legal research (read: cheap labor). Besides legal research, when you work at a firm, you'll also likely write memos and help file cases and other documents. Don't be surprised, however, when you're given nonlegal tasks to do, such as answering phones, stuffing envelopes, and writing nonlegal materials.

For some law students (especially those with mediocre grades), working at a firm part-time during the school year is the perfect opportunity to show your employers what you can really do in a summer or permanent position (see Chapters 14 and 15 for more on landing summer and permanent jobs). When they see how indispensable you are, they may start to think about making you a summer or permanent postgraduation offer. Furthermore, when you work at a firm during most or all of your second and third years, your employers definitely get a good sense of your attitude, work ethic, and competency, which can really make the difference when you're just a face in the crowd on paper.

Part V

Preparing for Your Future

The 5th Wave   By Rich Tennant

"What's the chance of settling this without getting attorneys involved?"

HARVARD LAW SCHOOL ALUMNI PICNIC

ANTS, GNATS AND BEES

In this part . . .

Find out how to discover what your dream summer and postgraduation jobs are. In this part, I share helpful techniques for determining where your career interests lie, networking with influential contacts, and narrowing down your area of practice options. If you're looking to take a nontraditional route, I also explain how to thrive in an alternative legal career.

Chapter 14

Landing Your Perfect Summer Job

. . . .

In This Chapter

▶ Deciding what type of job best suits you

▶ Preparing effective résumés and cover letters

▶ Mastering the art of the interview

▶ Considering thank-you notes

. . . .

*W*hen you're looking for your ideal summer jobs following your first and second years of law school, remember that the job you choose can significantly impact your future professional growth. That's because your summer jobs in the legal field help you narrow down your interests to specific areas of practice (see Chapter 16), gain valuable hands-on legal experience, and determine what type of practice settings (see Chapter 15) most interest you.

Whether you volunteer or find paid legal work during your law school summers doesn't matter — the *quality* of your summer job experiences is most important. Starting your summer job search early and having a strong grasp of the type of work you're interested in gives you a leg up in finding the best summer job fit. A great job is waiting for you, I promise. You just need a game plan for finding it.

In this chapter, I walk you through exactly what you need to know about summer jobs, including the most popular types of jobs, such as clerking for a judge, summer associateships, clerking at a firm, and working at nonprofits or governmental organizations. I also cover how to handle initial (on-campus) and call-back interviews. With perseverance and motivation, you'll not only land your ideal summer job but also gain a meaningful and instructive experience from it.

Considering Major Factors That Impact Summer Job Options

Law school differs from college in that summer jobs are no longer simply a way to earn money. Instead they're viewed as an important part of your legal education. Because much of what you discover in the classroom is theory-based, your summer jobs during law school are an opportunity to apply what you've learned in a hands-on legal setting.

Many rising 2Ls and 3Ls (second- and third-year law students) find paid work or volunteer at a variety of workplaces, including nonprofits, governmental organizations, law firms, and courts. The goal of your summer job needn't be to make the most money possible or work in the most prestigious setting. Instead, if you concentrate on finding work that fits in with your personality, your interests in an area of practice, and your career goals, you'll come out head-and-shoulders above peers who are more shortsighted in their summer job outlooks. If you haven't already heard from your career services office (CSO) or upperclassmen, the summer job picture changes dramatically according to these three factors:

- Your year in school
- Whether you're a part-time or evening law student
- Your academic record

Factor No. 1: Your year in school

As newly minted first years (1Ls), the goal of your summer job search is finding a *job* — not necessarily exactly what you'd like to do after graduation but something vaguely in line with your interests. If your goal is to work as an environmental attorney after you graduate, but all you manage to find during your first summer is a job clerking at a personal-injury law firm, hey, it's no big deal. Finding your dream job as a rising 2L is difficult, particularly paid work (which is a necessity for many students). My advice is, when you can't find your ideal job, just take whatever you can get, as long as it has a legal bent. Trust me, the employers you interview with as a rising 3L next summer will be bowled over that you took the initiative to get your feet wet in *any* area of the law.

I couldn't find a job in my preferred area of practice area as a rising 2L — intellectual property — so I took whatever I could get, which happened to be a summer job working in the field of *alternative dispute resolution,* which in my case is where a mediator tries to resolve an issue by talking things out. My job basically involved data entry (instead of actual hands-on legal work), but at least it was *something* and it was law-related.

As a second-year (2L) student, your summer job search becomes much more important in the sense that you must press more to find a job that's in line with your eventual career goals. Why? Many students parlay their 2L summer jobs into permanent offers. If you like your 2L summer job, and actually receive an offer, you're relieved of the pressure of hustling to find a permanent job during your third year. Likewise, when you interview for permanent jobs during your third year, know that employers prefer seeing a connection between your career interests and your second-year summer job, if at all possible. That way, when they ask you why you took that particular summer job in estate planning, your answer appears more focused and less undecided when that's actually the practice area you'd like to pursue.

Factor No. 2: Whether you go to school part time or in the evenings

If you're a part-time or evening law student, devoting three months to a traditional legal summer job may not seem feasible. Given the fact that you're probably working (and depending on the steady income from) a full-time job, you may not be able to take a leave of absence for the summer to work as a clerk, summer associate, or volunteer.

Many CSOs recommend that evening and part-time law students do one of the following to gain summer legal experience or the equivalent during the year:

- ✔ Leave their regular jobs to take permanent full-time jobs as law clerks year-round.

- ✔ Hold a series of temporary full-time jobs through law school to make summer legal jobs easier to arrange.

- ✔ Keep their current jobs but arrange their schedules so they can clerk or volunteer one half-day a week, year-round. One way to adjust your schedule is arriving an hour early or staying an hour later at your regular full-time job every day so you make accommodations for taking a half-day off each week.

  In this arrangement, you still get the same type of exposure to the real legal world that a full-time law student receives during the summer, only in a less-concentrated way.

Factor No. 3: Your academic record

The summer job picture also changes based on your academic record. The sad truth is that your grade-point average (GPA) matters somewhat in landing a plum summer job, but especially when you're aiming for a summer associate position with a large law firm. That's because summer associate positions for rising 3Ls often lead to permanent offers. As a result, those firms choose their summer associates judiciously. You often need to be in the top 10 percent of your class just to get an initial interview with a large firm; however, this requirement may be more lenient for students attending the top law schools.

GPAs also figure in when securing work as a law clerk at many firms, especially in big cities like New York or Los Angeles. Of course, your legal work experience and extracurriculars also figure in the equation, but firms are more eager to grant interviews when you have a strong academic record. That said, most law students with any GPA can find volunteer work with nonprofits, courts, and governmental organizations and clerking jobs in more out-of-the-way cities and towns.

The Early Bird Gets the Job

Because you have many factors to consider when searching for your dream summer job, I recommend that you start early. If you're a first-year law student, that means getting your application materials together by December 1. The National Association for Law Placement (NALP) mandates that 1Ls cannot send résumés or cover letters out to employers until after December 1.

Yes, I know that's awfully early — first years have barely gotten used to the Socratic Method (see Chapter 8) before they must start thinking about the summer, but because of the nature of large law firm hiring, an early start is essential. If you're not interested in a large firm job, 1Ls need to do the brunt of their summer job search activities for all other employers in January and February. Small and medium-sized firms, however, usually don't know their clerking needs very far in advance (see Chapter 15 for a discussion about applying to these kinds of firms), so you need to keep after them throughout the spring.

Second-year students who want to apply for summer associateships at big firms must start sending résumés and cover letters in August before their 2L year starts. The hiring timetable for 2L summer associateships is late summer to early fall, and decisions are generally made from Thanksgiving through Christmas. As for 2Ls who are looking for summer jobs with all other employers, they also need to focus the majority of their efforts in January and February, unless the particular employer they're considering has earlier or later posted deadlines.

Letting your passions fuel your career choices

Figuring out what you're interested in summer jobwise may be hard when you're a first-year student who hasn't yet had the opportunity to choose any electives. Although you can choose from a plethora of areas of practice (see Chapter 16) for your first legal summer job, knowing exactly what these practice areas entail is difficult, especially when you've only taken standard 1L courses like torts and civil procedures (see Chapter 6) and have no other pre–law school exposure to law. That's why visiting your CSO as soon as you have an opportunity is a good idea (see the following section for more on the CSO).

Regardless of your progress in law school or your stage of preparedness in the job search, you may want to think about the following questions to help you pinpoint your areas of interest.

> ✔ **What do you like to do in your free time?** Think about how you can incorporate your personal interests into your legal interests. For instance, if you like creating artistic masterpieces or playing an instrument, an intellectual property job may appeal to you, because you may be interested in the legal aspects of protecting creative work. Or, if you enjoy participating in environmental cleanup projects and learning about environmental issues, a summer job in environmental law may be a great fit.

> ✔ **What is your ideal work environment?** Try thinking about jobs that you held in high school or college. What did you like and dislike about those environments? Are you the type of person who prefers a slower, steadier pace? Or does it take a frenetic, looming deadline to really motivate you? Talk to your CSO counselors about what areas of practice or settings best fit with the characteristics of your preferred work environments.

Although shifting between the law school mind-set and asking and answering soul-searching questions like these is often difficult, it's nevertheless important that you do. That way, you can begin to have a better idea of what you're interested in and where your career path may lie.

Getting help from your CSO

Your law school's *career services office (CSO)* is your best friend throughout your job search. Face it — at what other times in your life will you have access to around-the-clock, *free* career advice? Probably never, so take advantage of it now!

Your CSO can help you in more ways than you can imagine. If you have no idea where the office is, you need to ask an upperclassman or your dean where it is in the law school. They're usually located right in your law school building, often near other administrative offices like the dean of students office. Stop by and ask for a tour of the facilities. Get acquainted with all the resources there that can help you, such as summer and permanent job postings, books about areas of practice, and alumni career directories.

Most career services counselors say that students often harbor the misconception that CSOs are in place only to help the top third of the class find jobs. That isn't the case. However, the reason some students may think that way is because the CSO usually is busy with on-campus interviews all fall. That's one of its major activities. Your CSO is there to help everyone find jobs, but keep in mind that some students are disappointed to find out is that the CSO is not a headhunter. CSO staff members cannot hand you a job, but they can give you all the guidance that you need to find one. If you make an appointment with your career services dean, you can find out how individualized the assistance that you'll receive can be.

Taking Stock of Your Summer Job Options

The good news about your summer job search is that everyone in your law school class can find a *job*. As long as you're willing to work for free, you'll be able to find *something* in the legal field (hey, everyone welcomes free labor).

When you're a 1L, the not-so-good news is that unless you're in the top 30 percent or so of your law school class, your finding a summer job that pays is unlikely. The key word here is *unlikely* — but not impossible. I managed to find a paying job after my first year, despite the fact that I wasn't in the top third of my class. It didn't pay much, but it was at least above minimum wage and enabled me to see a field that I rarely would've encountered in traditional legal practice — alternative dispute resolution — and provided me with a valuable experience working at a dynamic nonprofit.

As a 2L, you have a much greater chance of nabbing a paying job; however, many 2Ls still end up volunteering because in doing so they have a wider range of options. One reason why landing a paying job is easier as an upperclassman is that 2Ls are more in demand. Most summer employers prefer hiring them, because they have an extra year's experience under their belts and are more adept at research.

Getting a foot in the door by working for free

The main types of abundant nonpaying jobs include:

- ✔ Working at nonprofits like the American Civil Liberties Union (ACLU) or the Natural Resources Defense Council

✔ Working at government agencies such as the Environmental Protection Agency (EPA) or Department of Justice

✔ Working at a public defender's or prosecutor's office

✔ Clerking for a state or federal judge

You can do unpaid work in almost every specialty of law from environmental to wills and trusts to family law. The areas of law in which you're most likely to find unpaid work include criminal, poverty, environmental, civil rights, disability, and employment law.

Even if you dislike the idea of working for free, your job still will be a great means of gaining new skills and finding out more about a field that interests you. Many students who need a steady flow of cash during the summer volunteer during the day and work at service jobs in the evenings. On the bright side, if you volunteer, at least you have more freedom to structure your hours and plan around your summer vacations. As a bonus, most employers for which you volunteer your services are more understanding about accommodating part-time after-work job schedules. And some students even choose to work without pay in an externship arrangement (see Chapter 12) where they work for law school credit. That way, you can shave off a class and lighten your load for one semester. And there's no homework or exam to boot!

Making the grade when looking to get paid

If you're looking only for paid employment, your biggest obstacle in the job search will likely be your grades. Your chances of landing a paid job largely depend on what practice setting (see Chapter 15) you're aiming for and what your grades are. Large law firms, especially in big, glamorous cities like Chicago, Los Angeles, New York, and Boston, are the most stringent about grades. They look for students in the top 10 percent of their classes or who meet their class rank criteria. Most of these firms have pretty rigid cutoffs for grades, so even when you have impressive extracurricular or personal achievements, they may be brushed aside in favor of your raw GPA. Not fair, you say? It sure isn't. These large firms pass over hundreds of talented and bright future lawyers who happened not to have a good exam day (or several).

If that is off-putting to you, keep in mind that not all employers are so grade conscious. It's really only the large law firms with summer-associate programs that concentrate so heavily on grades. The rest — the small and medium-sized firms, judges, governmental, and nonprofit organizations — are more accepting of a diverse range of GPAs, but you still need to fight tooth and nail against many other students for any paid summer positions.

No matter where your grades place you in your class, you have plenty of options. If large firm jobs don't appeal to you, plenty of medium-sized and smaller law firms offer positions, and jobs with the government and nonprofits also are yours to explore. If working at a traditional legal job (as a clerk, volunteer, or associate) doesn't get you excited, consider an alternative summer job, such as in legal publishing or law school administration (see Chapter 17 for more about alternative permanent job options).

Picking Through an Assortment of Summer Jobs

Just like a kid in a candy store, after you find out about all the possibilities for summer jobs, your head will be spinning. You'll find that the phrase, "so many jobs, so little time," rings true. The summer job prospects for 1Ls or 2Ls include clerking for a law firm, nonprofit, government organization, or a judge. Whichever one you choose, you'll likely be doing plenty of legal writing and research.

Yes, you'll do legal research until you're blue in the face — everything from researching case law for briefs to writing pages and pages of memoranda. You'll spend hours rereading a single statute for nuances of meaning and days hunting down one elusive case for your supervising attorney's motion to dismiss. You'll become so familiar with the folks on the other end of the Lexis and Westlaw student research help lines that they'll know you by name before the summer's over. I called the Lexis toll-free help number at least five times a day during my 2L summer — those people are lifesavers! Good thing it's all free!

The appeal of a clerkship

The term *clerking* simply means a law student working for a lawyer or judge (even if it's for free). It's the legal summer job lingo. You can clerk at a law firm, for a judge, or at nonprofit or governmental organizations. Clerking at a law firm (or other paid practice setting) means you'll be a temporary, paid-by-the-hour employee who helps with legal research and writing. If you work for free, you'll do the exact same types of tasks, only for free.

Occasionally, clerking jobs for 2Ls can lead to permanent employment, depending on what the firm's needs are and how well you wow them. Some clerking jobs can last into the school year; others are only for the summer. Regardless of how long you'll be clerking, be sure to do your job as well as you can, so that you receive stellar recommendations that you can use in future job searches or even to score a permanent offer.

When you clerk at a *nonprofit* (meaning a business not conducted for the purpose of making a profit, including organizations such as Lawyers for the Creative Arts, a public defender's office, or the Natural Resources Defense Council), you'll likely be doing the same kinds of things that you would at a law firm, only you usually won't be paid. Many students like the more laid-back atmosphere of the nonprofits, especially when they've already sampled law firm life. See Chapter 15 for more about working at nonprofits.

Judicial clerkships involve plenty of legal research and writing for one particular judge in a sort of mentorship arrangement. The field for summer judicial clerkships often is competitive, especially at the federal level. To land one of these summer positions in either the state or federal court systems, you need outstanding legal research and writing skills and recommendations from your professors, especially when your grades are borderline. Many professors clerked for judges, so ask around to see whether professors at your school have any ties to judges with whom you may be interested in working. Check out Chapter 15 for an in-depth look at what clerking for judges entails.

The lure of a summer associateship

When you work for a large law firm, you're not considered a clerk. Instead, you're usually considered a *summer associate,* even though you do the same tasks as a clerk. In other words, in a summer associateship, you do the same work as a summer clerk, only you're paid not by the hour but rather by a flat rate — and that rate can run anywhere from $1,000 to $2,400 a *week*. In addition, summer associateships usually are offered only by *large law firms* (generally firms with more than 75 lawyers).

In general, large law firms are the only ones that can afford to offer summer-associate programs. In other words, you won't find a ten-person law firm paying its clerks $2,400 a week! The reason they're called summer associateships is that the term "associate" commonly is used to describe the more junior attorneys at large firms.

One option that you may want to pursue as a summer associate is asking whether you can split your summer. *Splitting your summer* means spending the first six weeks (or so) at one firm and the other six weeks at another. You may even be able to split your summer across different cities if you want, although housing can become an issue, unless, of course, you have friends or family with whom you can stay. Some firms strongly discourage this practice, because it means that you have less time to get to know their staff and operations, and vice versa. Others don't seem to care. You can find information about splitting the summer on the firm's entry in the *NALP Directory of Legal Employers* (free online at www.nalpdirectory.com or at your CSO).

Some summer associates are treated like first-year lawyers at large firms. Others are barely spoken to and are left to sink or swim on their own; it all depends on the firm. Talk to upper-class students about their experiences as associates at various firms and inquire at your CSO, which often maintains a file of students' perspectives on their summer employment that's categorized by firm. Finding out as much as you can about the firm before you start helps you know what to expect.

The only caveat to being a summer associate at a large firm comes at the end of the summer. That's because (depending on the particular year), some firms have poor summer associate-to-offer ratios. In other words, a firm may hire 40 summer associates but only plan to offer 10 of them positions. Or they may hire five associates but make no offers. That means many disappointed students will have to hustle with the rest of the class in September as 3Ls out looking for permanent jobs. Besides looking at the firm's past history of offer and acceptance ratios (which you can find in the *NALP Directory of Legal Employers*), you can't do much else to predict how this summer will turn out.

Readying Résumés and Cover Letters

Before ever starting interviews, you need to make sure that your résumé and cover letter are in tip-top shape. Because some of the most popular employers receive as many as 100 or more résumés a week, you need to be professional and meticulous in your presentation. Your CSO can help you develop your résumé and cover letter, and I highly recommend stopping by and going over these materials line by line with your counselor. However, don't stop there: As the old law school adage about cover letters recommends, "Show it to at least three people." Some main points to keep in mind as you begin crafting your résumé and cover letter are included in the sections that follow.

Crafting a successful legal résumé

Think of a good résumé as your ticket to an interview. If you don't have the right ticket, you won't get in. After all, many CSOs have something called a *résumé drop* for summer employers, which means they collect résumés from all interested students and the employer then determines to whom they'll make interview offers. That's why your résumé needs to impress from the moment the interviewer starts reading the first line.

A legal résumé is a little different from the one you used as an undergraduate, because:

✔ You want to make the law school section as meaty as you can, by including any extracurricular activities, leadership positions, and research assistantships you participated in or academic honors you received.

This section goes first on your résumé, so you want to make it as memorable as you can.

✔ You want to leave off any undergraduate or postcollege jobs that involved flipping burgers at fast-food restaurants or posing nude.

✔ Unlike your undergraduate résumé, your previous legal experience (summer jobs, part-time school-year jobs, and research assistantships) is one of the main reasons an employer is going to hire you. Thus, you want to write a brief but detailed description about what you did at each legal job you held.

But unlike the résumé you used in college, you want to tailor descriptions of what you did at each legal job to the *needs* of your future employer. For instance, suppose that you want to work at an environmental law firm this summer. Instead of crafting your résumé solely from the viewpoint of what *you* gained from your previous legal experience, like "learned about federal environmental statutes," you need to put yourself in the shoes of your prospective employer and write more about what your employer will gain from what you've discovered through your experiences.

So, the example can be rewritten as: "Researched and wrote memoranda on federal environmental statutes with little supervision." This more specific, employer needs–based second approach turns more heads than the vague, student-centered first approach. The latter shows exactly what you did (rather than what you learned) and demonstrates that you're a self-starter. The main benefit of preparing your résumé with your target employer in mind is that it tells the employer that you're sensitive to its needs and that you're thinking about what the employer can gain from you, and not vice versa.

The following are the ten most important elements of a legal résumé.

✔ **Perspective:** As I mentioned, write the résumé from the perspective of what you can do for the *employer*, not what *you* got out of each of your activities and jobs.

✔ **Action words:** Use action words whenever possible, in past tense. "Prepared," "wrote," and "collected" are all examples of evocative action words.

✔ **Page limit:** Limit your résumé to one page, unless you're a nontraditional student with an extensive prior career history. In that case, two pages is perfectly acceptable.

✔ **Section headings:** Make them powerful and specific. "Education," "Legal Experience," and "Publications" are good ways to begin a new section. Don't forget to list your law school name and college and (graduate) school names under "Education." If you're a 1L applying for your first summer job and you have no legal experience, listing your past work history under the general heading of "Professional Experience" is perfectly acceptable.

✔ **Personal interests:** Adding them gives a human dimension to your résumé, but they're usually only included when you don't have much else to put on your résumé. For instance, if you're a rising 2L who has only one summer legal job and an extracurricular activity or two to put on your résumé, adding a section at the very end titled "Personal Interests" keeps your résumé from looking too bare-bones. Plus, you never know when a recruiter will pick up your résumé as a fellow origami enthusiast and offer you an interview on the basis of your mutual passion. But use common sense when listing your interests — painting, tennis, and chess are safe bets — an activity like hunting may raise a few eyebrows.

✔ **GPA and class rank:** The general guideline is if your GPA is higher than 3.0, list it. If not, keep it off and wait until an employer asks you for it. Schools vary in how they report class rank, so talk with your CSO or dean of students to find out the best way to list it on your résumé.

✔ **Extracurriculars:** List all your legal extracurriculars under your law school name in the "Education" section.

✔ **Paper:** Choose a lightweight bond paper, rather than plain printer paper. Slightly textured, off-white stationary paper looks best, but avoid any colors other than off-white, pale tan, white, or gray. Make sure the envelopes match.

✔ **Printer:** Use a laser printer, whenever possible, because it provides the crispest look to your résumé (and cover letters).

✔ **Proofreading:** Proofread your résumé many times to make sure all information is factual and that no embarrassing spelling mistakes are evident. Don't rely on the computer's spelling checker alone. You don't want to be applying to a law "farm" or have researched federal "statues."

Tailoring your résumé to the employer for whom you want to work is a great idea. That's because the résumé you send seeking a job clerking for a judge isn't the exact same as the one you'd send to a family law nonprofit. The reason is that all employers stress different qualifications and characteristics in their potential hires. Judges, for instance, want evidence of your research and writing abilities, so you want to emphasize any research assistantships for professors and moot court or journal participation (see Chapter 13). A family law nonprofit, on the other hand, wants to see your commitment to public-interest and children's issues. In that case, you want to emphasize any practical public-interest experience you've gained, such as previous summer jobs at nonprofits or work at law school clinics (see Chapter 12). Having two or three versions of your résumé for such purposes is a smart way to go.

Creating credible cover letters

Your cover letter often is the first piece of information that employers read about you. So make it special! The best way to make yours stand out is to research the employer before writing the cover letter. Pack your cover letter with specifics about why you think the employer and you are a good fit: its clients, a lawyer or partner whose career you admire, its mission, recent or current cases it's handled, and tidbits that you read about it in the news. Then link what the employer does with your interests. For example, if you appreciate its mission to serve poor clients, describe your commitment to the public interest through your extracurricular and previous legal work experience.

Making your cover letter memorable is always key to getting an interview. If you had to read hundreds of them a week, which is what many law firm recruiters must do, you're more likely to remember cover letters that are well researched and thought out than the ones that are blatantly mass-mailed and generic (in other words, no "Dear Sirs").

Researching employers

Researching employers is essential when you want your cover letter to stand out from the letters of all the other applicants applying for a summer position. The Internet makes researching employers easier than ever, regardless of whether you type the employer's name into a search engine and read any articles that have mentioned it or simply browse the employer's Web site for any important nuggets of information. Spend half an hour per employer online and see what you can dig up. Talking briefly by e-mail or phone to alums who currently work for the employer is another excellent way of digging up the dirt for your cover letter. Prefacing your chat with "I'm very interested in applying for a summer job with your employer, and I was wondering whether you can spend a few minutes telling me what you think I need to know about your employer," is a good start.

Now, you may think, "Why should I spend the half an hour or more researching this one employer just to write a cover letter? Can't I use my time in a better way, given that my letter may just be tossed in the trash? But when you think about the thousands of dollars that an employer can spend interviewing, training, and (paying) you, spending a mere half an hour researching each of the employers that you contact doesn't seem so out of line. You can't expect employers to make an investment in you if you won't make a minimal investment in them. Scheduling your cover letter writing sessions for the weekend provides you with more time and less stress when doing them.

Writing the letter

As for the body of the letter, the traditional four-paragraph format works best.

- The first paragraph serves as an introduction, revealing who you are and how you found out about the employer (through a job posting at your CSO, online, or through a direct referral).

- The next paragraph describes why you and the firm are a good match, based on your interests and what the firm handles.

- ✔ The third paragraph discusses your qualifications for the position (be sure to mention information that's most relevant to that particular employer first, such as research and writing experience for clerking with a judge).

- ✔ The last paragraph directly requests what type of action you want to occur and informs the employer of your availability (such as "I will contact you next week to discuss summer intern opportunities. I will be returning to Chicago frequently throughout the spring and am available to meet with you at any convenient time for an interview.").

You may also want to mention any attachments that you're sending, such as a résumé and reference list.

Make your cover letter a knockout, and employers will take notice!

On-Campus Interviewing

During *on-campus interviews,* or *OCIs* (as your CSO likes to call them), employers visit your campus and conduct interviews with students they usually preselect from a résumé/cover letter drop. Many schools offer OCIs during the fall only; others have fall and spring OCIs.

A *résumé/cover letter drop* is the time and place that your CSO designates for all students interested in a particular employer to drop off their application materials (usually just a résumé and/or cover letter). Then, that employer wades through the stack of résumés and cover letters and contacts the students it wants to interview. Your CSO may also request that you do your résumé drops online through a special online service the CSO subscribes to. If that's the case, the CSO sends out notices to all students about how to log onto this service and upload your résumé.

The number of firms or other organizations that conduct OCIs at particular law schools varies significantly according to many factors. These factors, in turn, vary from year to year depending on such things as the state of the economy, but the prestige of your school also is a huge factor and so is its ranking as a national or regional law school (see Chapter 3 for a complete discussion). National law schools sport firms from all parts of the country, whereas regional law schools get mostly firms from that city or state coming to interview. Another important factor to note is that the more prestigious your school, the higher the likelihood that the employers that conduct OCIs will give out multiple offers for call-back interviews. Similarly, at less prestigious schools, the number of offers may be significantly fewer. Call-backs are the next step in the interview process, so be sure to check out the "Managing the Call-Back Interview" section later in this chapter. At many schools, an OCI is really a vehicle for only the top quarter of the class to secure call-backs; the rest of the class needs to make contact with employers on their own initiative.

Bear in mind that mainly large firms and some governmental organizations conduct interviews on campus. The smallest firms and nonprofits simply don't have enough people on their staffs to send lawyers out for the day to interview. You need to use a different strategy (other than OCI) when contacting these employers (see Chapter 15 for a discussion). Your initial interviews with these employers may occur over the phone or in-person at their offices; however, the choice varies from employer to employer. (When you volunteer, you're more likely to get an expense-free telephone initial interview rather than trekking out to their office.)

OCIs often are big sources of stress. Seeing your classmates come to school in suits often triggers inferiority complexes in many law students, because it's clear who got the interview that day and who didn't (unless, of course, your school is the type where students regularly come to class in suits). Because on-campus interviewing is so visible, many students fear that if they aren't selected for OCIs, they'll never get summer jobs. Many CSOs, however, routinely indicate that at many schools, only 15 percent of students in a particular class secure jobs through OCIs. The rest find them through networking, informational interviews, alums, and by responding to job postings.

Posting your résumé

The first step to getting an interview through an OCI is finding out your CSO's policy on how to submit résumés. Some career centers ask for paper copies of résumés. Others ask students to post them online through a service like eAttorney (`www.eAttorney.com`), where employers who subscribe to the service review résumés online and notify you online about interviews. Whichever approach your CSO takes, make sure that your résumé is polished and proofread, so you can make the best impression.

Dressing for success

Make sure that you have a professional-looking suit. Navy and black are the safest colors. For women, skirts rather than pantsuits often make the best impression on conservative interviewers, and men need to avoid loud ties. Additionally, jewelry and makeup need to be kept to a minimum. I'm often surprised that so many students seem to have no idea how to dress for an interview. I've seen purple suits, no pantyhose, hiking boots, and backpacks. Appearance makes an impression, especially when candidates have similar qualifications.

Honing your writing sample

Every lawyer has to write; it's in the job title. And to prove that you have a command of the English language, you need to bring a writing sample to your on-campus interviews (or any initial interview, regardless of where it takes place) for each employer that you plan to meet with. Although some on-campus interviewers won't even ask for a writing sample, many will, and having one ready makes you look thoroughly prepared.

You don't have to be an SAT-vocabulary spewing, Fitzgeraldesque prodigy, but your writing sample needs to make sense and read well. And just any old piece of writing won't do. That means no short stories, papers that you wrote in college, or submissions to the law school newspaper. Most first-year students use a sample (three to five double-spaced pages maximum) of the brief or memorandum they wrote for their first-year legal writing class (after making corrections or changes that their writing instructor suggested, of course). Most second- and third-year students use a piece of the same length that was written during their summer jobs or a piece from that same legal writing class (if they don't have anything more recent).

Whenever you use a piece of writing from your summer job, checking with your supervisor first is extremely important for determining whether you need to *redact* (cross out with an opaque black marker) the names of parties or other identifying facts. Otherwise, you may risk a breach of attorney-client privilege, and that can land you in serious hot water with the employer and your law school. Yes, that means your typo-free writing sample is covered with thick black lines, but employers are used to seeing these marks. Marking out text is better than retyping the whole thing and inserting Xs in place of the names or identifying facts. If you have a selection of potential writing samples to choose from, one that has fewer blacked-out pieces of information may be less distracting to read than one where every other word is crossed out.

Whatever type of writing you decide to use, make sure that it uses impeccable grammar and is typo-free. Although the number of interviewers who actually read the writing sample is open to debate, if your interviewer indeed decides to read it, you want to present the most favorable picture that you can. A sloppy, correction-fluid painted writing sample is not going to do that.

Another important tip is making sure that you know the contents of your writing sample inside and out. At nearly all of my call-back interviews (and a few of my initial ones), I was asked to explain in great detail the circumstances surrounding my writing sample (for example, the facts of the case, what the outcome was, and how I felt about that outcome). If I hadn't looked at my writing sample since the day I wrote it, I would've looked hopelessly unprepared as I fumbled for the answers to those questions. Luckily, I reviewed my sample the night before each interview, so I was able to field my interviewers' questions in a competent fashion.

Asking (and answering) tough questions

When you get to the actual on-campus (or initial) interview, which probably will last about 20 to 30 minutes, make sure that you have a list of questions to ask the interviewer either written down or committed to memory. If you don't have any questions, an interviewer may think you're not interested in the employer and, as a result, may end up passing you over for a call-back in favor of more enthusiastic applicants. Having thoughtful questions always signals that you've gone the extra mile to find out about a particular employer.

What kinds of questions should you ask? The best questions are tailored to the particular employer, but asking general questions is okay too. A good guideline is: If it's a really basic question, like how many offices the firm has or how many lawyers work there, skip it — otherwise you'll look like you just decided to interview with that firm on a whim (even if you really did). Use basic facts about the firm as a foundation for questions that probe a little deeper. For instance, you can ask, "Do you anticipate expanding beyond your current six offices?" A great place to find such fodder for your questions is the firm's Web site or promotional materials.

Finding out who your interviewers will be beforehand is also an excellent idea, whenever doing so is possible, because you can then learn some things about them ahead of time. Your CSO often can tell you who the interviewers are, and you can surf the employer's Web site and read the interviewers' bios, if they're available. Otherwise, you can try typing the interviewers' names into an Internet search engine and reading whatever comes up. Of course, you needn't go to heroic lengths just to find out this information, but anything you can find out can only help your chances of succeeding in the interview.

When the subject of grades comes up . . .

During an interview, the interviewer probably will ask you about your grades. This question is a big problem for some students whose grades are mediocre or poor. Students who fall into this category usually wait for the interviewer to mention their grades first, without volunteering the information themselves. That way, if the interviewer never brings it up, they assume that their grades just aren't a problem. Do you think this is the right way to approach grades that you'd rather not showcase? Absolutely not!

Instead, always mention your grades (even when they're poor) by offering a short, concise statement about them at the beginning of the interview — and preferably not something like, "I don't do well on essay, multiple-choice, or short-answer exams." For instance, you may say something like, "I know my grades aren't the highest, but I believe my work on the law journal and my job as a research assistant for Professor X speak more to my abilities." When you don't say anything at all about your grades, the interviewer is left to come up with explanations, like you're a slacker or you just can't handle law school–level work. Because that isn't the impression you want to present, take the time now to compose a solid explanation.

Additionally, you never want to make the mistake of pretending that your grades don't exist or hoping the interviewer forgets to ask about them. That's the kiss of death. Neither do you want to avoid explaining any inconsistent grades. Because the interviewer usually has your entire transcript anyway, that makes scanning first for inconsistent grades or semesters easy. For example, if you're usually an A– student, but you received a C+ in your property class, the interviewer will likely ask, "What happened in property?" Or, if you have a consistent B average, but one semester you received a straight 4.0, your interviewer will likely be interested in why that happened.

Most students normally have some idea of why they bombed a particular class or semester — "I hated crim law" or "I partied too much that semester." However, sometimes your grades are a total mystery. That's what happened to me. The classes I'd study hard for were my lowest grades, and the ones I was less diligent in were often my highest. It made my transcript into something of a conundrum. If you're unsure of why your performance is all over the map, make an appointment with your dean of students. Your dean may be able to point out patterns that you can't see. For example, the dean may discover that you do better on closed-book than open-book exams. After my dean helped me gain some insight into my haphazard grades, I was able to offer my interviewers an explanation much more coherent than "I dunno."

Other points of discussion to remember

Besides attending the interview with a prepared spiel about your grades, don't forget to talk about your work experiences, extracurriculars, and volunteer work. Don't ever assume that your interviewer actually has read your résumé and, as such, knows all about what you've accomplished in law school thus far. Many times, your interview is the first time that an interviewer has ever laid eyes on your résumé (that is if the interviewer even bothers to look it over at all).

Don't be surprised if the interviewers don't appear like they know what they're doing. Most law firms don't have any formal process for selecting lawyers to attend OCIs or even to conduct interviews on-site. These attorneys aren't human-resource professionals. Many are asked to go at the last minute and have not prepared at all.

Keep in mind that one of the more crucial interview questions you're likely to be asked is why you want to be a part of the employer's city. Retention is a huge issue, especially with law firms, and that's why you need to have a carefully thought out answer, especially when you can't show any tangible reasons for making a commitment to the city like having grown up there. If you want to work in a city where you don't have many ties, start by taking your 1L summer job there. That way, you have a great explanation for your 2L interviewers. You can say: "I worked in Phoenix my 1L summer, loved the city, and plan to settle here after graduation."

Managing the Call-Back Interview

Many employers require a call-back interview to complete the interview process. The *call-back* interview is when you travel (either at your own or the employer's expense) to the employer's offices for a final round of interviews. These generally last a half to three-quarters of a day, including one meal (usually lunch.) Many firms require call-backs, but nonprofits and governmental organizations tend not to require them. The general guideline is that if you're volunteering your services, you won't have a call-back.

The call-back is an opportunity for the employer to conduct more interviews with you, generally with several to many lawyers at the firm or organization. At my call-backs, I interviewed with between four and seven lawyers total. At half an hour per lawyer, that's a good half to three-quarters of a day of interviewing. Remember, however, that at the same time they're interviewing you, you also need to be interviewing them and deciding whether this particular employer is where you can see yourself working.

I found call-back interviews to be stressful. Why? When you're interviewing with a large firm, you may be traveling to another city, sleeping in a hotel for the night, enduring four to eight interviews in a short timeframe, and having a meal with your interviewers. After such a high-intensity day, I was always exhausted and ready to unwind.

When interviewing for a job at a small or medium-size firm, nonprofit, or government organization, you'll have a similar day of interviews, probably without the meal, but you'll often be expected to pay for everything yourself (travel and hotel). For all interviews, you'll be expected to be on your best behavior, have interesting questions to ask, and maintain the highest level of etiquette.

Reviewing your etiquette

The call-back letter or e-mail that you receive from an employer explains that you're invited to interview with the firm (at their expense or not) at the firm's office in the city you're interested in. If they're picking up the tab, the firm either pays you outright or reimburses you later for your travel, meal, lodging, and ground-transportation. That doesn't mean, of course, they'll cover the cost of the new suit you buy for the occasion or a dinner for you and your buddies at the most expensive restaurant in town.

If they're picking up the tab, the firm or its travel agent usually arranges your flight and lodging for you; all you have to do is show up. If you need to cancel, make sure you do so well in advance. I've heard horror stories about students at other law schools not showing up for call-back interviews and the firms they jilted deciding not to recruit at their schools ever again. Law firms, like elephants, have long memories.

Regardless of the size or type of the employer, before you leave campus for your interview, make sure that you've done your homework on the firm and the lawyers who will be interviewing you. Because you can often find out from the firm's hiring attorney or recruiting coordinator who your interviewers will be, you have ample time to dig up the dirt on them. Of course, things can change at the last minute, and you may be assigned different interviewers, depending on whether people are out sick or have a client matter crop up at the last minute. Look up their bios on the firm's Web site or type their names into www.martindale.com. Make sure to note whether any of them went to your college or law school and whether they practice in areas that interest you. Find out what kinds of awards they've won, whether they worked on a journal, and what cities they're from. This material will be invaluable whenever you face a lull in the conversation. Plus, it shows your enthusiasm. What interviewer wouldn't be wowed by a student who goes that extra mile?

Getting ready

When you're in your hotel room the night before your interview, make sure that:

- ✔ You go over your notes about the firm and lawyer bios
- ✔ Your suit is pressed and presentable
- ✔ You have your *portfolio* (leather or faux leather case in which you keep copies of your résumé, transcript, and writing samples) with you and many copies (at least one for each interviewer) of your résumés, writing samples, and transcripts
- ✔ You get a good night's sleep to be at your best the next day. Your sagging eyelids and those huge bags under your eyes make an unfavorable impression.

In the morning, be sure to allow ample time for getting to your call-back interview, because you don't want to be even five minutes late. Being tardy for a call-back interview (or any interview for that matter) is a bad idea. Leave at least 20 extra minutes more than you think you'll need, especially if you're not staying near the firm or if it's raining or snowing. If you're really worried, leave an extra half-hour. If you find that you have some extra time when you arrive at the employer, stand around in the building's lobby before going up to the firm. After all, you don't want to look too eager by arriving 20 minutes early and just sitting in the waiting area. Instead, park yourself on a couch in the building's lobby and review your lawyer bios and questions.

The call-back interview usually has two parts: the in-office interviews with attorneys and the lunch (or, less frequently, dinner) component. If you're interviewing with a large firm, lunch or dinner always is included, whereas at a small firm, medium-sized firm, or governmental organizations, a dining component is not always included.

Here's a quick rundown of how the in-office interview will (usually) go.

✔ When you arrive at the firm's office, greet the secretary pleasantly and, by all means, don't be brash or curt. Secretaries often have more influence in hiring decisions than you think, so if you're rude to the secretary, she may alert the hiring partner about it. Many career services staff tell tales about law students who were rude to the secretary and never received an offer, despite sterling qualifications.

✔ Next, you're directed to the recruiting coordinator's office, where you chat for awhile (small talk) and then receive a folder with your schedule for the day. But don't let your guard down at this or any point during your call-back interview — every conversation you have, no matter how big or small, is an interview, for all practical purposes. Your schedule lists attorneys with whom you'll be interviewing and the length of time you'll meet. The lunch portion of the interview also is listed on the schedule and so are the attorneys with whom you'll be dining.

Your interviews with the lawyers usually last a half-hour each. Keep in mind that each lawyer you meet with already has a copy of your transcript, résumé, and writing samples (which are either requested by the firm prior to the call-back or the ones you or had already provided to the initial interviewer). Although the lawyers ask some questions, particularly about your writing samples, the biggest part of those interviews will feature *you* asking questions. So, come prepared with a huge list of them. Make your questions meaningful; they need to be even more thought-provoking than the ones you asked during the initial interview.

Robert Harris, clerk for Justice Simeon R. Acoba of the Hawaii Supreme Court, says that his biggest recommendation for call-back interviews is remembering that the firm is trying to recruit you as much as you're trying to impress the firm. Harris noticed that firms are relatively serious about a candidate whenever they offer a call-back interview. He says at that point, they've probably moved past academics and résumé items to a stage where they're just trying to find out whether they like you and whether you'd fit in their workplace. Harris also advises that you need to be ready to spend plenty of time at a call-back interview. During several of his interviews, he was introduced to and spent more than a half-hour with virtually every partner at each of the firms. By the end of the process, Harris was completely exhausted and late for another appointment he'd scheduled. In other words, expect a marathon of an experience.

Munching Through the Lunch Interview

The lunch portion of the interview often makes students the most nervous; most students are puzzled by whether they're officially being interviewed during the meal. On the one hand, your interviewers won't be asking you typical interview questions, so the lunch will have more of a relaxed feel. On the other, remember that these are not like your friends, so don't become too comfortable with them. The best answer to whether you're being interviewed at lunch is always a resounding, "Yes."

No matter how friendly your interviewers may seem, they're still evaluating every move you make, from whether you order inappropriately to whether you're rude to the wait staff. Remember that certain topics like relationships or salaries are inappropriate for this lunchtime conversation. Treat the meal component the same as you would the other parts of the interview — formal, yet not stiff.

Many elements of good etiquette must be followed during an interview meal. Making a major faux pas here can greatly hinder your chances of receiving an offer. When you're at home, eating a meal seems like second nature. But in an interview situation, you need to think about strategy. Instead of reaching across someone's chest for the rolls, you need to ask someone to pass them to you. And instead of spitting an enormous glob of food from of your mouth directly onto your plate (or worse, on the floor) you need to slyly use your napkin. The main things to keep in mind are to be friendly to the servers, always say please and thank you, and generally mind your manners.

Ordering protocol

One area where many law students make their first big mistakes is when ordering. At first glance, ordering seems pretty straightforward — when the waiter asks what you want, you just choose something. But there's more strategy to it than that. When ordering, you need to follow the interviewer's lead, whenever possible. It sounds old-fashioned and stodgy, but this is the way things need to be done in the interviewing world.

If the waiter asks what you want first, say that you haven't yet made up your mind. That way, you can see what your interviewers order. The reason you want to wait? It's your job to order something in line with what the rest of the group orders — nothing too expensive or inexpensive. Sure, you may feel like this silly rule stifles your sense of self-expression, and that if you want to order the peanut butter and jelly sandwich then you should go ahead and do so. But when you're in a high-stakes interview scenario, playing it conservatively and following your interviewer's lead often is best.

In addition, when you choose your menu item, make sure that you steer clear of ribs, spaghetti, or anything else that's too messy. The last thing you want is to splatter your interviewer while twirling your pasta or get something nasty on your suit. You also don't want to be blanketed by 15 napkins and a bib. So stick with safe menu items and choose something that's easy to eat, easy to cut, and doesn't come with buckets of sauce. Fish always is a good choice. But watch out when you squeeze that lemon!

Table talk

One important lunch-interview technique is keeping up your end of the conversation by asking questions and showing initiative. You don't want to sit there like a bump on a log. The point of the lunch interview is seeing how you interact in a quasi-social setting (like when you'd be interacting with clients). You need to be alert, engaging, and inquisitive. Don't spend all your time eating or listening — break it up by throwing out some conversation starters. Ask the same sorts of questions you would in a regular interview. But, for variety, tossing in questions about where everyone grew up and in what neighborhoods yields intriguing responses.

Brushing up on your current events by reading a local newspaper (online or in paper) before your interview starts always is a good idea. That way, when the interviewers are talking about what the mayor said yesterday, or about the new building downtown, you may have something to contribute. Likewise, keep in mind that the lunchtime conversation may turn to subjects you know nothing about . . . whether that's sports, movies, or local politics. Whenever the discussion moves into uncharted territory, waiting a few minutes to get the gist of the conversation always is better than just jumping in. That way you won't look totally clueless by saying, "The Cubs are a really good football team," when everyone else is talking baseball.

Picking up the tab — Don't!

Whenever the check comes, if the waiter happens to place it in front of you, just wait until your interviewer picks it up. Paying the bill is never your responsibility, but picking it up yourself and placing it in front of the interviewer is bad form. Never check the bill to make sure it adds up correctly — your interviewers will be flabbergasted and it won't go over well, no matter how helpful you want to appear. After the bill is paid, be sure to thank everyone individually and make sure you know how you're getting back to your hotel or the firm and whether you'll be escorted.

Writing Thank-you Notes

Thank-you notes are the order of the day whether you're attending OCIs, other initial interviews, or call-backs. Everyone likes to feel appreciated, and, much to their detriment, many students omit this crucial bit of etiquette. Thank-you notes need to be typed in business letter format — no handwritten notecards — and addressed to each of your interviewers individually. E-mail is never a good option. Thank-you notes need to be sent as soon as possible after your interview, but if you receive your decision prior to mailing them out, it's your call whether to go ahead and send it. (If it's a yes, definitely do it; if it's a no, you may not feel like wasting a stamp.)

Thank-you note writing can be made as painless as possible by first composing a prototype thank-you letter. After that, you can prepare personalized variations of the prototype to send to each of your interviewers.

Chapter 15

Getting the Lowdown on Careers

*W*hether you're a rising 2L who wants to get a head start, or a second-semester 3L who's just getting around to it, the job search can be a tad overwhelming at times. With everything that you must do to find a decent job, from regularly sending résumés and cover letters to networking with alums, maintaining a successful job search can take on the same time commitment as a law school class (and a five-credit one at that).

But, nothing is more exciting than searching for your first real lawyer job! What makes it such an exhilarating process is that you never know where a lead may take you. One minute, you're set on a judicial clerkship, and the next, you've happened upon a different dream job as a public defender, perhaps. Whatever your current career plans (or lack thereof), the sky's the limit with your Juris Doctor (J.D.) degree.

Because I know how intimidating the job search can seem at first, in this chapter, I help you break down the process into manageable, easy-to-digest chunks. First, I examine the most common lawyerly job opportunities and how you need to approach each one. Next, I take you step-by-step through charting your job-search goals and provide you with insider information about employer hiring practices. So start your engine, put the pedal to the metal, and get ready to accelerate on a fast and furious job-search journey!

Exploring Practice Setting Possibilities

Finding a job can seem like the most important part of your law school career, and for jobless second-semester 3Ls, it seems like a *life-or-death* part of your law school career. Remember, however, that you've already won half the battle: Armed with a law degree (and eventually a pass from the bar exam), you have a ton of options for your first job within the legal field. Sure, most of your classmates will probably end up working in private practice at law firms, but you needn't follow that path. Branch out and discover that your options are nearly limitless: Imagine clerking for a judge, trying life-and-death cases as a prosecutor, or calling all the shots as a solo practitioner. And of course, you have dozens of areas of practice to choose from (see Chapter 16 for a complete discussion of these options).

If, out of this limitless sea of choices, you still can't find anything that tickles your fancy, consider an alternative career, such as legal publishing, law school administration, or law librarianship. See Chapter 17 for all you ever wanted to know about nontraditional legal jobs.

Sadly, many law students and new graduates never explore many of the diverse career options, because they're too caught up in what everyone else seems to be doing. And, much of the time, what everyone else seems to be doing is interviewing for positions with big firms. True, large firms are attractive workplaces, with their huge starting salaries and luxury offices, but positions like that are hard to get unless you have A+ credentials. Additionally, many large-firm lawyers burn out quickly because of the break-neck, 80- to 100-hour workweeks and having to put in *face-time* (showing up just so partners and other lawyers know you came in) during your precious weekends. Before getting caught up in the big-firm frenzy, take a peek at all your other options. You may be pleasantly surprised: Working with a nonprofit or governmental organization may be a more satisfying fit.

You really don't need to start thinking about your future until the summer before your third year. Any later than that, however, and you're setting yourself up for a major meltdown. That particular summer is when you need to conduct all your self-assessment (talking to your career services office [CSO], reading career self-help books, and thinking about what you really need in your career), job shadow, talk to alumni, and pin down a few areas of practice that truly excite you.

Taking the private practice route

The American Bar Association reports that 72 percent of young lawyers in its 2000 ABA Young Lawyers Division Survey, "Career Satisfaction" work in private practice. *Private practice* simply means that you work in the for-profit business sector rather than the governmental or nonprofit sectors.

Private practice, like any other job, has its benefits and drawbacks. Most lawyers enjoy higher salaries overall in private practice than they do in the public sector, but higher salaries often mean a correspondingly lengthy workweek. Lawyers like working in private practice for several other reasons, too. Here are some of them:

✔ They're able to engage in *client development*, which means recruiting new business and nurturing clients they already have. This activity is virtually nonexistent in the public sector.

✔ A greater variety and number of positions are generally available in private practice, and upward mobility (job advancement [ability to make partner] and/or increases in salary commensurate with experience) is generally faster than in the public sector.

✔ You have greater flexibility to *specialize* (choose a practice area that interests you) in private practice, whereas you tend to have a more definitive job description in the public sector.

On the other hand, a common complaint about private practice is that most lawyers are required to keep track of their *billable hours,* the number of hours a firm is able to bill a client in exchange for a lawyer's work. Billable hours aren't an issue in the public sector, because the client isn't paying the organization or agency. Most firms quote their billable hour requirements in terms of how many hours per year you must bill. Generally, firm billable hour requirements are within the 1700 to 2300 hour range. Of course, the larger the firm, the more likely you'll have to bill more hours (because you're getting paid more). As you can probably imagine, keeping track of your time with a billable hour system (which usually breaks down into keeping track of your time in six-minute increments), can be highly annoying.

Large firms

If obscenely high starting salaries, a posh working environment, general prestige, and a support staff working for you around the clock sounds like your cup of tea, consider tossing your hat into the ring for a job at a large law firm. Large firms are generally defined as having more than 75 lawyers. They usually boast dozens of practice areas; many of them are highly specialized. At a large firm, you generally have two ways to hook up with a particular area of practice. You either choose to specialize in labor law (or some other area) right away or rotate through different practice areas until you make up your mind.

One caveat before you begin: Expect plenty of competition in applying for a large firm job. Large firms have the luxury of choosing from the cream of the crop, so keep in mind that your odds of making it are generally slim unless you're in the top 10 percent of your class, or at a top-notch school. These are the employers to whom grades (and law review — see Chapter 13) matter the most; so if it's really your dream job, make sure to earn the best grades you can throughout law school so you'll be a competitive candidate come application time.

New lawyers with large firms often are known as *associates*; when you start, you're usually placed in an *associate class.* Yes, it smacks of your primary school days, but it's the lingo. Throughout your years at the firm, you're referred to by your class year. For example: "He's a seventh-year associate."

So, why are big firms known as sometimes having poor attrition rates? I can sum it up in one word: *burnout*. This problem is alternatively termed the *golden handcuffs dilemma*. When you have $80,000 in loans breathing down your neck, who wouldn't love a sweet $100,000 or higher starting salary? But this huge paycheck comes with a price. After their first few weeks, associates at large firms don't blink an eye at 80- to 100-hour workweeks, and putting in face-time on the weekends is usually expected. If your family situation or personal interests won't allow such a massive time commitment to your work, you probably won't last long at a large firm.

The people who do best at large firms are the ones who love to be part of a dynamic working environment. For instance, Harold Davis, Jr., an intellectual property lawyer at Katten, Muchin, Zavis, Rosenman in Chicago, specifically wanted to work at a large firm, so he'd have more opportunity to do the things he wanted to do: either to specialize in a niche practice or change focus to an entirely different area. He says that in a smaller office, you're more often constrained by the infrastructure of that office. In a firm with 100 or more lawyers, on the other hand, you have greater economies of scale in terms of availability of support and diversity of expertise than at a smaller outfit. He likes the fact that when he has a question about anything from agency law to wills, he knows he can always refer the client to another lawyer and still keep the business within the firm.

Applying for jobs with most large firms is easy because they generally have predictable hiring seasons that typically begin during the late summer or early fall. Many third-year law students start submitting résumés and cover letters beginning in August, and initial interviews usually take place from September through early November. You can find the deadlines for applying with large firms on their respective Web sites or in the *NALP Directory of Legal Employers*, which you can find in your career services office (CSO) or search free online at www.nalpdirectory.com.

But keep in mind that most large firm jobs are procured from offers by the firm during your 2L summer associateship (see Chapter 14). In other words, if you're not hired on as a summer associate during your 2L summer, odds are against your finding a large firm job during the fall application and interview season. That's because many firms won't be seeking additional new associates, because they'll have already filled their associate class from the summer associates who accept their offers.

Small and medium-sized firms

When you consider that only a small percentage of all lawyers in private practice in this country are at the big firms, you may be wondering where the heck the rest of them are. The answer: Most work at small and medium-sized firms. A recent study by the National Association for Law Placement (NALP) found that for the graduating class of 2001, 29.9 percent found work in firms with between two and ten lawyers. Medium-sized firms are generally defined as having between 21 and 75 lawyers, and small firms have between two and 20 lawyers.

Small and medium-sized firms have many things going for them.

- ✔ **Because they're not quite so behemoth, you won't feel like you're just another face in the crowd.** In other words, you get to know your fellow associates better and may form more long-lasting and personal relationships with them.

- ✔ **Their clients are typically individuals and small businesses, compared with largely corporate clients that large firms service, so you get to know who you're representing more intimately.**

- ✔ **They appeal to many law students and new graduates, because some offer a more balanced lifestyle.** You'll need to ferret out those that do, if that's important to you, but keep in mind that many small and midsize firms work you just as much as the big ones but don't have the prestige or the fat paycheck of the large firms.

- ✔ **Their lawyers tend to take on significant responsibility earlier, including representing clients and taking on your own cases much sooner than at large firms.** Generally, the smaller the firm, the quicker you gain responsibility, so don't be surprised when you're going to court by yourself your very first day at a four-person firm.

K. Bartlett Durand, Jr., a complex litigation lawyer at Bickerton Saunders & Dang in Honolulu, was intent on finding a firm where he could enjoy a balanced life. One thing he was determined *not* to do was join the legal career treadmill. Durand says he didn't go to school until he figured out a way to get out of school with little or no debt. That tactic enabled him to focus on jobs where he'd enjoy the work and be treated as a complete individual and not just a billable hours factory. When looking for jobs, Durand was able to focus on smaller, more aggressive firms and avoid the big, partner-track firms. One reason he took this approach was that too many of his friends did all the right things in school, landed the big, fancy, well-paying jobs at major firms, and then burned out in only a short time. He prefers living a balanced life and that strongly influenced his approach to school and finding work.

The upside of life at small and medium-sized firms can also be its downside, however: Being part of a closer-knit group can make having confrontations with your colleagues difficult. In other words, being part of the family can make conversations about a raise or about a problem colleague with the higher-ups at the firm more difficult. Another often-cited downside of small and medium-sized firms: They provide fewer resources than larger firms. For example, you probably won't have as extensive a network of support staff at a small firm, so you may find yourself doing all your own faxing, typing, and mailings. That's one reason small and medium-sized firms pride themselves on finding people who are willing to roll up their sleeves and get the job done.

Remember that having fewer working lawyers means small and medium-sized firms can't afford to pay their new associates $100,000 starting salaries. Thus, you generally find starting salaries in the range of $40,000 to $85,000 for small and medium-sized firms. Typically, the larger the firm, the higher the salary, but the size of the city factors in, too. In other words, Chicago pays more than Biloxi, Mississippi.

Who fits in best at small firms? The answer can be summed up simply: self-motivated people. Because smaller firms often don't have the resources to provide extensive training, working at one means that you must be a self-starter, because you won't be able to rely on as much supervision from the higher-ups. Medium-sized firms also value quick studies, but may offer more in terms of mentoring than very small firms. Either way, you need to be comfortable with the concept of business development, because small and medium-sized firms sometimes expect their associates to recruit new clients early on. At a large firm, this activity is largely left to the partners.

You may be thinking that small and medium-sized firms sound like a great fit and that you want to start off your job search as if you're looking for a job at a large firm. Using that tactic won't get you far. Small and medium-sized firms require a different approach for two reasons:

- ✓ **They can't always anticipate their needs far in advance.** They don't always know their hiring needs very far ahead of time and don't have demarcated hiring schedules. For instance, most of them don't hire a certain number of new lawyers each year; they tend to hire as someone leaves or they get an onslaught of new business. As a result, you'll need to keep querying them until you get a nibble.

- ✓ **They're often less visible than large firms.** You probably won't find many of them around for on-campus interviews (OCI). They simply don't have the time or the money to send a lawyer to your school for a day or two of OCI. Instead, finding them is up to you, and you do that through research.

Here are the job-search methods you need to undertake in finding a job at a small or medium-sized firm.

- ✓ **Putting your research skills to good use:** Small and medium-sized firms don't always have Web sites. And they're not usually in the news the way large firms often are, so you'll need to put your research skills into action to sleuth out their contact information.

  Start by browsing www.martindale.com, which is a free online legal directory, where you can search by firm size, location, and area of practice. You can also check your CSO for resources such as any local or state directories of small and medium-sized firms. Or, simply look in the Yellow Pages and start making some calls.

✔ **Writing a carefully tailored cover letter:** You want to distinguish your-self (and catch the hiring lawyer's eye) by making it clear that you didn't just pull the firm's name from the Yellow Pages (even when that's what you really did). Show that you've done your homework in your cover letter by mentioning either that newsworthy case the firm just won, a practice area they have that interests you, or a particular lawyer at the firm whom you admire. These firms are interested in finding lawyers who make a good fit, so don't forget to mention any ties you have with the city or town (such as having grown up there).

✔ **Including your résumé but making sure that your practical experience is explicitly emphasized:** Similar to your cover letter you want to tailor your résumé so that it emphasizes all the practical experience you've gained, such as working in law clinics, at summer jobs, and as a research assistant. Small and medium-sized firms are looking for lawyers who can handle significant responsibility early on, so they're particularly wowed by extensive on-the-job legal experience. Furthermore, they don't have the resources to spend much time on mentoring, so they expect you to be a quick study. Doing a good job at your past workplaces is evidence of that ability.

✔ **Turning up the schmooze:** Networking is of prime importance when approaching small and medium-sized firms, because jobs aren't usually advertised the way they are for large firms (on firm Web sites or at on-campus interviewing at your school). Attending local and state bar events, (see Chapters 16 and 19 for more on these functions) going to law school alumni mixers, and spreading the word to everyone you meet (see Chapter 19) are great ways of building a network of contacts.

Solo practice: A shingle of one's own

Not everyone wants to work with other people; many intrepid souls eventu-ally choose the solo route. In fact, The American Bar Association reports in its 2000 ABA Young Lawyers Division Survey, "Career Satisfaction," that 7.8 percent of young lawyers are solos.

Going solo certainly has its rewards: You call all the shots, you don't have to share the profits, and no one says you can't come to work in your pajamas or take a five-hour lunch break. And in spite of the popularity of Three Dog Night's song, one needn't be the loneliest number. Solo lawyers need to actively recruit business, so you'll be out and about and talking with poten-tial clients a good portion of the time.

On the other hand, very few people go *right* into solo practice as new gradu-ates for a very good reason: You have your work cut out for you. To put it bluntly, as a new graduate, you don't know what the heck you're doing. It's the rare person (unless you have plenty of pre–law school experiences work-ing at a firm) who can make it in a solo practice right out of law school. That's why most new grads interested in this path find a job and a mentor for at least two or three years before setting off on their own. But I mention it as a career option, so you can get a head start thinking about it and researching it.

Because the only person to whom you'll be applying for a job is you, several things that you can do *now* to knock the socks off yourself later include:

- **Taking relevant courses.** Forgo some of the theory courses in exchange for things like accounting for lawyers, negotiations, law school clinics courses (see Chapter 12), externships for credit (see Chapter 12), and any other practical or skills courses. You may find out later that doing so helps you out immensely when you're figuring out how to keep track of the firm's finances or need to negotiate with a difficult client.

- **Learning about business management and the mechanics of running a law office however you can.** Talk to current solo practitioners, job shadow them whenever you can, and focus your summer jobs (see Chapter 14) on working in small or solo law firms. Soak up all you can about the ins and outs of actually being an entrepreneur.

- **Taking a course or two at the business school, particularly those related to entrepreneurship or financial management.** Knowing how to write a solid business plan can be a key to obtaining the kind of start-up capital you need during your first few years out on your own. And knowing how to manage your finances will make you less dependent on outside help for this type of essential business ownership work.

Working in a boutique firm

Boutique firms are law firms that specialize in one particular area, such as intellectual property, tax, or environmental law. Boutiques are usually small and medium-sized firms. Working for a boutique is appealing whenever you have a burning interest in a particular area of practice and want to fully immerse yourself in it. You can find boutique firms the same way you'd look for a regular small or medium-size firm job (see the section, "Small and medium-sized firms" earlier in the chapter). Joining your local or state bar association and then joining specialized bar association committees is a wonderful way of networking with potential boutique jobs leads (see Chapters 16 and 19 for more on joining your friendly bar associations).

Becoming in-house counsel for a corporation

Working as *in-house counsel* means that you're a lawyer for a corporation. You have one client, and one client only: the corporation. Think of big corporations like Disney, General Mills, Simon & Schuster, and Boeing. All probably have several to many in-house lawyers staffing their legal departments. I'm including in-house counsel in this book, even though it's rare for new graduates to find these jobs, just to give you a head start in thinking about the possibilities. That's because most in-house positions generally require at least three to five years of experience. But it's certainly something to think about, and if you know there's a particular type of corporation you want to work for (like a media company or health-care organization), you can start gaining experience in relevant practice areas now.

Most in-house counselors will attest to the numerous benefits of working in-house. The first is that in-house positions tend to offer a better quality of life than firm jobs because the workweeks aren't as long and hectic and client development isn't really an issue (you already have your one client). Thus, lawyers can focus all their energies on solving legal problems of the corporation. On the flip side, you usually won't make as high a salary as in a firm, but at some corporations, stock options can be very rewarding.

Working in the public sector

Law students who explore working in the public sector are often amazed by the variety of choices that are available. Many attorney job titles are available in government, and you can find even more in administrative agencies and public-interest organizations.

Working for the government

You can find legal-related jobs at every level of government, from the city attorney's office to the U.S. Department of Justice. And don't think that you're limited to particular areas of the law when you work for the government. You'll find everything from environmental law to tax to torts. Working for the government will net you a salary somewhere in between public-interest and private practice jobs. NALP reports that for the graduating class of 2001, the median starting salary for government jobs was $41,000.

How do you find a government job? Many government jobs become available in predictable hiring seasons, so check the Web sites for departments in which you're interested. These job applications typically require reams of paperwork, so apply well before the deadlines. Another good way to find government jobs is to meet lawyers (particularly receptive alums) who work in the public sector and who can keep you informed of job openings before they happen and who can help get your name out. Informational interviewing (see Chapter 16) is a great way to go about doing this.

Working at a nonprofit

Nonprofit lawyers are some of the happiest around, because working at public-interest organizations is one of the most satisfying ways to change the world. *Public-interest* and *nonprofit organizations* are essentially the same thing; they're organizations often devoted to a particular cause, on whose behalf you represent people who can't otherwise afford legal services.

Nonprofit lawyers are advocates for battered women, animal rights, and human rights, just to name a few. You may work for an arts organization representing low-income artists and writers, a legal aid office helping people with such issues as landlord-tenant disputes, or an AIDS law organization helping people with disabilities overcome discrimination.

The pros of nonprofit work are many. You get

- ✔ Extreme job satisfaction — you're helping those who need it most
- ✔ A more relaxed working environment (no billable hours, client development, or partnership track concerns)
- ✔ Tons of client interaction and counseling
- ✔ Dedicated folks on staff

The cons to public-interest work include some of the lowest salaries around (starting salaries generally range from $30,000 to $50,000), which ain't good when you've got backbreaking loans to pay off. In fact, NALP reports that for the graduating class of 2001, the median starting salary at a public-interest job was $35,000. That's a main reason that many new graduates who'd otherwise love a public-interest job just can't afford to take one.

Finding a public-interest position as a new grad is challenging (but not impossible). Here's why:

- ✔ The number of positions is few.
- ✔ These organizations don't have much money to hire many new lawyers.
- ✔ Entry-level positions are hard to find because these organizations don't have the money to extensively train new lawyers.
- ✔ They want to see a high level of commitment, demonstrated via past public-interest work experience.

Set yourself apart from the crowd by garnering plenty of impressive public-interest experience as a law student. Try working as a summer intern or volunteering at the organizations you want to work for. If you show the staff lawyers what you can do, you'll be looked upon more favorably come hiring time.

Clerking for a judge

When you think of the term "clerk," you may imagine someone who works in a retail store at the mall. But a *judicial clerkship*, despite its funny name, is simply a mentorship arrangement with a judge — one where law school grads are hired to do legal research and writing for one particular judge.

Judicial clerkships are highly coveted by law students for two key reasons:

✔ **Prestige.** Clerking for a judge is considered an honor by the entire legal profession (especially firms seeking new lawyers). Not only are you working for one highly influential person, but all you do is legal research and writing, so when you finish the clerkship, you're assumed to be a highly competent researcher and writer. And that spells instant credibility.

Working so closely with a judge (and doing a good job) also ensures one heck of a reference after you're done, which is a powerful selling point in your future job searches. Finally, gaining all this valuable experience while clerking can open doors to you that otherwise would be closed because of your grades. You may find that firms that wouldn't even give you the time of day because of your grades are suddenly beating down your door to interview you after completing a clerkship. In fact, some firms require a judicial clerkship before they'll even consider hiring new lawyers.

✔ **Flexibility.** The flexibility of serving a clerkship can't be beat in terms of the period of the clerkship and your quality of life. That's because the job is normally a short-term job option. Most judges hire clerks for a period of one to two years, depending on the particular judge's policies. Many clerks view their jobs as good career bridges between law school and practicing law.

Because they're short-term by nature, many new graduates enjoy the opportunity to experience a new city, take some time to think about what they want to do after the clerkship, and focus on networking in their geographic locations. In fact, many law school graduates take clerkships to try out a new area of the country, without having to make a long-term commitment to it. Judicial clerks also have fairly set hours; it's typically a 9-to-5 job. Some judges even hire permanent clerks, and these positions are great for parents who have significant family obligations, because the job is an opportunity to use their legal skills and yet still have ample time for their families.

New graduates love clerkships because they're known to offer unparalleled practical experience. Because the main task of judicial clerks is engaging in legal research and writing, you'd better like it, because you'll do it 24/7.

Depending on the personality of your judge, you'll provide research for many different opinions, report the findings of your research (suggest the outcome) to the judge, and perhaps even outline or completely write the judge's opinions. Think of the power in that. You're the one writing the opinions and deciding which side should win! Of course, the judge has the final say in the matter, but you're doing quite a bit of the work.

Besides getting firsthand experience in potentially shaping the law, you also discover how to navigate in a wide variety of areas of the law. Regardless of whether you work at a firm, nonprofit, or governmental agency after graduation, clerks often say that you'll never be exposed to such a broad variety of law again (unless you later become a judge!)

Those who probably wouldn't enjoy the experience include people who:

- ✔ **Crave recognition.** Your name doesn't go on the opinions; only you and the judge recognize your good work.

- ✔ **Need a sky-high salary.** Pay for clerks is generally in the 40s to low 50s.

- ✔ **Dislike legal research and writing.** That's what your job description is, in a nutshell. Some view clerkships as the equivalent of writing a lengthy paper every few days.

- ✔ **Need constant social stimulation.** The work is usually just between you, the law library, and your computer screen.

- ✔ **Are not self-motivated.** You need to be a self-starter to meet tight deadlines and get your research and writing started.

You need to really flex those research muscles to get a clerkship, because although tons of judges are out there, few clerkship openings are ever advertised. So, after you decide to explore a clerkship, narrow down where in the country you want to be. Then, decide at what level court you'd like to clerk; your options include the state systems, with their district, appellate, and supreme courts, or the federal system, with its federal district courts, federal courts of appeals (circuit courts), or the Supreme Court of the United States.

Another clerking option is specialized courts within the federal system, which are often called *courts of limited jurisdiction*. They include courts that deal with bankruptcies, taxes, and intellectual property areas, among others. Of course, the higher you go in the court system, the more competitive it is to land a clerking spot. In other words, it's usually harder to land a clerkship with the state supreme court than with a state district court.

When you aren't limited by geographic location and want to clerk, start sending out résumés in the federal or state systems. Some clerking opportunities are publicized in CSOs, but most are discovered by individual students on their own initiative. You can find judges' names and contact information by going to state or federal Web sites.

When you're working on your cover letter, try working in a tidbit about what you know about the judge. If you're an admirer of the judge's opinions, say so. If you're impressed by something the judge wrote, mention it. If you can find out any personal data, such as the names of the judge's undergraduate and law schools or hometown, throw it in. Or, if you have an interest in the topic of their opinions, mention that. For instance, you can say something like, "You've authored the last five Missouri opinions on double jeopardy, and I'm highly interested in that issue."

The selectivity with regard to their clerks as a whole varies from judge to judge. Some judges, particularly in the federal courts, pay strong attention to class ranking and being a member of a law review (see Chapter 13); others are less concerned about grade-point average (GPA) and only want to know that you can research and write. Overall, judges have their own individual sense of what they want in law clerks. Generally, though, they're most interested in strong research and writing skills, strong analytical skills, and a degree of independence. Judges don't want people who can't make decisions on their own. Having outstanding writing samples, demonstrating your analytical and writing abilities, are paramount to include with your résumés and cover letter.

Setting Goals for Your Job Search

Setting concrete goals is one of the most overlooked but truly essential aspects of any respectable job search. I know, if you're like me, you're probably thinking, "C'mon, can't I just go with the flow?" But actually sitting down and setting goals helps you articulate what you want in a job, and lets you see on paper where your interests lie. When you merely go with the flow you risk conducting a scatterbrained, misdirected search. So take the time now to engage in some thoughtful self-assessment; doing so will save you migraines down the road! The next few sections pinpoint some key aspects to think about when setting your goals.

Determining where in the country (or world) you want to be

Figuring out first where you want to be makes your job search much less complicated. Think how much harder targeting your job search would be if you mailed out résumés to employers in Anchorage, Alaska, Grand Rapids, Michigan, Pittsburgh, Pennsylvania, and Pensacola, Florida, all at the same time. You probably wouldn't be as convincing about being a good fit in that many places as you'd be when concentrating all your efforts on only Kalamazoo and Ann Arbor, Michigan. That's because a golden rule of employer psychology is that all employers like to see some sort of tie with their cities; otherwise, they fear you'll leave if you find that you don't like it.

To make sure that you aren't disqualified because you lack a connection with your employer's city, it's better if you've worked in your target city during law school, lived there at some point, or gone to college there. The notion of a connection with the area is particularly important to small firms, because they're more focused on having associates bring in business, so any connection (such as having family there or graduating there) can sway the firm in your favor. Judges looking for clerks, however, usually aren't as concerned with any geographic ties.

Serving the public is clerk's biggest benefit

Robert Harris, clerk for Justice Simeon R. Acoba of the Hawaii Supreme Court, doesn't mention the tropical weather or Hawaii's beautiful beaches when describing what he loves most about his job. Instead, he says the feeling that you're doing something to help people is incredibly rewarding. Robert decided to work at the Hawaii Supreme Court for several reasons:

- It was an opportunity to meet and to work with judges at an appellate level

- He really wanted to see how the judicial process works

- It allowed him to learn about different types of law before going out into practice

More importantly, however, was the fact that clerking was an opportunity to work with a highly intelligent and experienced mentor for an entire year. In addition, Harris stresses the job of working at an appellate level. "Researching and writing cases is in some ways the purest form of law." Harris enjoys the opportunity to take abstract concepts taught in law school and apply them in real-life situations. Very few jobs, he states, allow you to figure how to resolve problems quite in the same way that a law clerk or a judge gets to do. Harris notes that he has met many people who have stressed that clerking was one of the highest points of their legal career.

As a clerk, Harris is assigned a number of cases and his chief responsibility is to brief his Justice about the important issues in each case and to assist in preparing the final opinion. Often, he and Justice Acoba will go through several drafts before the justice thinks the opinion is headed in the right direction. Then Justice Acoba will circulate it among the other justices on the Supreme Court until it receives a majority approval. In addition, Harris also has a number of other responsibilities, such as announcing oral arguments and reviewing recent decisions by other courts.

Harris says that the climate in Hawaii is a bonus, but he really doesn't get to enjoy it as much as he'd like. That's because appellate work entails a considerable amount of research and writing, and as a result, he simply doesn't go outside as often as he would with another kind of job. Clerks work pretty long hours, but Harris says perhaps not as many hours as at some firms. He usually gets to work around 7:30 a.m. and finishes around 6:30. He also works about half a day on Saturday. He gets two weeks of vacation. "To be frank," he says, "you don't do this job for the money or for the hours."

Looking back at the job search for his clerkship, Harris believes the greatest asset he had for landing this amazing job was the respect and trust that he developed among his professors, employers, and classmates during law school. Directly, this helped because his previous employer, and several of his professors, spent an enormous amount of time writing glowing letters of recommendation. Indirectly, the activities he participated in during law school helped create these letters of recommendation, because he interacted with his professors outside the legal community far more than most law students and thus had a better opportunity to work with these people. In addition, he states, the enjoyment he got from being active in law school clubs and activities helped him enjoy law school more, and thus be more successful at it.

If you positively must work in Seattle even though you've never stepped foot in the state of Washington, you'll need to come up with some pretty convincing reasons why you want to be there (and the weather ain't one of them). Having an area of practice that ties in with the geographic area will help in this department, such as wanting to practice maritime law in a coastal city like Seattle, for example. Also, planning ahead of time to register for and take the bar in your target city will help convince employers that you're 100 percent committed, because you're dedicated to the time and expense of sitting for the bar there.

Figuring out what type of employer you're looking for

Conducting a fruitful job search is awfully hard when you're *cross-pollinating* the gardens where jobs grow. In other words, when you're sending out résumés in search of clerkships, government jobs, large firms, and nonprofits simultaneously, your energies are split several ways, and your ambivalence can show in your cover letters. That's why I recommend focusing on one or two types of employers and really digging in by meaningfully researching those types.

If you're having trouble identifying the types of employers that fit your interests, consider job shadowing. *Job shadowing* is a fantastic arrangement in which you contact an alum (or a practitioner with whom you've had some sort of tie) and ask whether you can spend a half-day to a day hanging out in his or her workplace. Regardless of whether you just sit in a corner and observe or get to do something a little more active, you can get a firsthand look at the type of workplace, and all it entails — particularly when you've never been in one before.

Sizing up your employer

It's also important to determine what size of an employer you want to work for. This is really applicable only to firms; although when you're seeking a judicial clerkship, you want to decide whether you're going for a state or federal clerkship. After you've decided on small, medium, or large firms, you'll know how and where you need to focus your research efforts — on the appropriate methods for that employer size (see the section, "Exploring Your Practice Setting Possibilities" earlier in this chapter for more information).

Targeting your résumés and cover letters

Although the concept of the mass cover letter/résumé mailings may sound appealing (you just crank out a bunch of identical letters starting "Dear Sir or Madam"), these types of correspondences usually end up going directly into the circular file. Instead of using this broad-spectrum approach, you can increase your potential for job-search success by *targeting* your résumés and cover letters. That means you need to personalize your résumés and letters with useful information you've dug up online or through directories about particular employers from which you're soliciting work. Doing so may enable you to talk about why you're a great fit for that employer in your cover letter. For example, doing this ensures that your letter to the prosecutor's office won't sound identical to the one you draft to the public defender's office.

You may be thinking that your résumé surely can be mass-mailed, because how can a *résumé* be tailored to a specific employer? You'd be surprised! Applying for a job at a nonprofit calls upon a different skill set than applying for a job as a judicial clerk. For a nonprofit, you emphasize your nonprofit extracurricular and summer work experiences, perhaps by featuring them more prominently on your résumé. For a clerkship, on the other hand, you highlight any journal or other writing experiences and summer jobs clerking for a judge. See Chapter 14 for details of exactly what goes into a legal résumé and cover letter.

Making sure to always follow up

A polite phone call made about a week after the employer receives your materials can do wonders in boosting your application from the bottom of the pile to the top. All you need to say is something akin to: "Hi. This is Rebecca Greene. I'm just calling to make sure that you received the cover letter and résumé I sent last week, and to let you know that I remain very interested in your firm." Short, sweet, and simple. Ever heard the saying, "The squeaky wheel gets the grease?" Well, it's especially apt here.

Besides giving your materials a better shot at getting read, following up also sets you apart as someone with initiative. Only someone who's really interested takes the trouble to make a phone call. And you want to project exactly that kind of eager-beaver image (but not overly eager to the point of being irritating). After all, if you were the one doing the hiring, wouldn't you be impressed with someone who took the time to follow up? If you let your fingers do the walking, your acceptance letter will do the talking!

Figuring Out What Legal Employers Really Want

Welcome to the wide, wonderful world of hiring practices! I know from personal experience that as a law student, you often feel in the dark about what goes on behind the hiring committee's closed doors. And yes, many times hiring decisions seem extremely subjective, but that's why you need to arm yourself with as much information as you can about what legal employers want.

Recognizing the true weight of grades

Although it seems that every employer ideally wants to see the top third of the class, the law review, and top-notch work experience, that really isn't the case. Yes, it is the cold, hard truth that unless you're in the top 10 percent of your class or attend a top law school, you're unlikely to be hired at a *large* firm. But, after all, if only the top 10 percent ever got jobs, where would the other 90 percent of the class end up?

You'll find that every workplace has its own ideas about how grades and everything else fit into the picture. Many judges looking for clerks prefer that their applicants have stellar research and writing skills; some don't give a hoot about all those B-minuses on your transcripts. And small and medium-sized firms tend to place more emphasis on your extracurricular and work experiences, along with being a good fit, over grades.

The reason for these types of employers not being overly concerned about your grades is that these employers are selecting potential employees largely from the middle of the class, after large firms have snapped up the top people. Because distinguishing a B average from a B+ without more information is difficult to do, they want to see evidence of your legal competence outside the classroom. Solid work experience during summer jobs (see Chapter 14), work in a law school clinic (see Chapter 12), participation on a law journal/law review and moot court (see Chapter 13), and leadership experience in a law school club (see Chapter 13) all can catch their eyes.

Understanding the importance of attachments

As you can probably guess from any jobs you've ever held, your résumé and cover letter are important. These show your accomplishments and that you know something about the employer. But your attachments — your writing sample (s) and any references (either in list or letter form) — are equally, if not more, important, for some employers.

Some employers specify on their Web sites or employment information how many writing samples and/or references they want. Others don't specify, but you still need to send some anyway. The general guideline, if the employer doesn't specify how many it wants, is to include one writing sample that's about five double-spaced pages long. The standard for references is to provide one page, containing the names of three to five references. Law school professors and legal employers are your best reference bets.

Pay particular attention to your writing sample, because you can be sure the hiring attorney will go over it with a discriminating eye. Judges, in particular, scrutinize your sample for analytical skills and strength of your arguments.

Wayne Schiess, senior lecturer in legal writing at the University of Texas School of Law in Austin and author of *Writing for the Legal Audience* (Carolina Academic Press, 2003), says that when an employer asks for a writing sample, you shouldn't include the essay you wrote for your con law professor, nor the undergraduate paper that got an A. Instead, practicing lawyers expect to see the kind of legal analysis that you produce in your legal research and writing course. Schiess says that not all lawyers are good writers, but they're a persnickety bunch. They want a writing sample that deals with legal issues and analyzes them thoroughly: a memo or a brief. They expect to see a writing sample that's been edited and polished to the point that it contains no grammar or punctuation mistakes. And they don't have time to wade through something long. Five polished pages are better than 15 mediocre ones.

Preparing for an initial interview

You want to convey a certain message to all types of legal employers in your interviews. That message is "I'm interested, I know all about you, and I have what it takes to be a great addition to your staff." Beyond exuding this message in the three "p's" — preparation, presentation, and personal grooming (see Chapter 14) — you can astound employers in several other key ways (Chapter 14 also features detailed information on what goes on in the initial interview):

✔ **Before the interview, find out who your interviewers are and do some advance research on them.** You don't need to go digging up their FBI files, but you can enter their names in an Internet search engine, look up their bios on the employer's Web site, or type their names into www. martindale.com (a free legal workplace search engine) to find out where they went to school and any published law review/journal articles they have. Watch their expressions when you start out your interview with: "I noticed you went to my alma mater. It's wonderful to meet a fellow history major from Anywhere University!"

✔ **Do your research into what types of law the employer practices.** The last thing you need is to go into an interview prepared to expound on your commitment to employment law, only to find out that this is an estate-planning firm only. Review the firm's Web site, call up and anonymously inquire as to their areas of practice, or look around your CSO for any files on the employer.

✔ **Corral an alum who works where you're planning to interview, or contact one who used to work there.** One of the best ways to get the inside scoop for an initial interview is talking to someone who can provide you with the kind of insider information that makes it look like *you* did all the work! By talking to an alum, you can get the kind of juicy details that can impress your interviewers with what you know!

Acing the call-back interview

The call-back interview, in contrast with an initial interview, is something only some legal employers do. A *call-back interview* is where the employer invites you to its offices for a second (and last) round of interviews. These interviews are not so much interviews in the traditional sense as they are a mutual chance for both parties to check each other out. Call-back interviews give you an opportunity to get a feel for the employer. So, don't just sit there like a bump on a log, obediently answering questions. Instead, take the time to look — don't be shy, really look — at your surroundings. One question needs to run through your mind: Can I imagine working here?

You're generally expected to pay your own way to a call-back interview (for all but the largest firms). See Chapter 14 for detailed information on how to handle the call-back interview for summer employment, which is exactly the same for permanent employment.

1 Accept: Handling a Job Offer Properly

A hearty congratulations! You've done everything right, and you have a plum offer in hand for one heck of a job. Before you call everyone you know, whooping it up that you got a job, you need to seal the deal with style.

Responding to an offer with enthusiasm

Think about how you'd feel if you were an employer handing out an offer only to be met with a casual, "Hmm, let me think about that for a couple of days." Put yourself in an employer's shoes for a moment. You'd be pretty annoyed, right? Don't treat your offers with such casualness particularly in rough economic times. If you're ready right then and there to accept, then respond with an automatic "Yes! That's wonderful! I can't wait to start!" Clearly, you'll start off on better terms with your employer.

If you're not quite ready to commit, and you need a little more time, make sure to convey your needs with a positive attitude — not one that says this employer is the last link in your job-search food chain. If you're not enthusiastic, the potential employer may feel that it's made a bad decision and feel negatively toward you before you've even started! That's the last thing you want.

Finding out what's negotiable

After you receive an offer, you need to start talking turkey. Specifically, you need to find out exactly how much money you'll be paid, what the benefit setup is, how many hours you're expected to bill, what kind of clients you'll be dealing with, how much vacation time you'll get, and any other deal-making or deal-breaking stipulations you may encounter. If you're unsure about what exactly to ask for, talk with your CSO a few weeks before you expect to receive your offer. You want to write all these items down, because sometimes they're hard to remember when you're so excited about your offer.

As everybody knows, salaries can be touchy topics, and as a new lawyer, you may have little leverage. But negotiating is certainly worth a shot, particularly when you bring something highly desirable to the table (such as extensive work experience, fabulous grades, or a published journal article).

Dealing with Rejection

Alas, the worst has happened. You've been rejected — either as a summer clerk immediately applying for a permanent job at the firm or as an independent applicant. It happens to everyone at one time or another. The key to handling rejections with grace is to always act positively. I know — easier said than done, especially if all you want to do is sob under the covers or wring your former prospect's neck right then and there. However, because you don't want to burn any of your bridges, lest you want to work for this employer in the future, just grin and bear it, and save your outrage for a punching bag.

Playing the Waiting Game

If you're not accepted or rejected outright by your potential employer, you may be put on some kind of waiting list, similar to ones you may have been put on before you got into college or law school. As a result, you may feel that when you're in the no-man's-land of the dreaded waiting list, you can do little to propel yourself out of it and onto the acceptance list. But that isn't true!

If you present yourself as an enthusiastic, grateful candidate, and make sure the employer knows that it's your first choice, you'll be perceived better than the person who immediately gives up and withdraws or presents a negative attitude. Likewise, you want to show the employer that you're the right person for the job by asking whether you can do or submit anything else to bolster your case. These tasks can include providing an updated reference list, additional writing samples, or perhaps returning for an additional interview.

Chapter 16

Narrowing Your Focus: Choosing an Area of Practice

In This Chapter

▶ Keying in on a few specific areas of practice during law school

▶ Identifying the right area of practice for you

▶ Perusing some common areas of practice

Deciding on an *area of practice* (or specialty) is one of the most exciting aspects of the entire job-search process. For students merely beginning their job searches, focusing in on an area of practice can entail a great deal more time and work than you ever thought possible. That's why you need to start exploring practice areas as soon as you're ready to explore your career options by thinking about your personal strengths and skills, talking to practitioners in fields that interest you, and working summer jobs or finding part-time school-year jobs (see Chapter 13) in particular areas of the law.

To start you off right in this chapter, I examine why focusing in on a few specialty areas in law school may benefit your job search later. I know, you're probably like me, and just want to accept the first bona fide job that comes your way, regardless of specialty, but I show you why doing so is a bad idea and how to come to an epiphany about your particular area of practice based on your law school experiences. Finally, I list the 18 most popular areas of practice and point you in the right direction to get more information about them.

Focusing on Some Key Areas of Practice during Law School

Take the time during law school to gather as much information as possible about the areas of practice that interest you. Although you don't need to select a single specialty area, narrowing the field to only a couple helps focus your job search (see Chapter 15 for more about the job-search process).

Some people fall into an area of practice by chance, usually whatever area they happen to get into with their first postgraduation jobs. Others have a more personal reason for their choices: For example, they take a civil rights class and positively fall in love with the subject matter, or they've known from birth that they'd become estate planning lawyers because of their fondness for counseling people about financial issues. However, the majority of law students don't have a clue what their area of practice will be until they've gone through at least a semester of law school. More realistically, you won't really know what you enjoy until halfway through law school, after you have the chance to sample a few electives.

Choosing a practice area is a major decision

Although many law schools don't have anything like college majors, (the ones that do have something called certificate programs) some are known for their specialization and expertise in particular areas, such as Vermont Law School's link with environmental law. In other words, when you graduate, your law school diploma normally doesn't say "J.D. in Internet law," nor is your area of practice denoted on your transcript (unless you're participating in a certificate program).

Some prelaw students choose their law schools because they've heard or seen that the school excels in a particular area, such as corporate or entertainment law. These schools typically offer plenty of courses in the specialty areas, well-known professors in their respective fields, and sometimes even semiformal concentrations, or tracks, in them. Many students, however, decide to take matters into their own hands and informally specialize in an area of practice while attending law school. I was one such student. I informally specialized in intellectual property law, taking nearly every course that my school offered on the topic. Of course, some students prefer the liberal arts approach to law school, taking as diverse a schedule as they can without focusing on any one area. Whatever approach you take is completely up to you.

David M. Marquez, a third-year student at Northwestern University School of Law in Chicago, knew going into law school that pursuing work and experiences related to his personal interests would be crucial. For him, that meant legal work related to natural resources. "Growing up in Los Angeles," he recalls, "I was continually aware of the importance of resources like clean water and usable land." After completing the required first-year courses, he enrolled in every resource-related class offered by Northwestern, researched eminent domain for a professor writing a book, interned at the U.S. Environmental Protection Agency, and wrote a senior research paper about water issues in California's San Fernando Valley. Although he sometimes worries about being typecast as an environmentalist, Marquez finds that he often seems more certain about his chosen career path than many of his class-mates. "The old adage is true," he says. "You've got to love what you do, or at least not hate it!"

Understanding how employers view specialty applicants

Most employers don't expect you to choose an area of practice while you're still a 1L or 2L in school. But when they come across students who have, and who've also demonstrated their commitment by excelling in the relevant classes, choosing summer jobs in the field, and holding leadership roles in relevant clubs, they're going to be bowled over. In other words, showing this sort of focus can set you apart during the hiring process.

In fact, some employers value highly those applicants who show initiative in a particular area. They think that because you're this focused already, you're probably a better employee than someone who hasn't yet taken the time to figure out what he or she wants to do. Regardless of whether that's really the case, having an employer view you as more focused and committed never hurts. Keep in mind that boutique firms — the ones that concentrate in a par-ticular practice area only — may be more receptive to students with a strong grasp of their practice area interests.

One of the best ways, as a rising 2L, to sample a practice area in-depth is to land a summer job (paid or unpaid) in that area (see Chapter 14). When I was a 1L, I just wanted to find a summer job — any summer job. I wasn't too focused, sent my résumés to every legal employer I could find, and as a result, I wasn't as successful as I could have been at finding a job in my pre-ferred practice areas. By contrast, while looking for work during my second summer, I had two practice areas in mind and targeted legal employers only within those two areas. This time I ended up with a much better summer job-search experience, because I was better able to articulate in my cover letters the reasons I was interested in the specialty and I had built up relevant extracurricular experience in both areas. The benefit of being focused also translates into the search for permanent jobs (see Chapter 15 for more on the search for permanent jobs).

Putting On Your Career Counselor Cap

Because law schools (generally) don't have the equivalent of majors, you're more or less on your own to figure out which areas of practice interest you. I always thought it was too bad that law schools don't offer advisors in the dif-ferent practice areas, the way colleges do. However, you *can* form an informal advising relationship with a professor who teaches in your area of interest and can serve as a valuable resource.

No one expects you to be completely in the know about areas of practice right off the bat. I didn't even know that such a thing as areas of practice existed until after my first semester of law school, for heaven's sake! So don't beat yourself up whenever you don't have the slightest clue about what different practice areas entail. When you start doing research, particularly informational interviews (see "Informational interviewing with practitioners" later in this chapter), you get the idea soon enough.

You can, however, take matters into your own hands by figuring out exactly what the specialty of your dreams is. All it takes is a little self-assessment and self-reflection, as the following sections explain. Keep in mind that starting your self-assessment journey by analyzing all areas of legal practice is fine, as long as you're able to cross off the areas that don't interest you. Otherwise, your job search may grow too far out of control to be helpful.

Deciding what courses you liked best

Identifying your favorite classes sounds like a no-brainer, but you'd be surprised how difficult making these determinations actually is for many students. Some law students love everything; they can't decide from among the choices of family, real estate, or health law. Other students have it easy: They readily identify one or two courses that inspire them. A few, on the other hand, make it through law school without ever finding their true legal passions (see Chapter 19 to find out what to do when that happens). If that's the case for you, try very hard to narrow down the courses you've taken to at least one or two that weren't quite as bad as (or maybe were a little better than) the others. (I know, sometimes that's hard to do.) If you find that you can't even do that, then check out Chapter 17 for some honest advice about alternative careers in the legal field that may be more what you're (consciously or subconsciously) looking for.

The key to finding the best area of practice for you is being able to figure out what courses really get you excited every time you think about them. Did you ever read ahead in any courses, because you were so interested in the subject matter that you just can't wait to get to it? Have you done outside reading on your own initiative, such as law review or journal articles, based on topics you learned about in a particular class? Whenever you go the extra mile to find out more about what you've covered in class, that's a sure sign that class is an excellent candidate for being a legal specialty.

Nevertheless, when you're still stumped, try focusing on whether you enjoy *litigation* or *transactional* matters more. Briefly, litigation involves adversarial work, such as preparing for and going to trial, while transactional work involves making deals, negotiating contracts, and often making use of counseling skills. Identifying which of the two camps you fall into can make identifying the classes that you enjoyed much easier. For instance, when you prefer litigation, estate planning and wills and trusts probably weren't among your favorite subjects, but trial advocacy or criminal law probably were.

K. Bartlett Durand, Jr., a complex litigation lawyer at Bickerton Saunders & Dang in Honolulu, was interested in complex litigation even before law school. He worked as a litigation paralegal for eight years before going to law school, which obviously helped him a great deal in school, particularly because he already knew that he enjoyed litigation. Because he was focused on litigation, he took plenty of practical classes — negotiations, advanced civil procedure, pretrial practice, prosecution clinic, and mediation — to develop the tools he needed for the actual practice of law (as opposed to the scholarly development that is the focus of most classes).

Recalling impressions of your summer employment

Summer and part-time school-year jobs are useful for giving you an inside look at particular areas of practice. You gain up-close and personal experiences with the kind of work you'd be doing, with practitioners who are involved, and perhaps even with the types of clients you'd encounter.

Similarly, these jobs are particularly helpful in your finding out the truth about an area of practice. For example, as a 2L, I loved my classes in environmental law and thought it would be a great practice area for me. However, my summer externship (see Chapter 12) in environmental law confirmed just the opposite, that it wasn't for me at all. I found dealing with the nuts and bolts of environmental statutes rather tedious and couldn't see myself enjoying what I found to be its extensive theoretical and abstract side, each an aspect of the area that I hadn't gleaned from class. You may also find out that your summer job either confirms your interest or disinterest in an area of practice.

Bree H. Kame'enui, a 3L at the University of Washington School of Law, decided on her area of practice — the public sector — based on law school and pre–law school work experiences. Prior to law school, she worked in a children's service agency and in bilingual education. Kame'enui also had experiences volunteering with farm-worker labor rights campaigns, homeless youth camps, and tutoring English as a second language. She chose law school as a means for her to address the large gaps in service to low-income and indigent populations and to become an advocate for social justice. What further solidified her interest in and dedication to public-interest legal service was her public-defense work with juveniles, asylum defense proceedings, and Social Security benefits advocacy during law school. She hopes to continue working in the public sector in the legal aid services area or in public criminal defense, so that she can focus on the incredible legal needs of so many.

Determining what practice areas fit best with your desired location

You can find the more common areas of practice — corporate, securities, real estate, and wills and trusts — in virtually all locations. Other areas, however, are more location-specific. For example, when you want to be an *admiralty* (navigation and shipping) lawyer, you probably won't bring home much bacon in land-locked Omaha, Nebraska. Instead, you'd want to make a run for the East or West coasts, focusing your job search in cities like Seattle, Boston, or Miami. Or, if entertainment law is your bag, you probably won't have as much luck in Tuscaloosa or Phoenix as you would focusing your job search on New York, Los Angeles, or Chicago.

The best way to find out what cities are prime prospects for which specialties is by checking with people in your CSO, alums, and other practitioners. That's how I found out that Chicago isn't the best spot for practicing the type of intellectual property law that I'm interested in. By talking to several alums in the field, I found out that New York and Los Angeles, on the other hand, are. Whether such a realization makes you decide to switch target cities or areas of practice is entirely up to you.

Informational interviewing with practitioners

Conducting *informational interviews* is one of the most successful approaches to figuring out what you want to do. Essentially, an informational interview is when you make an appointment (usually lasting 30 to 45 minutes) with a practitioner to get information and advice about a particular field. In an informational interview, you're not soliciting for a job — instead you're just asking questions about the practitioner's field and finding out more about it.

Informational interviews, as opposed to formal interviews (see Chapter 14), have a laid-back and relaxed feel to them: No one is judging or scrutinizing you. However, you still need to bring along a portfolio with your résumé, a transcript, and a writing sample, just in case your interviewer asks for them (but don't provide these materials to them unless you're first asked to do so). You never know when your informational interviewer will remember that a colleague at another firm is looking for a new summer clerk or permanent associate and wants to pass on your résumé.

I discuss the concept of informational interviewing last in this section, because finding the right people to interview is made easier after you narrow your choices for an area of practice to three to five contenders.

Finding people to interview is easy: Just ask your career services director to point you to alums, look at the comprehensive (and free) online database at www.martindale.com, where you can search by area of practice, city, and even law school, or simply start rifling through your rotary card file of contacts. The key to conducting a useful informational interview is asking probing questions such as: "How did you choose this area of practice over all the others?" and "What courses do you recommend I take to best prepare myself for your field?"

Peeking at 18 Popular Areas of Practice

The range of practice areas you can enter today is diverse and ever changing. In fact, as areas of practice merge and overlap, dozens more are bound to become available in years to come. In this section, I give you a quick peek at the most popular areas of legal practice right now. This listing by no means represents *every* practice area (that would fill another entire *For Dummies* book). If you want to delve further into any of these areas, talk with your CSO and conduct some informational interviews (see the previous section for details). You can also check out an exceptionally helpful book, *The Official Guide to Legal Specialties: An Insider's Guide to Every Major Practice Area*, by Lisa L. Abrams (Harcourt Legal & Professional Publications, 2000).

Unlike doctors and medical specialties, lawyers and legal specialties tend not to have different salary rates based on how technical or prestigious they are. Instead, differences in lawyers' salaries are linked more to sizes and types of practice settings and number of years in practice. The only exception to this rule is the intellectual property field, where patent lawyers are often paid more than any other lawyers, mainly because they're required to take a separate bar exam, the *patent bar,* and usually required to have a bachelor's or advanced degree in a science, such as chemistry, engineering, or computer science (see Chapter 4 for more about how science-related majors can aid you in law school).

- **Admiralty:** *Admiralty* (also known as *maritime law*) is the law of navigation and shipping. An admiralty lawyer may encounter issues regarding shipping accidents, the regulation of cruising and yachting, nonpayment to boatyards and marinas, oil spills, water pollution, piracy, and commerce issues.

- **Art:** Art lawyers represent artists, museums, artists' foundations, and nonprofits in copyright, tax, and estate issues.

- **Aviation:** As an aviation lawyer, you deal with laws regarding aircraft operation and aviation facilities maintenance. You also deal with regulations for air traffic.

- **Banking:** When you enjoy dealing with finance, consider banking law, where you work closely with banks and advise clients on financial legal issues. You'll be involved in mergers and acquisitions, general corporate counseling, commercial lending, and litigation.

- **Bankruptcy:** Bankruptcy lawyers are involved with helping companies or individuals declare or recover from declaring bankruptcy. They also advise companies going through reorganizations and liquidations and assist them in structuring transactions to minimize risks in cases of bankruptcy.

- **Communications:** Communications lawyers deal with First Amendment, defamation, invasion of privacy, and libel laws, among others. As a communications lawyer, you deal with print or electronic media. The Internet is a huge part of a communications lawyer's practice.

- **Corporate:** Corporate lawyers are often involved in transactional work that involves negotiations and drafting contracts. You may help companies with the initial stages of selecting how they want to operate their businesses, with tax planning, and with mergers and acquisitions. Many corporate lawyers work in large law firms.

- **Criminal:** The two types of criminal lawyers are prosecutors and defense lawyers. Prosecutors hold government jobs; defense lawyers either work in law firms or for the public interest (for the government), often in public defender's offices. As a prosecutor you take the position represented by federal or state laws, prosecuting people charged with crimes. As a defense attorney, you defend people charged with federal or state offenses, including crimes that involve drugs, embezzlement, sex/pornography, various forms of misconduct, and homicide, with penalties ranging from a slap on the wrist to the death penalty.

- **Employment (Labor):** Employment lawyers handle work-permits, matters dealing with employee restructuring, hiring, termination, safety, and welfare. You may also deal with equal employment practices, affirmative action plans, sexual harassment, confidentiality agreements, and non-compete clauses.

- **Entertainment/Sports:** Entertainment lawyers work with musicians, actors, writers, and artists. You're involved in negotiating contracts, translating deals, and managing careers. You may also be involved in various aspects of motion picture and television finances and production. As a sports lawyer, you negotiate contracts and manage the careers of professional athletes. Sports lawyers work with amateur, professional, and international athletes.

- **Environmental:** As an environmental lawyer, you cover issues addressing land use, regulatory compliance, toxic substances, and potential environmental liabilities. You work heavily with federal environmental statutes and may be involved in policy work.

- **Family:** Family law deals with divorce, adoption, prenuptial agreements, alimony, and child custody. You can also represent the interests of children in family court, protecting them from abusive or neglectful parents.

- **Healthcare:** Health-care lawyers deal with medical malpractice suits filed against doctors and hospitals, Medicare and Medicaid disputes, and interpretations of the Americans with Disabilities Act. You may work with pharmaceutical companies, hospitals, educational institutions, health maintenance organizations (HMOs), and industry associations.

✓ **Intellectual property:** Intellectual property (IP) lawyers are involved with the enforcement of trademarks, patents, copyrights, and other forms of intellectual property rights. You can work on the transactional or litigation side in IP. You may also work in the areas of trade secrets, unfair competition, entertainment, and computer law.

✓ **Internet:** Internet lawyers deal with domain name disputes and are involved in litigation relating to cybersquatting (when another person uses or registers a domain name to profit from the bona fide holder of a trademark). You may also advise clients in need of help with registering trademarks, trade names, and service marks. And you may deal with computer software licensing, development agreements, and distribution agreements.

✓ **Personal injury:** Personal injury lawyers deal mainly with automobile and other catastrophic accidents, product liability, and medical malpractice. They are exclusively litigators who frequently are in court.

✓ **Real estate:** Real estate lawyers represent clients needing assistance with real estate finance, acquisition, closings, development, and ownership. They're also experts on regulatory issues that affect real estate activities.

✓ **Tax:** Tax lawyers help clients (companies, nonprofits, and individuals) navigate their tax returns, deal with tax problems, tax exemptions, and tax disclosure issues.

Chapter 17

Thinking Outside the Box: Considering Alternative Legal Careers

*H*ave you ever wondered what working in legal publishing, in law school administration, as a law professor, or in mediation is like? Ever wonder whether using your J.D. in an alternative way suits you better than a traditional legal job? If you have, you're in good company. Every year, hundreds of law school graduates forego practicing law with firms, the government, or nonprofits, in favor of opting for a nonpracticing alternative career. Such careers can offer you benefits that many traditional ones cannot, including flexibility, creativity, and variety.

In this chapter, I explain why some people choose alternative careers and point out the benefits and drawbacks of this option. I take you step by step through the process of determining whether you need to look outside the box and try something different. I also take a closer look at a handful of the more popular alternative legal careers.

Bucking Traditional Legal Careers

Even if you went to law school bound and determined to practice law, no rule says that you can't suddenly change your mind. Many students do. In fact, the National Association for Law Placement (NALP) reports in *Jobs & J.D.'s: Employment and Salaries of New Law Graduates* that 6 percent of the class of

2001 obtained jobs where a J.D. is preferred. Will you be one of those 6 percent? Although getting out of the mentality that law school equals practicing lawyer isn't easy, knowing that a traditional legal career isn't your only destiny can be comforting.

If you don't intend to practice law, you can use your J.D. in two alternative ways:

- ✔ **By entering a career related to the legal field that uses the skills you learned in law school (or where your law degree comes into play) as an important credential, such as teaching law, legal publishing, or law school administration.** This option often requires a J.D., prefers one, or makes having one a major selling point in your getting hired. These careers are easier to find while you're in law school, because the majority of nontraditional alums you'll contact for advice and networking chose this route.

- ✔ **By entering a career that's completely unrelated to the law, where you'll probably never use your law degree again (and be proud of it!), such as marine biology, teaching high school math, or investment banking.** This second option is a bit tougher to pinpoint because your options are endless, and including a discussion of the entire world of jobs that you can find is beyond the scope of this book (check out *Cool Careers For Dummies*, Wiley Publishing, Inc., as a good starting point). But your J.D. probably won't help you out much in these completely unrelated careers, and in some instances, can even prove to be a hindrance (when you have to keep explaining your J.D. away to suspicious employers). But when you're intent on pursuing a career completely apart from the legal field, go for it!

Amy Cook, a literary agent in Chicago, chose a career that utilizes legal and business skills, although a J.D. isn't formally required. She enjoys serving as an agent, because it involves a more creative component for those who enjoy writing and editing. Amy became an agent via practicing intellectual property law and then working in a publishing house. She believes the most important benefits she offers her clients are her experience with IP law and her contract negotiating skills. She recommends that students who are interested in becoming literary agents focus on IP law, contract law, and negotiating skills, and then go to work as an editor for a couple of publishing houses to learn the business from the inside.

As you can imagine, most J.D.s who decide to go outside the box choose a job that's related to the legal field. They do so for several reasons:

- ✔ After enduring three (or four) years of law school, knowing that your degree is being put to good use is nice, even when you're not actively practicing law. In other words, you can be content knowing that you're making good use of your J.D. but that being a practicing lawyer won't be part of your identity.

✔ Your starting salary for a job that prefers or requires a J.D. is likely to be higher than the nonlegal, entry-level positions you may find.

✔ People who go to law school are usually already interested in the law in some fashion, so they tend to pursue careers where they have some contact with the profession or practicing lawyers.

The best way (besides reading this book) to find out about the breadth of available alternative careers is talking with people, particularly alums. Although it may not have a *directory* of nontraditional alums (because the majority of students seek traditional legal jobs), your career services office (CSO) is probably able to put you in touch with some alums who are doing interesting and unique things with their J.D. degrees. Hearing their stories helps you reinforce in your mind that anything is possible when you're willing to think outside the box. Also check out the wide variety of books that specifically address alternative careers, such as *Nonlegal Careers for Lawyers*, by Gary Munneke and D.K. Tooker (ABA Publishing, 2002); *What Can You Do with A Law Degree?: A Lawyers' Guide to Career Alternatives Inside, Outside & Around the Law*, by Deborah Arron (Niche Press, 1997); and *Alternative Careers for Lawyers* by Hillary Mantis (Princeton Review, 1997).

Practicing law isn't an absolute necessity

No one says that you must practice law, especially if you don't like it or don't *think* you'd like it. But when you go straight into a career that's unrelated to the legal field after graduation, many people may harass you with the proverbial, "Why don't you at least give law a chance?" speech. The problem: Giving it a chance has its own set of problems down the road, such as getting trapped by a high-paying position or feeling like you're too caught up with clients and business to leave, even when you really want to.

People considering alternative careers generally fall into two camps:

✔ Those who knew before law school, or shortly thereafter, that's the route they want to pursue

✔ Those who went all the way through law school without a clue as to how they'd eventually use their degrees

When you fall into the first camp, you may have decided to go to law school just to get the legal education or to use your J.D. in an alternative career where it's required or preferred. That's wonderful; I applaud everyone who fits this description. You can move on to the section "Sampling Nontraditional Legal Jobs" later in the chapter, because you've probably engaged in all the self-assessment that you need to reach a decision about your preferred career path.

On the other hand, when your situation is more in line with the second camp, trust your gut instincts. If you're having serious doubts about your future as a practicing lawyer, it's probably because you never found a true legal calling, no matter how much you wanted to. If an alternative career is what feels right, then go for it, no matter what your friends, parents, dean, or CSO advisor may tell you.

How nonlegal employers value J.D.s

As everybody knows getting into law school isn't easy. You need to do well in college, take and ace the LSAT (see Chapter 4), and have a few personal or extracurricular achievements to round out your application, among other things. Because only a small percentage of the American population has a graduate degree of any sort, you've already distinguished yourself by showing motivation, the smarts to succeed, and the desire to continue your education.

Getting into law school is impressive, but making it *through* law school is entirely another animal. Just getting through those three (or four) years of blood, sweat, and tears signals that you have outstanding research abilities, can write pretty well, and are capable of quickly learning large quantities of information, all of which are attributes many employers outside the legal field cherish.

Proceeding toward an Ideal Alternative Career

If you're considering an alternative career, you know there's much to think about. You can't just say, "I don't want to be a practicing lawyer," and expect that your new job search will simply fall into place. So many options are available in the alternative arena that you're going to have to do the same kinds of self-assessment and soul-searching that are needed for finding a traditional legal job. (See Chapters 15 and 16 for more about finding traditional legal jobs.) Additionally, you must consider the many tradeoffs and compromises that result from deciding not to use your J.D. to practice law. For instance, you need to:

> ✔ **Think about whether you need or want to take the bar exam.** If you don't plan on maintaining an active license, you may want to forego the bar exam altogether (see Chapter 18 for suggestions about when to forego the bar exam). If you're going into a career that's completely unrelated to law, think deeply about whether the costs of the exam and prep courses, extensive studying involved, annual bar dues, and requirements for maintaining continuing legal education (CLE) credits after passing the bar are worth the benefits of taking the exam.

✔ **Consider what you're getting and giving up.** Sure, an alternative career is likely to offer you increased flexibility, better working hours, and more creativity in your work, but you must give up some things, too, such as a (usually) better salary, the prestige of being a lawyer, and the ability to enter the practice of law with ease after you've been out awhile. If you decide to enter business, an avenue that many J.D.s pursue, keep in mind that although you may make more money than a practicing lawyer, your hours are likely to be as long or longer, commensurate with your sky-high salary (especially in investment banking or management consulting). Politics may offer better working hours (overall) and more creativity in your work, but may require large amounts of personal (and other) capital to fund your campaign(s).

Pinpointing why you don't want to practice law

The first component of a good alternative job search is figuring out why you decided against practicing law. The reason: You want to avoid duplicating what you don't like about practicing law in your alternative career. If you don't figure out now what you like and dislike about practicing law, you won't have much luck determining what *exactly* it is that you want in your new career.

Although it may seem like a no-brainer because you're shelling out the big bucks to go to law school, at some point you probably entertained the notion of practicing law. If you decided before law school that you wanted to go into an alternative career, you've already covered this base, but I highly recommend that everyone else give this question some serious thought.

For example, here are some of the most common reasons that law students cite for deciding not to practice law:

✔ I hated law school, and didn't find anything about the experience that attracted me to become a lawyer.

✔ I didn't like any of my legal summer jobs and couldn't see myself performing the tasks of a lawyer day in and day out.

✔ I thought that an alternative career would better enable me to make a difference in society.

✔ I don't like what lawyers do; I find legal research, writing memos and briefs, and interacting with clients boring or distasteful.

✔ I went to law school because I didn't know what else to do with myself, but I still haven't found a passion in the law.

✔ I decided that I want to move up in a leadership position at my previous (or another) company.

> ✔ Through my discussions with lawyers, I became disenchanted with the legal profession and decided that being a lawyer is just not for me.
>
> ✔ I thought the legal profession would accommodate my creative spirit, but I was wrong.
>
> ✔ The income potential in another career is greater than what I can make as a lawyer.
>
> ✔ I need to work a normal 40-hour workweek or work part time.
>
> ✔ The legal market is so bad right now that I couldn't get the type of legal job that I want or be in the city that I want to be in.

If you're judging the entire legal profession on what you observed or discovered in your legal summer jobs, make sure that your experience was representative enough for you to honestly make such an important judgment. In other words, if the reason you don't want to practice law is because you hated both your summer jobs in labor law, the solution may be in finding an area of practice that better suits you rather than abandoning the thought of becoming a practicing lawyer altogether. Be sure that you consider your overall experience, including law school, legal jobs, and your conversations with practicing lawyers, when evaluating your feelings about the law as a career.

Pondering your personal likes and dislikes

Next, you need to think about your personality type and what sort of career is the best fit for you. Are you someone who can't stand sitting still (so a legal job behind a desk would drive you crazy)? Do you think you wouldn't like law because it lacks creativity? Do you need constant and varied stimulation, which repetitive legal research often lacks?

Here are some important questions that you need to ask yourself to clarify specifically what you like and dislike about the law:

> ✔ **In what situations have I performed supervised lawyerly tasks?** Think about the legal summer jobs you've worked (see Chapter 14), your work in law school clinics (see Chapter 12), or your job as a professor's research assistant (see Chapter 13). What have you liked and disliked about these experiences? Are they factors like writing memos and briefs, which you probably won't find in an alternative career? Or are they things like writing in general, which you probably will find in many nonlegal careers?
>
> ✔ **Do you want to be associated with or interact with people in the legal profession?** Do you enjoy being around lawyers? Or would you prefer a career that's more or less disassociated with lawyers and the legal profession?

> ✔ **When you think of yourself as a practicing lawyer, what feelings come
> to mind?** Pride? Prestige? Or irritation and disenchantment? Think
> about how your identity in an alternative career may differ from your
> present feelings toward lawyers.

Of course, if you discover through this self-assessment that you really are
interested in a traditional legal career, be sure to check out Chapter 15, which
provides everything you need to know about finding a fulfilling traditional
legal job.

Sampling Nontraditional Legal Jobs

As someone seeking an alternative job, many different options are open to
you. What follows are some of the most popular opportunities open to
(mostly) new graduates who don't plan on practicing law. Bear in mind that
this list isn't an exhaustive list; for more possibilities, talk to your CSO, nontraditional alums, or flip through some alternative career books your CSO
may have on hand.

Legal publishing

When you enjoy writing and reading and like to work on other people's written work, legal publishing may be a good fit for you. Legal publishing is a
wonderful career for bibliophiles (book lovers) and people who want to work
in a congenial, flexible environment, with optimum lifestyle considerations
(most jobs are 9 to 5). It's also a good fit for people who like working with
legal issues but don't necessarily want to be practicing law.

You have two main options here: legal book or periodical (including directory
and other legal resources such as loose-leaf service) publishing. Legal publishing may also involve positions in electronic media, such as developing CD
ROMs and other products, where you find innovative media formats that help
others learn about the law. General trade book publishers may also have
legal sections that you may want to look into, and commercial book publishers sometimes publish legal how-to books for the public.

Positions in book publishing may include *acquisitions editor* (someone who
acquires new book projects), *project editor* (one who oversees general editing
and coordinates all facets of the writing process), and *managing editor.*
Additionally, people in book publishing may work directly with authors of
casebooks and hornbooks (see Chapter 10), or may focus more on the product development side of the business. Periodical publishing positions include
periodical editors (who edit magazine, encyclopedia, or journal text),
researchers and *newsletter or magazine article* writers.

No single set way exists for finding out more information about the legal publishing field. One option is taking a look at your commercial study aids (see Chapter 10) and law casebooks to find out who publishes them. Or, check in the "law" section of a bookstore and look for the contact information of these publishers on the inside cover of the books you find there. Then you can do an online search for that company and find out their application policies or job openings. Alternatively, you can find out from your CSO whether any alums are in the field and contact them for informational interviewing to find out more about how to land a job in the field.

Law school administration

If you enjoy the university environment and want to work with students, consider a career in law school administration. Some of the positions that are open to new graduates who haven't practiced law include working in the admissions office, the CSO, the alumni affairs office, or as an assistant dean of students or dean of international programs. Some dean of students positions require a few years in legal practice, so that the person brings real-world experience to the job when counseling students.

Having a fairly regular workweek (usually close to 40 hours) is one of the best parts about jobs in law school administration. You'll also be working with talented, interesting students in a noncompetitive working environment and enjoying a more relaxed pace than in legal practice. In addition, many of these positions require or prefer a J.D., so you'll feel positive that you're bringing many of your law school skills into play on the job.

A good way to find out about law school administration jobs is through the *Chronicle of Higher Education*, (search online at chronicle.com), NALP (www.nalp.org), the *AALS* (American Association of Law Schools) (www.aals.org), and in the job postings often found on the Web sites of many law schools and universities.

Teaching law

All you need to be a law professor is a J.D.; no formal preparation is required of anyone who teaches at a law school; however, landing a teaching job at a law school is not as easy as it sounds. Although teaching law is an extremely competitive career, one in which you pretty much need a sterling law school transcript and a degree from one of the top five to ten law schools in the country to be able to choose from the best selection of positions, it's nevertheless a popular ambition for many new graduates.

Besides an amazing academic record, people interviewing for teaching positions also need stellar academic references (from their law school professors). Academic references don't have nearly the weight in other careers that they do in teaching law. If teaching law is something you're considering, start making the appropriate contacts before you graduate, particularly with highly revered and esteemed professors with whom you've taken courses. You want to shine in your classes so these professors can later trumpet your abilities to faculty hiring committees. Taking small seminars with research papers is particularly valuable, so that your professor comes to know you more intimately and can comment on your research and writing abilities more concretely.

If you aren't in the top echelons of your graduating class, aren't a member of the law review (see Chapter 13), or haven't done a prestigious clerkship (see Chapter 15), your prospects of getting a teaching job are doubtful but not altogether lost. If you didn't graduate from one of the top law schools, take comfort in the fact that law schools increasingly are looking for people who bring a special perspective to the study of law, which translated means a Ph.D., in a related discipline, such as economics or political science. Thus, getting a J.D. and a Ph.D. can help give you an edge when your academic record can't. Sometimes, getting an LL.M. (Master of Laws) in the area in which you hope to teach also helps.

Pure intellectual firepower also is valued in teaching the law; that's why only the cream of the crop generally are selected. The reason for this practice is that as a law professor you need to be able to think quickly on your feet in class, respond to students' questions and interrogatories with an immediate critique, and generate original ideas for scholarly research and publication purposes.

People love teaching law because it's a rare opportunity to read, think, and write about interesting things, work with smart young people, and get paid for all that. In addition, the pace is relaxed, because you're usually teaching only one or two courses a semester, and that gives you time to research and publish.

The best way to find out about teaching positions is through *The Chronicle of Higher Education* (chronicle.com) and the AALS (www.aals.org).

Legal journalism

Imagine writing stories about cutting-edge cases or legal developments in your community for a local newspaper, or freelancing articles for a legal magazine or newspaper. Welcome to the world of the legal affairs journalist. Although the need for a J.D. isn't a strict one when specializing in legal affairs journalism, having one serves as a huge benefit for most employers.

Legal journalists generally fall into two categories: those on staff at a particular publication (legal or nonlegal but covering legal affairs) and those who freelance. When you work for a publication, such as a newspaper or magazine, you're usually assigned articles to go out and write. When you freelance, you pick and choose your own projects by sending *query letters* (letters introducing you and the topic you want to write about) to publications. Some legal journalists do a mixture of both.

Because jobs in legal journalism are not likely to be posted in your CSO, you need to do some sleuthing work to find them on your own. One way to go about that task is sending résumés and cover letters to legal newspapers and magazines you'd like to work for, along with some *clips* (photocopied examples of your writing). You can find these publications by searching online or by thumbing through the extremely helpful *Writer's Market*. You can start getting clips as a law student by contributing to legal publications.

Mark Curriden, now a legal media strategist with the Dallas law firm of Vinson & Elkins, went to law school specifically to be a legal journalist. He was always fascinated with the law and with legal issues but never had any intention of actually practicing law. Curriden started working on his career early. As a third-year law student, he started freelance writing for the *ABA Journal* and built up a solid reputation. Right after law school, he landed a plum legal reporting job with *The Atlanta Journal-Constitution*. After spending seven years there, he moved to Dallas and worked for *The Dallas Morning News*. He also was at that highly ranked newspaper for seven years, until he changed gears and went to work for a law firm. As a legal media strategist, Curriden now gives advice to lawyers at his firm about how to deal with the media. Looking back, he believes his law degree was instrumental in advancing his legal writing career to where it is today. He says that anytime you're writing about legal issues, having a J.D. is significant. Curriden offers one piece of advice to law students contemplating a nontraditional career: "If you don't want to practice law, don't practice law. Do what you love instead."

Law librarianship

As traditional paper law libraries slowly dwindle and instead head into the electronic realm of computer technology, law librarians are gaining an even more sought-after set of skills: knowing all about the latest technology. As a result, today's law librarians are savvy electronic gurus who can help streamline your research time enormously with their vast knowledge of databases and other online resources. Because technology is ever changing, to be a law librarian, you need to enjoy learning about technology and be able to keep up with the newest developments.

Law librarian jobs are coveted because you're always:

- ✔ Working in a pleasant and quiet location
- ✔ Receiving immediate satisfaction from helping people dig up hard-to-find information
- ✔ Developing a better reputation for knowledge in your subject area
- ✔ Working hours that can't be beat (usually 9 to 5)

In addition, teaching opportunities in law school libraries are common, because someone has to teach all the first-year legal and research library portion classes or advanced legal research classes to 2Ls and 3Ls. Talking to law librarians at your school's library and other academic or law firm libraries is the best way to find out the range of duties law librarians perform.

Law librarians aren't limited to working in only law school libraries: They're also found in law firm and government libraries. Law librarians in each work-place specialize in different things and different areas of the library. Some specialize in government documents, while others focus on teaching law students or lawyers how to conduct legal research.

At many universities joint J.D./M.L.S. (Master of Library Science) programs are offered, which are generally four years duration. Most law library jobs require at least a master's degree, and although you don't need the J.D. to get a good job with a law library, the two combined enhance your options.

When you're looking for a law librarian job, check out the American Association of Law Libraries' Web site. Don't miss AALLNET's extremely informative section on Education for a Career in Law Librarianship, which can be found at www.aallnet.org/committee/tfedu/education.html.

Modifying Your Job-search Tactics

Your alternative job search isn't radically different from a traditional job search, but it may be slightly more difficult. This section takes a look at a few of the reasons why.

Convincing leery employers of your interest

One unfortunate fact of life for someone with a J.D. who's seeking an alternative career is that employers sometimes are suspicious when they know you've gone to law school but aren't practicing law. They may think that you couldn't get a job in law, and that you're just "making do" with them. As a result, you need to turn up the volume on your sales skills like never before.

Show them that their job *is* your first choice to allay their fears. Volunteering in a related capacity somewhere else helps you accomplish that feat, and then you can add that experience to your résumé and submit it to the employer you really want to work for. The volunteering can be done in law school, after you graduate, or even while you work another job. Another way to help convince an employer of your sincerity is to learn all you can about that employer and its work through informational interviews (see Chapter

15). That's where you meet with a person with whom you have some sort of connection (like an alum) and get advice and information about a career. Armed with the knowledge you glean from your informational interview, you can wow any employer into realizing that you're serious about this career commitment.

Touching up your old law school résumé

Your old law school résumé won't cut it when you're seeking an alternative career without some retouching. When you go this route, you need to look at your résumé from the perspective of your potential alternative employer rather than from the viewpoint of a traditional legal employer.

For example, if a job as a legal affairs journalist is what you want, play down the moot court and chairing the Bankruptcy Law Association and play up your writing experience. In fact, you'd want to include a special section on your résumé titled, "Writing Experiences" or "Publications" where you list all the relevant activities you did in law school and college.

The key is to always think about how your new employer is going to view your application materials. Using the same old law résumé when applying for a jury consultant position as your 2L summer job isn't going to fly; you need to specifically tailor your old résumé to your new alternative position.

The poster child for using a J.D. nontraditionally

Michael Uslan, an Emmy award–winning producer for *Where On Earth Is Carmen San Diego?* and executive producer of the *Batman* movie series, is an enthusiastic proponent of alternative uses of a J.D. He should know: The prolific executive and authority on comic-book history followed his passion and used his own law degree while working toward a successful career in the entertainment industry. It all started with his lifelong interest in comic books. Not only does he love reading them; he loves owning them, and he once amassed a collection of 30,000! Michael's path to law school began after he graduated from Indiana University–Bloomington with a degree in history, and, like many people, didn't know quite

what to do with it. Deciding to attend law school was the last option he concocted in a plan that potentially would start him on a pathway into the movie and television business. Then, he hoped his J.D. would enable him to inch his way from the legal/business side of the business over to the creative side, "when no one was looking." Although he had a great plan in place, he says getting into the law school mind-set was tough at first, but his friends and family convinced him to stick it out.

Uslan soon earned the nickname, "Phantom," in law school, because when everyone else was rushing back to study at the end of the day, he was rushing back to his apartment to write the next issue of *Batman* or *The Shadow* for DC Comics. Writing *Batman* comics had always been his dream, and he wrote them all throughout law school, which, he says, was "great therapy." During law school, Uslan came up with the idea of producing the definitive *Batman* movie, one featuring Batman as a creature of the night, the true Batman of the 1930s and '40s. This dream started him down the road that ultimately took him a total of 14 years to travel, obtaining the rights to *Batman*, raising money for the film, and pulling everything together when the picture was finally made.

Although Uslan says he was the only law student in his class with a burning passion for the entertainment industry, the Indiana University School of Law–Bloomington was extremely supportive of his unique interests. As a result of his alternative career aspirations, the law school allowed him to take and receive full credit for courses in libel and invasion of privacy through the school of journalism. He also took a copyright course and wrote a 104-page paper on the effects of copyright and unfair competition laws in the comic book industry. Uslan's masterpiece won an award for best paper, and he soon was busy devising a special curriculum in which he took an unprecedented six hours of independent study in copyright law.

Like many law students, Uslan went out into the real world and started looking for a job without any contacts in the entertainment business. But he got a lucky break, landing a job as a motion picture production attorney at United Artists in New York. At that job, which he refers to as, "the greatest training I could possibly get," he discovered everything essential to film production, including how to make contracts with stars and finance films. Later, he found out that he'd beat out 200 people for the job, including many Ivy League law graduates, because the person who hired him had "never seen anyone graduate with nine credit hours of copyright law."

With the equivalent of graduate school under his belt, Uslan went back to DC Comics, where he was known as an expert on Batman, and was able to raise the money for the movie option independently and acquire the rights to the character. The rest is history: *Batman* the movie series took flight. Uslan doesn't deny that he had completely different interests and passions in law school compared with his more traditionally minded classmates. He never wanted to hang out his own shingle and always saw law school as a means to an end. But he credits law school with giving him several key qualities that he still uses in his line of work. "Without law school," he says, "I wouldn't be where I am today."

Part VI
Wrapping Up Your Law School Career

The 5th Wave   By Rich Tennant

©RICHTENNANT

"I always assumed elves just naturally dressed like this. I never imagined it was a condition of employment."

In this part . . .

*W*ith graduation looming, the concept of the real world takes on a whole new meaning. In this part, I lead you step-by-step through the bar exam and take you through the exciting days leading up to and through graduation.

Chapter 18

In a Class of Its Own: Preparing for the Bar Exam

*T*he first thing you need to know about the bar exam is that it's completely *doable*. Sure, you've probably heard many horror stories about the bar exam throughout law school (or even before), focusing on how hard it is and how much it takes out of you. The truth is that in spite what people say, the majority of test-takers pass every year. And you can be one of them!

You've made it this far (either deciding to apply to law school or already succeeding in law school); don't let the bar exam be the one hurdle remaining between you and your dreams of becoming a practicing attorney. To ensure that you don't, I introduce you to the four sections of the bar exam in this chapter and show you what you need to do to ace each one. Then I explore in detail the features of bar review prep courses and explain how to decide whether they're the right tools for you. Finally, I discuss how to best use your study time and ways to increase your productivity as the exam date draws near.

Deciding Whether to Take the Bar Exam

Not every graduating law student takes the bar exam. If you decide against taking it, you're still a bona fide law school graduate (J.D.); you just won't be able to call yourself a lawyer (see Chapter 19 for a complete explanation of properly using that term). Although some graduates like to have the bar exam under their belts as something to fall back on, paying the test fees, taking expensive prep courses, and using three quarters of your summer preparing for it makes little sense when you're not ever planning to practice law (see Chapter 17 for more about alternative careers).

If you do not pass the bar exam and are not admitted to your state bar, you cannot practice at all. But if you're entering a career where practicing law isn't a component, thinking deeply about the pros and cons involved in undertaking such a time-consuming and expensive endeavor is wise.

The main purpose of the bar exam is to ensure that all of a given state's lawyers have the same minimal level of legal knowledge. Because they've all passed the bar, they have at least a passing knowledge of fundamental legal concepts, regardless of the quality of their respective law schools. And that's comforting for anyone seeking the advice of an attorney.

The Bar Exam, Explained

The bar exam is the final frontier for law students. It's the last obstacle you need to overcome before becoming a lawyer. The main point of taking the bar exam is so that you can formally be admitted to the practice of law. After you're admitted to a state's bar, you're all set to hit the ground running in your new career.

Familiarizing yourself early (such as in the first month of your final year of law school) with your state's bar exam application deadlines and registration procedures is important. States vary in how early you need to register with their bar offices so that you can take the bar exam. Some deadlines are so early that you need to start getting your application materials together many months before the actual exam. Although it is possible to register for a state's bar exam after the regular deadline has passed (by registering before the late deadlines), *substantial* fees often are associated with this procedure. In a similar vein, if you have a disability, make sure that you check with your jurisdiction early-on so you can find out what you need to do to receive accommodations for the bar exam.

The bar exam is a two- to three-day event, depending on your state, and that doesn't include the professional responsibility exam, which is given on other dates. The bar exam always takes place twice a year in late July and late February. Most people take it in July, right after graduation, but the small number of people graduating in December usually opt to take the February bar exam.

Although each *jurisdiction* (state, U.S. territory, or Washington, D.C.) gives its own bar exam, across the board, they're generally verisimilar. Because some particulars — requirements, fees, registration dates, and parts of the exam — differ between jurisdictions, you need to go to the Web site of your state bar to find out the specifics. For a comprehensive listing of state bar offices, check The National Conference of Bar Examiners Web site and click on "bar admission offices" for a complete listing (www.ncbex.org).

If you want to practice law in a state that's different from the one where you take the bar exam, you need to check with the new state to determine its policies regarding admittance.

The bar exam officially can have four parts. Some jurisdictions employ all four and others only two or three. The National Conference of Bar Examiners administers all parts of the exams, including:

- **Multistate Professional Responsibility Examination (MPRE).** A two-hour, 50-question multiple-choice test given three times per year (not corresponding to the bar dates) in March, August, and November. It tests your knowledge of ethics and professional responsibility.

- **Multistate Bar Examination (MBE).** A six-hour, 200-question multiple-choice test that focuses on core legal subjects, such as contracts, property, and torts, among others. You know, the stuff you learned — and have forgotten — from first year.

- **Multistate Essay Examination (MEE).** A three-hour, six-question essay test. It covers 2L and 3L topics, such as corporations, family law, sales, and secured transactions, to name a few. Only some jurisdictions require test-takers to take this particular test.

- **Multistate Performance Test (MPT).** A 90-minute per question test featuring three skills questions. Besides answering questions about fact analysis and problem solving, expect to actually review a client file and answer questions about it.

Always keep in mind that exactly what you'll be tested on depends on your particular state. States differ in terms of how many of these parts they test, and how much time (for example, a half-day versus a whole day) they allot to each part. To find out specifically what you do and don't need to take, contact the state where you're seeking admission.

Multistate Professional Responsibility Exam

The MPRE is the only oddball part of the bar exam, because it isn't given at the same time as the three other parts. In fact, you can take it while you're still in law school. Many people take it either in November or March of their final year, but it's also offered in August. The MPRE also is graded separately from the other parts of the bar exam, so your score on it won't affect your score on the other parts. Each jurisdiction also determines its own passing score.

Taking the MPRE while in law school has its benefits; however, some jurisdictions require you to take a certain number of law school credits before sitting for this exam; check with your state. For starters, taking it then gets it nicely out of the way. The timing also is good for another reason: The exam tests you on standards regarding a lawyer's professional conduct, which is the kind of information you find out about in your professional responsibility and legal ethics course. Most people take that course during their upper-class years (see Chapter 12), so the information should be relatively fresh in your mind.

Only three states do not require the MPRE: Washington (state), Wisconsin, and Maryland.

Multistate Bar Exam

The MBE features questions specific to the fundamentals that all lawyers need to know and most of which you discovered as a 1L.

The subjects tested include contracts, constitutional law, criminal law, property, torts, and evidence. You're asked 34 questions each in torts and contracts and 33 questions each in criminal law, evidence, property, and constitutional law. Each subject, in general, is weighted equally.

The overall multiple-choice exam is a hefty six hours long, but at least it's divided into two three-hour periods with a hundred questions during each period. You're also permitted a lunch break between the two parts of the exam, which you definitely need to take. Make sure that you:

- Walk around a bit, because you're likely to feel quite cramped after sitting through a tense, three-hour block of time
- Don't overdo lunch and wind up sleeping through the second part

As for the nitty-gritty of how to answer the questions: Each question is followed by four potential answers from which you choose the dreaded best answer. I always hated those best-answer questions, because my answer always seemed to be second best. Although you're not marked off for wrong answers, you receive credit only for correct ones.

Besides the immense amounts of law that are covered, the tricky thing about the MBE is that the questions aren't straightforward. Instead, they're written by professional test-makers who plot how to throw you for a major loop. That's why just knowing the law isn't good enough. You also need to know how to deal with how questions are written, and that's why taking a bar review course is a good idea (see the "Recognizing the Advantages of a Bar Review Course" section later in the chapter). After you discover the fundamentals of interpreting the question, you can better determine how examiners want you to answer.

If you're planning to practice in Louisiana or Washington (state), you're in luck, because you don't have to take the MBE!

Multistate Essay Exam

The MEE tests the same skills that are tested in law school exams, such as identifying legal issues raised by a fact pattern and deciding what is and is not relevant in that fact pattern, among other skills. (Check out Chapter 11 for more about fact patterns.)

The MEE is a three-hour exam made up of six questions about the following areas of law: agency and partnership, commercial paper, conflict of laws, corporations, decedent's estates, family law, federal civil procedure, sales, secured transactions, and trusts and future interests. Questions can test more than one topic, so jurisdictions can choose all or some of these topics to test in their six questions. Other jurisdictions come up with and administer their own additional essay questions, which can mean more or fewer than six essays to answer.

The MEE is not administered by every jurisdiction. As of this book's initial printing, only 15 jurisdictions require it.

Multistate Performance Test

The MPT is an interesting phenomenon; it's a 90-minute-per-question, three-question skills test that asks you to perform the kinds of functions that a lawyer encounters on a daily basis. It doesn't test knowledge of substantive law. Instead, it tests skills such as accurately interpreting documents in a client file and analyzing a fact situation from a hypothetical client problem. You'll be asked to produce an end product for each question, such as a memorandum, client letter, or brief, among others.

Many students often find this portion to be the least stressful of all bar exam components, because it doesn't test your knowledge of the law. By the same token, because it tests how well you can work with different factors, such as statutes, case law, and a client's facts, and then engage in a lawyerly task, many students think it's easier to handle.

As of this book's initial printing, 28 jurisdictions required this test.

Looking at the Character and Fitness Review

When applying to take the bar exam, you go through a screening process (background investigation) to determine whether you're morally fit enough to become a member of the bar of a particular jurisdiction. In some jurisdictions, you can't take the bar exam without first passing this review. Often, a personal interview also is required.

The character and fitness exam usually isn't too hard for most law students to pass; generally you're provided with several pages of questions, asking things like whether you have a criminal record or ever were fired from a job.

Remembering that you must fully disclose any past transgressions (such as an arrest or DUI) is important, because not disclosing is often viewed worse than the transgression itself (because you're lying now, and you committed the transgression in the past). In fact, the most common reason for applicants failing the fitness review is that they fail to disclose a transgression during the fitness process. Check with your particular state to find out whether a felony on your record creates a presumption that you're not qualified to practice.

Recognizing the Advantages of a Bar Review Course

The purpose of commercial bar review courses is plain and simple: to get you to pass the bar. These courses are generally six- to seven-weeks long and are like an intensive boot camp at which you'll probably learn more actual *black letter* law (straightforward rules) than you did in law school. Bar reviews usually begin about two months before the start of the bar exam and end right before it.

Much like commercial SAT or LSAT test-prep courses, bar review courses market themselves heavily on the rates of their students passing the bar exam. They don't teach you how to think like a lawyer (see Chapter 8), the way law school does. Instead, they focus mainly on tricks and tips for conquering each question you may encounter. One of the benefits of taking a bar review course is that you don't have the stress of taking all the bar courses (see Chapter 12) in law school — because you know you'll get all the information you need about the subjects tested on the exam during the review course.

Many students believe that taking a bar review course is a no-brainer. Much is riding on your passing the exam and sticking to a hard-and-fast study schedule is nearly impossible without the structure of a review course. Although they can be expensive (around $2,000 or more), many students are able to take advantage of early registration discounts that some courses offer.

When you already have a job offer in hand, you want to make sure to find out whether your firm is willing to pay for the cost of your taking the bar review course. Many large law firms do, but smaller firms and other organizations and companies generally aren't willing to. Some students take out extra loans to cover their bar review tuition and living expenses while studying for the bar exam. If you can't take time off to attend bar review classes during the day, you can take a home study program, or combine home and away programs, to get ready for the bar exam.

Bar review courses generally give you books of outlines for each subject area that's tested. These outlines are invaluable for getting the essence of the laws and concepts that are actually on the test.

Making you stick to a schedule

As everyone knows, tackling huge quantities of information is much easier when you have a schedule, and bar exam prep courses give you that kind of structure. They also provide you with an actual schedule so you can chart your studying and thereby know exactly how much time you can afford to spend on each topic that you need to study.

Scott Hairston, a corporate lawyer in Chicago, found that sticking to a tight schedule became easier the more that the pressure increased. During the entire first month of bar review, class was a breeze. He woke up, went to class for the morning and didn't touch a book the rest of the day. That all ended, however, four weeks before the exam, when he took a scored practice test and (like everyone else who blew off their studies) did miserably. The experience was a big wake-up call that forced Hairston to adopt a daily study routine, which began at 8:00 a.m. and usually ended about 11:30 p.m., with no days off, right up to test day. By comparison, when taking law school exams, he typically thought about studying the week beforehand and then devoting about a day or a day and a half to each test. It isn't that the bar is so much harder, but rather it's just that so much more is riding on it. The test itself was a big relief, if only to bring an end to that nightmarish studying. And, yes, he passed (and got to keep his job)!

Allowing you to take simulated practice exams

The other great thing about bar exam prep courses is that they make you take simulated practice exams. If left only to your own devices, can you really say that you'd sit down and take a six-hour test on your own time? Probably not. And taking these practice exams is one of the best ways to gain valuable experience: by answering the practice questions in a timed format. When you have experience doing multiple exams in a timed setting, you find out how well you can handle time-pressured questions, and that's key to doing well on the exam!

Using What You Know and Other Tricks to Prepare for the Bar Exam

Studying for the bar exam involves plenty of advance preparation. You need to prepare for it like the penultimate academic challenge that it is. Although courses that you took in law school, especially during the first year (see Chapter 6), help you to a certain extent, the exam features ways of testing with which you just won't be familiar at all. For example, bar examiners may phrase questions differently than you've ever heard or read in law school, and because most law school exams are essay (see Chapter 11), you may not be used to the multiple-choice format of the MBE and MPRE.

 When your bar review course begins, you definitely want to follow its recommendations for how many hours a day you need to study, but in general, several hours a day is highly recommended for the first month; thereafter, most students kick into high gear and study between six and eight hours per day until the test.

By far, the key to doing well on the bar exam is preparing far in advance. The bar is a far cry from law school finals where you can cram the night before and pull off a decent grade. With the bar, you shouldn't put off studying until well into the review course.

Chapter 19

Moving toward Graduation — and Beyond

*H*ave you ever noticed how enormous law school diplomas are? They make your college diploma look like an index card by comparison. Soon, that baby, complete with your new title, "Doctor of Jurisprudence," will be in your hot little hands! That magical time you've waited for is almost here — the day you can finally call yourself a law school graduate! Your three (or four) years of hard work have paid off, and soon you'll start a new life and a new job, maybe even in a brand-new city. If that's not exciting — and even a little scary — I don't know what is.

Although daydreaming about your graduation day can be a real blast, you need to take care of some more mundane business first. In this chapter, I walk you through satisfying your final graduation requirements, acing your graduation photo shoot, and keeping in touch with classmates. I take a closer look at the feelings of insecurity and doubt (graduation jitters) that hit many law students during their final year, and what you can do about them. I also discuss the all-too-common realities of postgraduation unemployment, and give you some simple tips for landing your dream job.

Winding Up Your Law School Career

As scary as it may seem, your days as a student are numbered. Soon, you'll leave the protective shell of academia and head into the unknown abyss of the real world. If you've been in school for 20 (full-time) or 21 (part-time) consecutive years, this realization can come as a real shock, and you may be nervous about what lies ahead. Taking things slow and tying up loose ends in a methodical fashion is the best way to gradually cut the scholastic apron strings. The first thing you want to do is make sure you won't have any nasty surprises on graduation day (such as your name not being called — imagine the embarrassment). That means checking with the registrar and dean of students to confirm that everything is all set before the big day.

Fulfilling all your requirements

Rarely do law schools not have several graduation requirements. As a result, you need to make sure that you've satisfied all of them before you ever begin thinking about walking down the aisle.

Some graduation requirements are easy to forget about, such as the common perspectives requirement (see Chapter 12), so grab a copy of your transcript and scour it to ensure that you've covered them all. If you still need to fulfill one or two graduation requirements as a second semester 3L, register early or alert your registrar, so as not to be closed out of courses that fulfill these requirements.

Making sure you graduate on time

No awakening is more rude than realizing you're one credit short, a few weeks into your 3L spring semester. If that happens, unless you have an understanding registrar or dean of students, there's probably little you can do besides making up that credit during the summer or next semester. Avoiding this problem at all costs means ensuring that everything is in order creditwise long before your 3L spring semester starts. Set up a short meeting with the registrar to make sure that what you're registering for second semester gives you enough credits to graduate on time. At this meeting, don't forget to review any courses you've taken outside your law school to ensure that your residence requirements have also been met.

Getting a Professional Graduation Photo

Strike a lawyerly pose, and show those pearly whites, because your graduation photo's going to serve you well for a long time. Almost all schools offer a graduation photo opportunity, usually in the fall semester of your third year.

The main purpose of this photo shoot is often to provide the school with a picture for its class composite, which the school usually hangs in a special hallway (or room) with all the other class composites of yesteryear.

Remember that you get something out of smiling for the camera, too. Most of the time, you can purchase your own photos from the proofs the photography company sends you, which are fun graduation gifts to give to friends and family. Plus, having something tangible (besides your diploma) that you can look at and that commemorates your three (or four) years of hard work feels good. Compare it with your high school senior year photo, and you'll see how far you've come!

Taking a picture-perfect photo

When having this photo taken, you want to put your best headshot forward because you're unlikely to get a retake when you don't like the outcome. To ensure that no one mistakes yours for one of those bad passport photos, check out the following list for some picture-perfect tips:

- ✔ **Wear a dark-colored suit.** Navy, dark gray, and black are good bets. Because your photo will be positioned in alphabetical order with the other members of your class in the composite photo, you'll stand out when you're the only one in the fuchsia suit. However, a purple blouse or brightly patterned tie can be a stylish contrast against a dark suit.

- ✔ **Sit up straight.** Your photographer will likely pose you on a stool, adjusted for your height and the height of the camera. Whenever you slouch, it's magnified in your photo, and you probably won't like the result.

- ✔ **Bring a small mirror and comb with you.** Your photographer probably won't provide items like these and probably won't notice whether you have a cowlick or a big chunk of spinach in your teeth. A quick check in the mirror enables you to properly arrange yourself before the shoot.

- ✔ **(Mostly for women) Ensure that your makeup looks natural.** What looks pretty in the bathroom mirror can look ghoulish on film. Especially beware of lipstick, which can look muted in real-life but like plastic clown lips on camera. Your best bet is to apply your makeup for photo day in natural light, standing next to a window. Doing so gives you the best possible idea of how your makeup will turn out in your photo.

- ✔ **Figure out which is your better side and face it toward the camera.** Almost everyone has one side of their face that they think looks more photogenic. For me, it's my left side. If you're not sure which side is your better half, peruse some photos of yourself, and compare. If your "better" side faces the camera at an angle, you're bound to like your photo more.

Making time for fun

Although your last year tends to become a little hectic with bar exam applications (see Chapter 18), fulfilling all your graduation requirements, and searching for a job (see Chapters 15 and 17), you still need to make time for fun. Don't get me wrong — all these necessary activities take up plenty of your time and are essential for moving forward in your professional life, but fun is equally important in satisfying your spirit.

As a new employee, in whatever work environment you choose, you're likely to be logging 50- to 60-hour workweeks, at a minimum. You'll think back wistfully to your 3L days when you had much more free time, and wonder why you didn't live it up while you had the chance. So, use your final year as the time to do it all (see Chapter 7 for details). Take advantage of all the opportunities a university setting has to offer. Remember that you probably won't have this much free time all at once again until retirement.

Putting your photo to good use

If you're temped not to order any copies of your photo for yourself, think twice. Even when you don't want to give them as gifts, you'll probably run into a few situations in your professional life when they come in handy.

For example, your employer usually features a bio page on its Web site (or promotional materials) and may request a professional photo from you. Your law school photo is a great one to use for this purpose, because it's recent and shows you in a suit and in a professional pose. Order some wallet-sized prints, and set aside several for this purpose. Besides, what else are you going to give them — a snapshot of you on vacation?

Reflecting on Your Law School Years and Looking Forward to Your Future

Your final year often is a time for deep self-reflection and assessment. For example, you can

- ✔ Look back on all you've learned and try to put it into a larger context.

- ✔ Think about the legal jobs you've worked and how they have or haven't contributed to your professional growth and development.

- ✔ Draw some conclusions about what the law school experience has meant to you overall.

As graduation nears, some 3Ls get a case of the graduation jitters. On one hand, you're excited about starting out fresh; but on the other, you're worried about leaving the nest. After all, this is probably the last time you'll be a student *ever again*. For students who enroll in law school straight from college, next year is your first foray into the real world, and that's a scary proposition. Even students who took some time off before law school may have forgotten what punching the timecard is like.

The final year for some law students also is marked with nagging feelings of self-doubt and insecurity. For example:

- Some students wonder whether three (or four) years and $80,000 was really worth it for a degree that they may be ambivalent about.

- Nontraditional students who sacrificed a previous career or family obligations to attend law school may be stressed when they realize that a law degree doesn't always equal the job of their dreams.

- The lucky ones with job offers in hand may start to wonder whether they can hack it in the dog-eat-dog legal world.

- Others doubt how much they've actually learned and wonder how good of a lawyer they're really going to be.

If you still haven't found your legal passion, or if you disliked your summer jobs in the legal field (see Chapter 14), and still don't know what you want to do, you may feel like you're floundering about. This situation can lead to anxiety and even panic, as you realize that your grace period is about to come to an end. Hearing classmates talking with excitement about their recent job offers and the *new lives* they'll be starting after graduation is hard to do when your future still is uncertain. Nevertheless, the next few sections explain some simple ways for sorting through these complicated feelings.

Figuring out what you want to do on your timetable

If you're unsure about your career plans in your final year, take your time in figuring things out. The end of the world hasn't come even if you're still unemployed at the end of the summer or even six months down the road. In fact, taking some time off between law school and your new job is an empowering way to recharge your batteries and find yourself. After all, when will you get such an extensive break again once you're gainfully employed? The following list details some productive methods for figuring out what you want to do in your final year, at your own pace:

✔ **Continue (or start) doing informational interviews.** *Informational interviewing* is best described like this: You meet informally with a practitioner to get information, advice, and further contacts. You're not actually announcing that you're looking for a job, but you are making known the fact that you're looking for advice and networking opportunities, so your interviewer (and anyone else) thinks of you when any new job openings arise. Informational interviewing also is an excellent way to gain general information about a field. See Chapter 16 for more details about this topic.

✔ **Job shadow as many people as you can.** *Job shadowing* is when you spend a half or whole day on the job with a job-shadow host. You observe what that person does during a typical day. In the process, you discover valuable information about how much time that person spends on paperwork or client contact. A day of job shadowing, although not conclusive, helps you determine whether you're well suited to a career. Chapter 15 has more information about job shadowing.

✔ **Research careers that are outside the box.** Whenever you're unsure whether you really want to be a lawyer, start considering the myriad jobs out there where a J.D. is an asset but also where you're not practicing law. Ask your career services office (CSO) to put you in contact with alums from your school who are working in alternative careers and then arrange to job shadow and conduct informational interviews with them as much as you can. Check out Chapter 17 for more details about careers outside the box.

✔ **Talk with as many people as possible regarding any doubts about the law.** If your career plans are uncertain in your final year because you're just not sure whether the law is for you, share your concerns with caring CSO staff, your dean of students, or alums. You'll soon find out that many people with J.D.s have (or had), doubts about whether law is really the right career for them. Keep in mind that you're far from alone when you didn't know from the first day of torts that the law was definitely for you.

✔ **See a new career counselor.** When your law school's CSO just isn't doing it for you, for whatever reason, take matters into your own hands. Perhaps it's time to seek out a different career counselor, either in the undergraduate CSO (if you're at a university) or through a private career counselor. Of course, private career counselors don't work cheap, but if you're truly undecided in your career plans or professional path, discussing your situation with a career counselor is an investment you at least need to think about. Spending a few hundred dollars now on professional advice can save you thousands in heartache and job changes later.

✔ **Read plenty of job-advice books.** This tactic is a good (and cheap) substitute for hiring a live private career counselor. You can find these books in your local bookstore in either self-help or careers sections.

Many great books of this type are available and can be helpful in getting your juices flowing by identifying

- Jobs that match your personality type
- Characteristics you need in your ideal job
- Names and descriptions of job titles that are available

In fact, you may want to check out *Cool Careers For Dummies* (Wiley Publishing, Inc.), which features a comprehensive list of many unique-sounding careers, including a section on jobs that are related to the legal field.

Ignoring people who think they know what's best for you

As tempting as it is for parents, friends, and significant others to *tell* you what they think is best for you, I suggest kindly thanking them for their advice but then ignoring them. Although doing so is difficult, it's really in your best interest, particularly when people close to you are saying negative things about your plans to pursue a nontraditional (or unrelated) career or when they're urging you to give law a fair try before giving up on it.

At this point in your life, you need to make your professional decisions based on what *you* think is best for you and not on other people's opinions. When their comments get out of hand, politely tell them that you appreciate their advice, but that as an adult, your life decisions are yours alone to make. That's the best way to get them to pipe down.

Avoiding feelings of guilt about wasting your degree

Some students in their last year know already that the law absolutely isn't for them, and that they want to pursue a completely different path (see Chapter 17). Whether you opt for a nontraditional or completely unrelated career, never feel guilty about wasting your J.D. After all, you're not *wasting* it; you're just using it in an alternative and creative way.

No one disputes that spending three (or four) years and tens of thousands of dollars on a rigorous education only to say *sayonara* for another career path is difficult, regardless of whether it's entrepreneurship, legal publishing, or medicine. However, saying sayonara is much easier when you have a positive attitude about what earning your degree gives you and how you can parlay it into your new career.

The following list may help put these benefits in better focus:

- ✔ **When you're not using the degree in the typical way (you're going to be an artist, dentist, or musician), view law school as a three-year detour.** You came, you saw, you tried, but you just didn't like it. That's perfectly okay, and don't let anyone try to convince you otherwise. Your legal education has added to your intellectual knowledge base, which is a valuable commodity in and of itself. The skills you learn in law school will always be helpful to you, regardless of whether you're negotiating your own contracts or speaking in front of a crowd.

  Keep in mind that most people work in an average of seven different careers during their lifetimes. Law school counts as one of those careers, and it puts you in a much better position for knowing what you do and don't like about jobs in general.

- ✔ **Although you may feel that you're in *exactly* the same place that you were before law school, you're not.** You've grown in many ways that you just can't identify right now. For instance, you've discovered

  - The nature of American society

  - The justice system and how it works

  - The art of logical thinking and advanced problem solving

  - How to conduct extensive research and writing projects

  - The challenge of speaking in front of large groups

  These few examples probably don't even begin to skim the surface of what you're taking away from your law school experience, consciously or not. Make your own list, and internalize it, so you can remind yourself exactly how far you've come.

Treasuring the Magic of Your Graduation Day

The light at the end of the tunnel is finally here — your graduation day! If your school is like most, graduation takes place on a weekend, and you're scheduled to attend dinners and other festivities planned by the school, such as a mix-and-mingle cocktail party for friends and family.

Make sure to purchase (if required) enough tickets to these events well ahead of time; your Aunt Millie won't be too pleased if she's left out.

On the day of the actual ceremony, make sure that you:

✔ Know where to be for any school-sponsored group photos and at what time

✔ Note when and where you actually have to line up to march

✔ Make sure you've brought your cap and gown (You wouldn't want to march without them, and you usually pick them up a few days before the ceremony.)

✔ Find out how you need to shake hands with your presenter as you receive your diploma

At many law schools, you won't receive your actual diploma on graduation day — instead, you'll get a plain old piece of paper that says "Congratulations!" or the equivalent. At these schools, diplomas are mailed in July or August after the spring semester exams are graded and overall credits are tallied. If you didn't pass your exams or satisfy all your graduation requirements, you won't receive a diploma at that time.

Although these may seem like fairly simple things to remember, you'd be surprised how many students are tripped up by the distractions of all the graduation activities and events.

Can you call yourself a lawyer now?

Many law students wonder about the following question: When you become a law school graduate, are you actually considered a lawyer yet? Although the term "lawyer" is thrown around causally, you technically shouldn't refer to yourself as a lawyer until you actually pass the bar exam and are admitted to the bar of your state. Until that glorious day, you should refer to yourself only as a "J.D." or "law school graduate." That's because people who haven't passed the bar exam and aren't admitted also aren't permitted to perform lawyerly tasks (see Chapter 18 for more details).

After you pass the bar exam and are admitted to the bar, you're a bona fide lawyer or *attorney at law*. With both titles, you can also add "Esquire" (or "Esq.") after your name. If you work in a nonlegal position after you pass the bar exam and are admitted, you can call yourself a lawyer but not a practicing lawyer (more specifically you're a nonpracticing member of the state bar). In other words, only when you're actively engaged in the practice of law are you a *practicing lawyer.* But no matter what you go on to do in life, you'll always be able to write "J.D." after your name.

On graduation day, and up until you pass the bar exam and are admitted to the bar, you're a J.D. or a law school graduate, no matter how frequently your parents brag about you as "my daughter (or son), the lawyer."

Saying goodbye to your home

Saying goodbye to your friends, your professors, and the campus is difficult. You've called this place home for three (or four) years, and now it's time to pack up and leave. Make sure that you take plenty of photos of your classmates, the law school, and the surrounding campus. So many students leave without having even a single photo of the school. Even if you don't want to make a scrapbook, you'll appreciate having a few mementos of your time there.

Keeping in Touch with Classmates

Regardless of whether you loved or didn't care for your classmates, the reality is that you'll probably never see most of these people ever again. Everyone disperses to various parts of the country and sets out on their own professional paths. You included.

So, even if you're ambivalent about missing your peers now, you may want to try to maintain ties with them. In a few months, you'll want to compare battle stories, talk about how your jobs are treating you, and find out what life is like in other cities. In that case, you need to start collecting contact information soon.

Starting a rotary card file of classmate contacts

Because graduation is too hectic a time for gathering new contact information from your classmates, you need to take care of that task a few weeks beforehand. If you don't have an actual rotary card file, make notes on index cards and store them in an index card file. Don't forget to take down e-mail addresses, because the computer probably is the best way to get ahold of busy, fledgling attorneys.

Remembering they're your colleagues now

That guy who used to show off at all the 1L parties? Yep, he's working across the hall from you now. Your former study-group partner may soon start referring you business. Your old roommate may be your opposing counsel on a case. After graduation day, the folks who used to be your classmates are your colleagues, however mind-boggling that prospect may seem. When you first start thinking about your future as a real lawyer, it kind of blows your mind, but pretty soon, after seeing your old buddies in suits everyday rather than jeans and a T-shirt, reality starts sinking in.

Dealing with the Prospect of Being Unemployed at Graduation

Being unemployed at gradation (or beyond) isn't the unheard of situation that it was before the dot-com bubble burst. In fact, you'll probably find that many of your classmates are in the same predicament as you.

Looking through the Web pages of many law school CSOs, you're likely to find some sort of statistic showing what percentage of the school's students were *employed* six (or nine) months after graduation. Interestingly enough, some of the time that statistic isn't broken down to say in what *types* of jobs those graduates were employed. That should comfort you, because it means that even when the percentage is high, the likelihood that every single one of last year's graduates found *legal* positions right after graduation is not that great. Some of them are probably working in nonlegal positions, legal temping, and maybe even a few are at fast-food joints, I'll bet.

Donna Gerson, former director of career services at the University of Pittsburgh School of Law, and author of *Choosing Small, Choosing Smart: Job Search Strategies for Lawyers in the Small Firm Market* (NALP, 2001), advises you not to panic when graduation day is drawing closer and you're still without a job. She says that this situation isn't unusual, particularly in a down market. Gerson points out that you can take some positive steps to harness your anxious energy and position yourself for full-time employment. Specifically, she recommends that you:

✔ **Focus on passing the bar exam the first time you take it.** Many legal employers, particularly small and mid-sized firms, hire only licensed attorneys. Thus, passing the bar exam can be the key credential that helps you get hired.

> ✔ **Continue searching for a job throughout the summer by checking job postings through your CSO on a weekly basis, arranging informational interviews, and attending networking events.**

After the bar exam is over, Gerson recommends that you consider working for a legal temp agency to make use of your skills. Not only can temp positions turn into full-time positions, but the structure and routine of work keeps you focused on your ultimate career goal of finding a full-time position, helps build your résumé, and generates some income.

Despite trying to maintain an optimistic outlook, it's hard to ignore the fact that being unemployed at graduation doesn't feel all that great. Being in that position can take some of the joy out of a festive occasion, especially when you realize that you're moving right back in with mom and dad after the ceremony or starting your new job as a waitress the next day. But, as the next few sections explain, you can do many proactive things to improve your job prospects.

Start spreading the news

If you're planning to stick around the city in which your law school is located, use your last semester to make contacts in your field of interest. Find every single local alum and talk them into having coffee. Be as aggressive as possible in making sure that your name is circulating, even when you feel like you're being a pest. Keeping in frequent touch with these alums or other contact you come across may help them suddenly remember your name the moment a colleague mentions that he or she is looking for a new associate.

When you plan to move to a new city, you want to do the same types of things, but in this case, you'll rely more on e-mail and the telephone while you're long-distance job searching during your last semester of law school. Again, find out the names of all your school's alums in your new city, e-mail them, and set up meetings with them when you're in town. During your last semester's spring break is a prime time for doing this vital task, so be sure to schedule a week's worth of appointments in your target city whenever possible.

When you let everyone with whom you come into contact know that you're looking for advice and information about a field in their city, opportunities start happening for you. After all, when people don't know that you're looking, they can't present you with the opportunities that do come around.

Moving to your desired city and getting involved

If you're still unemployed after graduation, you may want to move to your new city and take the bar exam (if you're planning to practice law) or start getting involved (for all jobs). If you're not busy studying for the bar, you can at least get a few months' head start.

As you settle in, you have many options (besides alumni networking) that you can use to improve your chances of landing your ideal job. These suggestions are also good even if you need a bit of a breather after law school (or the bar exam), and don't want to start work at your permanent job right away:

- ✔ **Work as a legal temp.** Yep, that's right, they have temps in the legal field, too. Just sign on with a legal temping firm (many cities have them, but they tend to cluster in the larger cities). You'll do short-term projects for as long as you're available and be paid by the hour. If you've passed the bar exam, you get bigger and better projects, but you can still be a temp even without passing the bar exam at most temp agencies.

  Although you won't receive any perks or benefits, your pay will surely net you more than if you work in some other service type of job. The main benefit of temping is that you can sample a variety of workplaces and areas of practice, and if you impress an employer, that can be your back-door ticket to a full-time job!

- ✔ **Volunteer to do the kind of work you'd really like to do.** Move to your desired city, and if there's a nonprofit that's in your ideal area of practice, spend a few months helping out wherever you're needed. That way, when any of the organization's attorneys hear of openings, you'll be perched right under their noses and first on their minds.

- ✔ **Get a random, temporary job.** Working as a temp to make ends meet is okay, but during your free time be sure that you continue to send out cover letters and résumés, attend local bar association functions, and get your name out within the legal community.

- ✔ **Join your state or local bar association and start attending functions.** Mixing and mingling with lawyers (and potential employers) is another important way of getting your name and interest in a particular practice area out there. Sign up for a committee or two in your area of interest and attend continuing legal education seminars. Don't be shy — go right up and introduce yourself! You may want to get some inexpensive business cards made up to hand out on the spot.

Part VII
The Part of Tens

In this part . . .

If you're familiar with the *For Dummies* series, you know that you can find a bunch of amusing and informative top-ten lists toward the end of the book. In this part, I've put together lists of useful law school resources, the best and worst things about law school, and little-known law school secrets.

Chapter 20

Ten Plus User-Friendly Law School Resources

. . . .

In This Chapter

▶ Knowing where to find the most useful resources

▶ Checking out various Web sites, magazines, and newsletters

. . . .

*F*or most people, using the Internet on a daily basis has become second nature (not to mention a great method of procrastination!). In fact, all through law school I spent countless hours checking out various law-related Web sites when I needed to be reading contracts or finishing up a legal research assignment. But never fear — all my surfing didn't go to waste. As a result, in this chapter, I'm able to provide you with some of the best law school–related Web sites. Just promise me that you won't surf with those newfangled wireless Internet devices in class; they're a new pet peeve for professors! In addition to Internet resources, I fill you in about various magazines and newsletters that you can read to find up-to-date information about law school culture, issues pertaining to women and minority students, and working in a legal career.

Perusing Ten (or So) Useful Web Sites

Besides Lexis and Westlaw, the two legal research Web sites that you'll no doubt use extensively during your law school career (see Chapter 10 for more info), you have myriad other great Web sites at your disposal. For example,

> ✔ **Cornell Law School's Legal Information Institute** (www.law.cornell. edu): Been asked to research an unfamiliar area of the law? Never fear, the Legal Information Institute site steers you in the right direction. It offers links to many primary law sources, including court opinions, constitutions and codes, and it provides context for whatever area of the law you're looking up. Trust me, you can't go wrong by bookmarking this site and referring to it often.

✔ **NonTradLaw.com** (`www.nontradlaw.com`): If you're a nontraditional law student, in whatever permutation, be ready to dig in to this Web site! Tailor-made just for you, it features a discussion forum (where you can read postings and post your own) and a chat room.

✔ **HierosGamos** (`www.hg.org/students.html`): Although its name sounds unusual, this site is not to be missed. Browse around and discover information about law school rankings, the bar exam, and preparing for law school exams. You can spend days surfing this site and still not read everything!

✔ **Jurist: The Legal Education Network** (`http://jurist.law.pitt.edu`): This comprehensive and impressive site gives you law school news, law school admissions information, and a great section on graduate programs in law.

✔ **The Boston College Career Center Law Locator Matrix** (`www.bc.edu/bc_org/svp/carct/matrix.html`): After seeing this site, my only question is: Why didn't anyone think of this before? This gem of a site offers a chart that helps you figure out which schools you're more likely to be admitted to based on your LSAT scores and grades. Click on the handy chart for a listing of likely schools.

✔ **Preparing for Exams by Professor Barbara Glesner Fines** (`www.law.umkc.edu/faculty/profiles/glesnerfines/bgf-ed5.htm`): A useful site for getting the lowdown on what exams are all about, you can find details about how best to prepare, how to outline, and how to set goals.

✔ **FindLaw for Students** (`http://stu.findlaw.com`): This site is comprehensive, bursting with information for law students. In fact, I recommend bookmarking it because you'll refer to it so often. Inside, you find information about law schools and law reviews, job listings, and bar exam information.

✔ **Greedy Associates** (`www.greedyassociates.com`): I didn't come across this site until my second year, but it was well worth the wait. It features a forum in which you can find helpful information concerning all aspects of lawyers' lives, including a message board where people discuss salaries and jobs, job postings from around the country, and links to legal information resources and relevant books for law students and lawyers.

✔ **The National Conference of Bar Examiners** (`www.ncbex.org`): A one-stop shop for all your bar exam needs. Here you can find out about where bar admission offices are located, read all about bar admission statistics, and discover more about the character-and-fitness determination procedures.

✔ **Careers in Law from the University of Minnesota Law Library** (`www.aallnet.org/sis/ripssis/careers.html`): A fantastic listing of career resources, including books for people considering alternative careers (see Chapter 17), information on judges and courts for people applying for judicial clerkships, and resources on government employment.

- ✔ **Lexis Nexis's Martindale-Hubbell** (www.martindale.com): A useful link to keep handy during job searches, use it to find employers or individual lawyers. You can search by practice area, lawyer name, law firm name, or law school attended, among others.

- ✔ **New York Lawyer . . . For Lawyers on the Verge** (www.nylawyer.com): Although the name of this Web site suggests that it's aimed at lawyers in New York, law students and lawyers from across country find this hip, humorous, career Web site eye-opening. That's because it has unparalleled advice (Q&A) columns that you can read concerning alternative legal jobs, job search dilemmas, getting into law school, interviewing, and more. These advice columns are not to be missed, because they cover questions you may not feel comfortable asking your dean or career services director. Be sure that you also check out the site's up-to-the-minute information on (law firm) associate's pay, layoffs, and other general information about law firms.

- ✔ **National Association for Law Placement** (www.nalp.org): This site focuses on legal careers and legal education research. When you like browsing research and statistics on interesting topics related to legal education or careers, be sure to click on the "NALP Research" section. You'll also find a link to the "NALP Directory of Legal Employers" (a more direct route is at www.nalpdirectory.com), which features contact information and useful job-search data on more than 1,500 employers throughout the country. There's even a section for pre–law students, with helpful information about choosing a law school, rankings, and more.

- ✔ **The American Bar Association** (www.abanet.org): This site has a wealth of resources, including ABA news, legal and professional resources, law student resources, and links to the association's many publications. You can also find detailed information on study abroad, legal education statistics, and post-J.D. programs. You definitely want to consider becoming a student member of the ABA, which features a free subscription to the ABA's *Student Lawyer* magazine and access to the ABA's many sections and divisions (interest groups for various legal specialties and topics).

Surveying Magazines and Newsletters

Law school magazines help you find out more about law school culture and show you how to survive and thrive during your three (or four) years. What follows is a listing of several widely read magazines, complete with contact information.

The American Bar Association's Student Lawyer magazine

Student Lawyer is the magazine of the American Bar Association Law Student Division. Inside, you find regular columns featuring information on jobs and careers, articles profiling interesting law students and lawyers, legal educational trends, and law practices. You receive a full year's subscription with your $20 annual membership fee in the American Bar Association's Law Student Division. Individual one-year subscriptions are also available for $22. The magazine is published monthly from September through May.

ABA Service Center
ABA Publication Orders
P.O. Box 10892
Chicago, IL 60610-0892
Phone: 800-285-2221
Internet: www.abanet.org/lsd/stulawyer

The American Bar Association's The Young Lawyer newsletter

The American Bar Association Young Lawyers Division publishes this newsletter 11 times per year. Although targeted at lawyers ages 36 and younger and lawyers in practice for five or fewer years, *The Young Lawyer* may also be of interest to law students for its practice-oriented information and tips. You find information about quality of life issues, women and minority lawyers, and advice about ethics and professional conduct. As part of your membership in the ABA Young Lawyers Division, you receive *The Young Lawyer* free, or you can order it for $29.95 per year through the contact information provided in the previous section.

The American Bar Association's Perspectives: For and About Women Lawyers newsletter

Perspectives is a publication that covers issues and topics unique to women lawyers. Inside, you'll find career-building tips, profiles of women lawyers, and significant developments that affect women lawyers. *Perspectives* is published quarterly by the American Bar Association Commission on Women in the Profession. Partners of the ABA Commission on Women in the Profession receive the newsletter with their membership, but all others may subscribe for $35 per year through the contact information provided earlier in "The American Bar Association's *Student Lawyer* magazine" section.

The American Bar Association's Goal IX newsletter

Goal IX, a quarterly newsletter, is published by the American Bar Association Commission on Opportunities for Minorities in the Profession. Members of the ABA Commission on Racial and Ethnic Diversity receive the magazine free. *Goal IX* informs its readers about programming, federal policies, and ABA initiatives important to minority lawyers. Individual subscriptions to *Goal IX* aren't available. Back issues are available, however, through the contact information provided earlier in "The American Bar Association's *Student Lawyer* magazine" section.

JD Jungle

Published four times a year, *JD Jungle* is a hip magazine aimed at young lawyers and law students. In it, you get an inside look at law school life, careers, recruiting, lawyerly fashion and accessories, and travel. You also may want to check out the magazine's companion Web site (www.jdjungle.com) for more great articles and information about the law school experience. If you'd like to subscribe to the magazine, follow the links to the magazine section, and receive a trial issue. If you enjoy the trial issue, you'll get an accompanying subscription of eight issues for $24.97. You can subscribe online or get a printable form that you can fax or mail to:

JD Jungle Subscriptions
P.O. Box 997
Bellmawr, NJ 08099
Fax: 212-352-9282
Phone: 212-352-0840

Chapter 21

Ten Best and Worst Things about Law School

After you're a bona fide law student, every new experience puts you in a better position for determining what you like and don't like about law school. Like all things in life, this educational bonanza certainly has its positive and negative aspects, and you'll need to take what you don't like in stride. This chapter takes a look at the good, the bad, and the ugly about law school, and gives you tips about how to accentuate the positives and minimize the negatives. If you anticipate some of the potential negatives and plan your strategy to deal with them in advance, you can have a more satisfying law school experience.

Gaining Valuable Public Speaking Skills

One of the best parts about law school is that even if you enter it terrified of uttering a single word in class, by the end of the first month, you'll be a public-speaking pro. Unlike in college, where you can hide in the back row of a 700-seat lecture hall, in the typical law school classroom, you sit in stadium-style seating, where the professor has an unobstructed view of every single student. Crouching low in your seat just won't cut it because you can't hide, but see Chapter 5 for strategic seating arrangement tips to minimize being called on.

You've probably heard it a dozen times already, but law school really does teach you to think on your feet. Even if you aren't a good public speaker when you start law school, the law school faculty makes sure you are by the time you leave through their unrelenting Socratic questioning. It's a major part of their job. When you want to get even more public speaking experience, make it a point to volunteer in class on a regular basis, participate in the moot court competitions, or try out for the mock trial team (see Chapter 13 for the lowdown on both these extracurriculars).

Becoming a Better Writer

Because students come to law school with a variety of writing skills and competency levels, one goal of your first-year legal research and writing course is getting everyone up to roughly the same speed. Achieving that goal may mean that former math majors may have to work much harder than former English majors, but achieving a higher skill level in writing is something that all lawyers must do.

Why must lawyers have a mastery of the written word? Writing is to lawyers what science is to doctors; you use it on a regular basis to practice your craft. The majority of most lawyers' work is made up of writing briefs, memos, and letters, and writing is the way lawyers communicate with clients, other lawyers, and judges. That's one of the reasons that, in addition to legal research and writing in the first year, many law schools have additional writing graduation requirements, such as an advanced writing course in the second year and a research paper seminar course in the third.

Besides writing courses that are required in law school, you have several off-the-beaten-path ways of gaining more writing experience (see Chapter 13 for more traditional ways, such as writing a law journal note or authoring a moot court brief). Specifically, you can

- ✔ **Seek out legal writing competitions.** Tons of these competitions are advertised every year on bulletin boards in virtually every law school; many of them include a monetary prize and/or publication in a law journal.

- ✔ **Hook up with a professor and become a faculty research assistant.** You'll probably find yourself copy-editing the professors' books or articles, and catching their writing mistakes naturally strengthens your own writing skills.

- ✔ **Find practitioners in your field of interest and coauthor articles with them for the newsletters of your local or state bar association.** Not only will you get to research and write a scholarly or popular article on a topic of interest to you, but you also gain valuable feedback on your writing from a seasoned pro. I coauthored an article on an intellectual property case with another lawyer for a newsletter of the Illinois State Bar Association the summer before my second year, and found it to be one of the highlights of my law school career.

Discovering How American Society Works

The nonlegal stuff that you learn in your years of law school is kind of like majoring in political science, civics, and American history, all rolled into one. By reading the assigned cases, you find out how the courts, political process, and justice system work. The cases also expose you to the seamier side of societal relations, such as bitter divorces, horrific surgical mishaps, and toxic waste dumping, which is an education in itself. Overall, the amount of knowledge that you can gain from law school about American society in general makes you a more informed citizen.

When you want to delve more into how American society works, consider taking courses with names such as legal thought, law and political theory, or law and society.

Developing Practical Legal Skills That You Can Use Regardless of Whether You Become a Lawyer

Even if you decide not to take the bar exam and become an attorney, the legal skills and knowledge that you gain in law school can benefit you throughout the rest of your life. For instance, before you came to law school, you probably signed contracts for credit cards and leases without thoroughly looking them over. As a law school graduate, however, you'll scrutinize each and every last word with a lawyer's trained eye. Not only that, but you'll also have at least a rudimentary understanding about provisions in a contract that are okay and the ones that are suspect. And you'll have the research skills to look up what you need to know in a law library.

Similarly, if you ever find yourself being pulled over for a speeding ticket (or worse, sitting in jail), you'll have a much better knowledge than the average person of your rights in that kind of high-pressure situation. If you're involved in a spat with your landlord, you'll know when to seek legal counsel. In other words, you've not only gained legal knowledge that will come in handy after law school, you'll also know how to find lawyers and ask them the right questions whenever you eventually need formal legal assistance.

Finding Out How to Look at Both Sides of an Issue

One invaluable skill that you discover in law school is being able to consider both sides of an issue, not just the one to which you're emotionally or initially drawn. Even if you decide not to become a lawyer, this skill is useful to have, regardless of whether you're arguing with your parents or trying to empathize with a co-worker. When you want to hone this skill, make sure that you participate in moot court in law school (see Chapter 13 for details). Thinking quickly on your feet and writing the required brief help you find out how to argue and analyze both sides of virtually any issue.

Spelling Disaster: A Lack of Discipline

One of the worst things about law school is that it takes more than just intellect and desire to succeed. You need a strong dose of motivation, discipline, and excellent study skills, too (see Chapter 9 for tips about acquiring good study habits). Although many qualified and talented people are admitted, not everyone does as well as they'd like because some soon succumb to slacker-like behaviors. In other words, you can arrive in law school from the top of your undergraduate class, but unless you put in the required hard work, you won't enjoy similar success in law school.

Although it sounds trite, the one key attribute that the most successful law students possess is self-discipline. There's just no getting around the fact that you need to keep up with your reading and assignments; otherwise, you sink into an unforgiving abyss from which it's hard to pull yourself out.

One of the best ways to prepare yourself to exhibit this kind of discipline is to gain it in college or on the job (if you're a nontraditional student). If you still have problems when you get to law school, then you may need to try the more radical boot camp–style approach, which basically means that you must force yourself to make a schedule and then stick to it (see Chapter 9 for tips on making and sticking to a study schedule). Practice sitting in the library and reading for long periods of time, so that you gradually improve your stamina.

Being with the Same People 24/7

One unfortunate fact about law school is that it's kind of like being in high school again. Besides the lockers, assigned seats, and a communal lunch and lounge area (at least there aren't hall passes), you're with the same people virtually all the time (particularly as a 1L). As a result, you may actually feel like you're regressing back to the ninth grade. For nontraditional students, this type of high-school environment can really tax your nerves.

Being with the same people all the time has its good and bad points. It's good because it's somewhat comforting to be surrounded by familiar faces when you're all going through the drama of the Socratic Method for the first time. You also build up an ample degree of tolerance for loud-mouthed know-it-alls, which comes in handy when you must deal with annoying clients as a lawyer. The downside is that it's hard to make new friends when the only people you know are in your assigned section (the one you're assigned to at the beginning of the year). Plus, when you see the same people nearly every waking hour, gossip (as you can imagine) runs rampant. Having everyone know your business gets real old, real fast. But you can't escape it, because you're stuck with the same section for the entire year.

Making new friends through participation in a variety of extracurricular activities really helped me break out of the section mentality. Check out Chapter 13 for all the activities you can participate in as a 1L.

Not Getting Enough of a Hands-On Education

Law school differs greatly from say, medical school, in the sense that nearly all your class instruction is theoretical, rather than clinical. In other words, theory, and not what lawyers actually do, is largely what you learn about in the classroom. This emphasis on the theoretical, instead of the practical, is a major drawback for some law students who learn better by doing than they do by just sitting in class absorbing material.

The way you can gain hands-on experience while in law school is by signing up for clinics and skills-based courses, such as mediation and negotiation (see Chapter 12 for information on both these topics). Doing summer and school-year externships for credit (also covered in Chapter 12) and jobs (paid or unpaid; see Chapter 14) also gives you more of a realistic sense of what lawyers do.

Facing Stiff Competition from Classmates

Law school is made far less pleasant by the fact that you're always competing directly against your classmates for grades and jobs. Because of stiff grading curves that many law schools impose, how well you do depends on how everyone else in your class does on a particular exam. That's why you're bound to hear a plethora of stories (some of them true) about pages being ripped out in library books and people refusing to share notes. Some people's attitude is that too much is at stake when another person gets a leg up. This constant reminder that your fate rests on the performances of other people sometimes taints the law school environment with an adversarial and cut-throat air.

The best way to avoid being sucked into this kind of competitive environment (that is, if you don't want to be in it) is maintaining a healthy outlook on life. See Chapter 7 for tips about "not sweating the small stuff" to keep everything in perspective.

Part-time and evening law students tend to report that their classmates are not nearly as competitive as those in the full-time programs. Perhaps this is because these programs attract more older students simultaneously working full-time jobs, who thus have less time for the immature and petty acts that sometimes characterize relations among full-time law students.

Realizing That the Law Is a "Jealous Mistress"

Everyone knows that being a student generally is easier than working a full-time job, because you have much more free time during the day (and can sleep in when your schedule allows). However, all the studying that you need to do, particularly as a 1L, can really eat into your free time. Non–law student friends and families may become jealous of how much time your law school studies and activities are taking up. That's why a well-known quote attributed to Supreme Court Justice Joseph Story that "The law is a jealous mistress . . . " is especially fitting.

Whenever you have a significant other or a family depending on you, you may especially need to prioritize your time. Reassuring them that you're still committed to them, but that you have to devote a lot of your time right now to law school because of its demands may help ease their concerns. Although the law may be jealous, it needn't become an out-of-control, green-eyed monster.

Chapter 22

Ten Little-Known Law School Secrets

One of the best parts about writing this book is the opportunity I have to share tips about law school that I gleaned during my three years of studies. Some of these facts I discovered the hard way as a brand-new 1L; others I realized only through hindsight. So, what follows are ten especially important tips that can save you time and money as you progress through law school.

Working Part-Time during the School Year Helps with Your Financial Aid

The American Bar Association regulations limit law students to no more than 20 hours per week of part-time employment while they're taking more than 12 credit hours in a semester. On top of this, many law schools discourage 1Ls from working at all. However, within these parameters, you can easily make enough money from 2L and 3L school-year part-time work to at least offset some of your living expenses.

Depending on your city (bigger ones tend to pay more) and what type of part-time work you do (working as a clerk pays more at a large firm than at a small one (see Chapters 14 and 15 for more on workplace options), you can average a decent salary to pay for rent, shopping, or food (but keep in mind you'll be paid by the hour and won't have benefits). Although most students prefer finding jobs in the legal field, working in nonlegal settings, such as retail or food service, can also be profitable. And, because you're offsetting your living expenses, you can take out fewer loans. The less you need to pay back later, the better!

Choosing Best-in-Class Study Group Members

As a 1L, you probably won't initially know anyone with whom to form a study group (see Chapter 9 for more on study groups). If you don't have any friends who you can ask to join you early on in the first of your classes, then focus on figuring out who are the more competent members of your class and corral them into your group as early as you can. The best way to do this is to listen intently in class. Who seems to know what's going on? Who provides insightful and well-thought out comments? You could approach them after class or in an e-mail and say something like, "I really appreciate your comments in class. Would you be interested in forming a study group with me and/or a few others to toss more ideas around?"

Using a Laptop in Class Saves Time Come Exams

Although lugging a laptop to and from class every day can be a pain, the time that you save when exams roll around is well worth it. That's because when you bring your laptop to class, you won't have to put much effort into making an outline, because all your class notes are already neatly typed and organized (see Chapter 9 for more on making outlines). Likewise, with a laptop, combining your reading or study-group notes with your class notes is easy, provided you keep it up and running during these meetings or while you read. When you have everything saved as different computer files, cutting and pasting into one outline document is a snap. Plus, typing everything out makes it much easier to insert headings or rearrange material.

Using Commercial Study Aids Throughout the Semester

As a 1L, falling behind in your classes right from the beginning is an easy thing to do. Your best bet for avoiding that problem is taking a few weeks to get a feel for each of your classes, diagnosing your problem areas, and then talking to upperclassmen about which commercial study aids work best for the courses you're taking (see Chapter 10 for more on choosing commercial study aids). After you've done that, you can purchase the study aids within the first month. That way, you can follow along in your commercial outline all semester, which helps you clarify confusing concepts before they get out of hand. One mistake I made was waiting until the last two weeks of my 1L fall semester before purchasing any commercial outlines. What do you think that says about wishing I knew then what I know now?

Not Giving Your Classmates Fodder for Gossip

The fact that gossip spreads through a law school like a wildfire through a dry forest should come as no surprise. Most law students don't enjoy being the target of such gossip, so they maintain a low profile at parties and other social events. Law students have long memories; don't forget that after graduation your classmates become your colleagues. If that isn't a good reason for keeping your personal life under wraps from everyone except your closest friends, I don't know what is.

Nontraditional students who aren't as much involved in the party/social scene usually have an easier time staying out of the law school rumormill. They may not be as keen as younger students to jump on the gossip bandwagon, and as a result, are better able to separate their law school and outside lives.

Getting Friendly with Professors Early Ensures Good References Later

Every law student needs references when applying for summer jobs, permanent jobs, or clerkships. Because most law classes are large, and you don't really get to know your professors in class, you need to work at cultivating good relationships with them outside of class. A few tips for getting started are

- ✔ **Making yourself stand out in class in a good way.** Raise thoughtful questions; doing so impresses professors more than someone who's perpetually eager to answer their every question.

- ✔ **Attending office hours frequently.** Because so few students ever take advantage of this opportunity, you won't only stand out, but you'll also spend valuable one-on-one time with your professor.

✔ **Trying to land a research assistantship position.** A *research assistantship* is the ultimate opportunity for cultivating meaningful relationships with your professors, so they can comment on more than your achievement on one final exam or classroom participation. Check out Chapter 13 for more about the value of a research assistantship.

Killing Two Birds with One Stone: Externships for Credit

Many schools offer opportunities to participate in externships for course credit. An *externship* involves working at a public-interest organization, courthouse, or governmental organization for credit but no pay. You can often take externship courses during the summer and during the school year. Not only do you gain hands-on work experience, but you're also afforded a refreshing break from classroom-based theory. On top of that, you can cultivate another valuable reference from your supervising attorney or judge. Another plus about serving an externship in summer is that it can enable you to take a lighter course load one semester in the next year. In short, externships are a great way to inject variety into your course load while doing something new and different.

Getting Course Outlines by Joining a Club

An added bonus of joining a law school club (see Chapter 13 for more on all types of law school extracurriculars) is the opportunity it offers for gaining access to a bevy of course outlines — a juicy tidbit that I didn't discover until my second year. Many club officers maintain a club folder of outlines from past members and make them available to all current club members, as long as they pay their annual membership dues (which usually amounts to only a nominal fee). With outlines, the more you have, the merrier, so don't overlook this fabulous opportunity to score some extras.

Graduating in December Sometimes Gives You a Leg Up

Only a handful of students elect to graduate in December at law schools that make doing so an option. Those who do often find more receptive job markets. Students who graduate in December, after 2½ years of law school, usually have taken summer school, studied abroad to gain extra credits (see Chapter 12), or started early, in the summer before their first full year at schools that offer summer starter programs.

Understanding why December graduates often have a leg up isn't hard. Competition for jobs during winter months is much less than in the late summer and fall. December grads may have a better shot at responding to postings in their schools' career services offices and want ads in the paper, because fewer people are likely to be job-hunting at that time of year.

Making Use of Alums while Job-Searching

The majority of jobs are found through connections; not through want ads or job postings at your career services office. This is true for both traditional legal and alternative jobs. Employers like to hire people who are personally recommended to them, rather than taking a chance on some unknown entity whose résumé just happens to land on their desk. If you have an alum (either who works there or who is known to the hiring staff member) pulling for you, it can make all the difference between an offer and a rejection. This is true regardless of whether you're looking for summer jobs after your first and second years or permanent jobs (see Chapters 14, 15, and 17 for more on finding jobs).

The best way to find alumni connections is to sit down with your career services staff and tell them what type of work you're interested in and in what geographical location. Using information in electronic or paper alumni databases, they can match you up with alums in your area of interest. Alternatively, on your own, you can go to www.martindale.com (legal jobs and law school faculty only), and use this extensive free database to type in your law school's name, your preferred practice area, and your geographical location. In the search results you'll find names and firms of lawyers who went to your law school. Just compose a quick e-mail requesting an *informational interview* (more on these in Chapter 16) to find out more about their work and gain advice on entering that field.

Index

Notes

FOR DUMMIES®

The easy way to get more done and have more fun

PERSONAL FINANCE

0-7645-5231-7

0-7645-2431-3

0-7645-5331-3

Also available:

Estate Planning For Dummies
(0-7645-5501-4)

401(k)s For Dummies
(0-7645-5468-9)

Frugal Living For Dummies
(0-7645-5403-4)

Microsoft Money "X" For
Dummies
(0-7645-1689-2)

Mutual Funds For Dummies
(0-7645-5329-1)

Personal Bankruptcy For
Dummies
(0-7645-5498-0)

Quicken "X" For Dummies
(0-7645-1666-3)

Stock Investing For Dummies
(0-7645-5411-5)

Taxes For Dummies 2003
(0-7645-5475-1)

BUSINESS & CAREERS

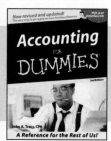
0-7645-5314-3

0-7645-5307-0

0-7645-5471-9

Also available:

Business Plans Kit For
Dummies
(0-7645-5365-8)

Consulting For Dummies
(0-7645-5034-9)

Cool Careers For Dummies
(0-7645-5345-3)

Human Resources Kit For
Dummies
(0-7645-5131-0)

Managing For Dummies
(1-5688-4858-7)

QuickBooks All-in-One Desk
Reference For Dummies
(0-7645-1963-8)

Selling For Dummies
(0-7645-5363-1)

Small Business Kit For
Dummies
(0-7645-5093-4)

Starting an eBay Business For
Dummies
(0-7645-1547-0)

HEALTH, SPORTS & FITNESS

0-7645-5167-1

0-7645-5146-9

0-7645-5154-X

Also available:

Controlling Cholesterol For
Dummies
(0-7645-5440-9)

Dieting For Dummies
(0-7645-5126-4)

High Blood Pressure For
Dummies
(0-7645-5424-7)

Martial Arts For Dummies
(0-7645-5358-5)

Menopause For Dummies
(0-7645-5458-1)

Nutrition For Dummies
(0-7645-5180-9)

Power Yoga For Dummies
(0-7645-5342-9)

Thyroid For Dummies
(0-7645-5385-2)

Weight Training For Dummies
(0-7645-5168-X)

Yoga For Dummies
(0-7645-5117-5)

Available wherever books are sold.
Go to www.dummies.com or call 1-877-762-2974 to order direct.

FOR DUMMIES®

A world of resources to help you grow

HOME, GARDEN & HOBBIES

0-7645-5295-3

0-7645-5130-2

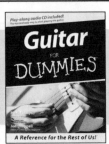

0-7645-5106-X

FOOD & WINE

0-7645-5250-3

0-7645-5390-9

0-7645-5114-0

TRAVEL

0-7645-5453-0

0-7645-5438-7

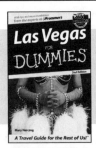

0-7645-5448-4

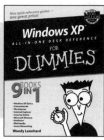
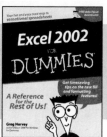

FOR DUMMIES®

Helping you expand your horizons and realize your potential

INTERNET

0-7645-0894-6

0-7645-1659-0

0-7645-1642-6

Also available:

America Online 7.0 For Dummies
(0-7645-1624-8)

Genealogy Online For Dummies
(0-7645-0807-5)

The Internet All-in-One Desk Reference For Dummies
(0-7645-1659-0)

Internet Explorer 6 For Dummies
(0-7645-1344-3)

The Internet For Dummies Quick Reference
(0-7645-1645-0)

Internet Privacy For Dummies
(0-7645-0846-6)

Researching Online For Dummies
(0-7645-0546-7)

Starting an Online Business For Dummies
(0-7645-1655-8)

DIGITAL MEDIA

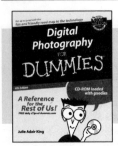

0-7645-1664-7

0-7645-1675-2

0-7645-0806-7

Also available:

CD and DVD Recording For Dummies
(0-7645-1627-2)

Digital Photography All-in-One Desk Reference For Dummies
(0-7645-1800-3)

Digital Photography For Dummies Quick Reference
(0-7645-0750-8)

Home Recording for Musicians For Dummies
(0-7645-1634-5)

MP3 For Dummies
(0-7645-0858-X)

Paint Shop Pro "X" For Dummies
(0-7645-2440-2)

Photo Retouching & Restoration For Dummies
(0-7645-1662-0)

Scanners For Dummies
(0-7645-0783-4)

GRAPHICS

0-7645-0817-2

0-7645-1651-5

0-7645-0895-4

Also available:

Adobe Acrobat 5 PDF For Dummies
(0-7645-1652-3)

Fireworks 4 For Dummies
(0-7645-0804-0)

Illustrator 10 For Dummies
(0-7645-3636-2)

QuarkXPress 5 For Dummies
(0-7645-0643-9)

Visio 2000 For Dummies
(0-7645-0635-8)

Available wherever books are sold. Go to www.dummies.com or call 1-877-762-2974 to order direct.

FOR DUMMIES®

The advice and explanations you need to succeed

SELF-HELP, SPIRITUALITY & RELIGION

0-7645-5302-X

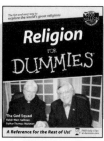

0-7645-5418-2

(Religion For Dummies)

0-7645-5264-3

Also available:

The Bible For Dummies
(0-7645-5296-1)

Buddhism For Dummies
(0-7645-5359-3)

Christian Prayer For Dummies
(0-7645-5500-6)

Dating For Dummies
(0-7645-5072-1)

Judaism For Dummies
(0-7645-5299-6)

Potty Training For Dummies
(0-7645-5417-4)

Pregnancy For Dummies
(0-7645-5074-8)

Rekindling Romance For Dummies
(0-7645-5303-8)

Spirituality For Dummies
(0-7645-5298-8)

Weddings For Dummies
(0-7645-5055-1)

PETS

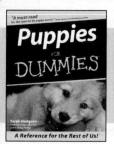

0-7645-5255-4

0-7645-5286-4

(Cats For Dummies)

0-7645-5275-9

Also available:

Labrador Retrievers For Dummies
(0-7645-5281-3)

Aquariums For Dummies
(0-7645-5156-6)

Birds For Dummies
(0-7645-5139-6)

Dogs For Dummies
(0-7645-5274-0)

Ferrets For Dummies
(0-7645-5259-7)

German Shepherds For Dummies
(0-7645-5280-5)

Golden Retrievers For Dummies
(0-7645-5267-8)

Horses For Dummies
(0-7645-5138-8)

Jack Russell Terriers For Dummies
(0-7645-5268-6)

Puppies Raising & Training Diary For Dummies
(0-7645-0876-8)

EDUCATION & TEST PREPARATION

0-7645-5194-9

0-7645-5325-9

(The ACT For Dummies)

0-7645-5210-4

Also available:

Chemistry For Dummies
(0-7645-5430-1)

English Grammar For Dummies
(0-7645-5322-4)

French For Dummies
(0-7645-5193-0)

The GMAT For Dummies
(0-7645-5251-1)

Inglés Para Dummies
(0-7645-5427-1)

Italian For Dummies
(0-7645-5196-5)

Research Papers For Dummies
(0-7645-5426-3)

The SAT I For Dummies
(0-7645-5472-7)

U.S. History For Dummies
(0-7645-5249-X)

World History For Dummies
(0-7645-5242-2)

Available wherever books are sold. Go to www.dummies.com or call 1-877-762-2974 to order direct.

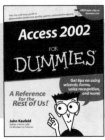

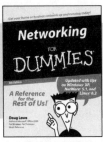